East Asian National Identities

East Asian National Identities
Common Roots and Chinese Exceptionalism

Edited by

Gilbert Rozman

Woodrow Wilson Center Press
Washington, D.C.

Stanford University Press
Stanford, California

EDITORIAL OFFICES

Woodrow Wilson Center Press
One Woodrow Wilson Plaza
1300 Pennsylvania Avenue, N.W.
Washington, DC 20004-3027
Telephone: 202-691-4029
www.wilsoncenter.org

ORDER FROM

Stanford University Press
Chicago Distribution Center
11030 South Langley Avenue
Chicago, IL 60628
Telephone: 1-800-621-2736

Library of Congress Cataloging-in-Publication Data

East Asian national identities : commonalities and differences /
edited by Gilbert Rozman.
   p.   cm.
  Includes bibliographical references and index.
  ISBN 978-0-8047-8117-6
  1. National characteristics, East Asian. I. Rozman, Gilbert.
DS509.3.E19 2011
950—dc23
                                         2011045219

Woodrow Wilson
International
Center
for Scholars

The Woodrow Wilson International Center for Scholars is the national, living U.S. memorial honoring President Woodrow Wilson. In providing an essential link between the worlds of ideas and public policy, the Center addresses current and emerging challenges confronting the United States and the world. The Center promotes policy-relevant research and dialogue to increase understanding and enhance the capabilities and knowledge of leaders, citizens, and institutions worldwide. Created by an act of Congress in 1968, the Center is a nonpartisan institution headquartered in Washington, D.C., and supported by both public and private funds.

Conclusions or opinions expressed in Center publications and programs are those of the authors and speakers and do not necessarily reflect the views of the Center staff, fellows, trustees, advisory groups, or any individuals or organizations that provide financial support to the Center.

The Center is the publisher of *The Wilson Quarterly* and home of Woodrow Wilson Center Press and *dialogue* television and radio. For more information about the Center's activities and publications, please visit us on the Web at www.wilsoncenter.org.

Contents

Acknowledgments

This project began as a course comparing great power national identities. Having recognized a dearth of systematic comparisons and having struggled with how to assess a mixture of similarities and differences in the evolution of Chinese and Japanese identities as well as how to incorporate parallels in South Korean identity, I planned a multistage project. I owe my greatest debt to Princeton University students who pioneered in writing comparative papers on the identities of two great powers and kept raising intriguing insights that merited further investigation. Several advisees wrote senior theses applying the comparative approach, and I am pleased that one of them, Andrew Kim, joined me in contributing a chapter to this volume.

A brainstorming session on comparisons of East Asian national identities was graciously funded by the Princeton Institute of International and Regional Studies and hosted by Keio University's Institute of East Asian Studies. Separate workshops followed at Princeton, focusing respectively on Japanese, South Korean, and

Chinese national identities. They were well supported by the Mercer Trust and the East Asian Studies Program at Princeton. The Korea Foundation's generous assistance enabled the contributors to this book to take time to prepare and revise their papers.

The final product benefited from comments by two anonymous readers and fellowship support from the Woodrow Wilson International Center for Scholars as well as backing from Joe Brinley, director of the Wilson Center Press, and the Center's Publishing Committee. For responding in a thoughtful and timely fashion to suggestions, the contributors deserve credit. I want to thank them and all who assisted with this book for their unstinting support.

Gilbert Rozman
June 2011

East Asian National Identities

Part I

The Six-Dimensional Approach

Introduction

Gilbert Rozman

This two-part study of national identities in Japan, South Korea, and China seeks to put a subject that has been treated haphazardly with little sustained analysis on a track for comparative scholarship. Despite many interesting observations in earlier works, there has been little agreement on what is included in national identity, how the identities of nations differ, and what is necessary to develop the field of national identity studies. If tantalizing observations have referred to the struggle over constructing identities in flux in the three countries under scrutiny, attention has yet to center on what is similar and different in their challenges. By assessing many aspects of national identity and tracing its evolution, this book highlights the distinctive features of East Asian states. It defines national identity as what a state, explicitly or implicitly, regards as distinctive in contrast to other states deemed important. What differentiates part I of this book is not the definition but the framework for specifying dimensions of national identity and generalizing about them.

1

Part I utilizes a six-dimensional approach to scrutinize national identity. First, it applies the approach to Japan, South Korea, and China, offering parallel presentations of how each of the dimensions shapes identity formation in these states. Then it proceeds to comparisons of the three cases on the basis of each dimension, exploring similarities and differences for their significance in understanding what makes East Asia distinctive. Even as national identity studies have been popular for two decades, touching on many aspects of East Asian states, this approach stands apart as a systematic, comparative, regionally focused, relatively comprehensive framework. With due regard for the distinctive nature of the national identities of each of the three states, part I concludes by identifying what I call the East Asian National Identity Syndrome (EANIS). It finds fundamental similarity across the region, noting also sharp differences in the intensity of the syndrome over time and across states. Thus, this inductive approach does not obscure divergence in identity formation with far-reaching consequences. Commonalities noted in EANIS should in no way suggest easier paths to forge mutual trust. On the contrary, as a planned second book on how identities shape bilateral relations will demonstrate, EANIS is a principal factor behind intense regional distrust along with difficulties in relations with the United States.

Above all, I argue that spikes in national identity since the 1980s have occurred when the six dimensions are aligned and give impetus to arrogant notions of national uniqueness and superiority on the international arena. Thus, in the late 1980s, Japan's spike coincided with its "bubble economy"; in the early 2000s, South Korea's spike capitalized on the Sunshine Policy; and from 2008 to 2011, China experienced the most hyperbolic spike as it calculated that its rapid rise was accelerating due to the abrupt decline of the United States in the global financial crisis. Such exceptionalism is not just a consequence of short-term forces. It is, this framework demonstrates, inherent in EANIS. Saving analysis of the impact of national identities on international relations for a second volume, this book examines the three countries separately and through comparative study of how identities are shaped.

Changing Perspectives on National Identities in East Asia

A single narrative took center stage during the Cold War. It contrasted the United States, democratic and leader of the free world, with the

Soviet Union, abuser of human rights and intent on establishing world domination through a ruthless dictatorship. Little attention turned to shades of gray, appearing in a more complicated world in which states took sides with one or the other adversary despite inconsistent overlaps in values. The situation in East Asia also saw the totalitarian regime in North Korea reinforce the most extreme version of the Stalinist image, while South Korea, under a dictatorship until 1987, and Japan, not entirely free of charges of harboring revisionist aspirations with regard to its historical depredations in the region, enjoyed the advantage of the contrast. By switching sides in the 1970s, China blurred the picture. Although some tried to refocus on its dark spots to reaffirm the black-and-white overview, others reconciled this reality to the big picture by explaining its Communist profile as merely a transitional phenomenon until it became integrated into the world economy with a middle-class society. Sharply polarized global identities overshadowed images of variant national identities, even in complex East Asia.

In the 1990s, states lost any raison d'être from the struggle against a global enemy. Interstate ties were divorced from the global struggle, obliging each side to perceive the other in terms of history, current bilateral ties, or anticipated regional cooperation. In East Asia, the foundation for all-around regionalism remained weak; current conditions left a mixed picture of booming economic ties and contested security interests. The door was left open for Confucian-derived predilections about history and the still-unresolved postwar normalization with Japan to shape national identity debates. In this new context, the once-unchallenged national identities of earlier decades also were shaken, leaving countries to grasp for ways to reestablish clarity, notably by means of contrasting bilateral images.

China struggled to supplement or, perhaps, gloss over its Communist identity with a different self-image as an economic miracle, a rising power, and the heir to a great tradition. In this process, the Communist movement could be associated with the liberation struggle versus Japan and the resistance against Western imperialism in which the United States was implicated. Japan had been shaken by the collapse of its economic miracle and social harmony image, as it too groped for a facelift to national identity, reasserting its great power significance and finding renewed merit in its history. Yet, as in the case of China, invoking a positive national identity could not be separated from reassessing the nation's principal partners amid efforts to clarify new threats to security and, it was argued, to the national identity. South Korea faced a strikingly new environment, interacting not only with additional great powers but also more directly with compatriots in North Korea. In the midst of this flux, bilateral relations became contested arenas for honing identities. Apart from Central and Eastern Europe and the former Soviet Union, no other region of the world forged such a caldron of change stirring up questioning about existing national identities.

In 2005, relations between Japan and China and between Japan and South Korea went into a sharp tailspin. The history issue gained increased prominence. Territorial disputes rose in importance, acquiring unexpected immediacy. South Korea's president cast doubt on the entire process of normalization with Japan since 1965. Demonstrators in Shanghai objected to Japan becoming a permanent member of the United Nations, brushing aside its postwar support for peace. The Japanese public gravitated to alarm about a "China threat" and tended to dismiss South Korean leaders as pandering to raw emotionalism. Although differences had surfaced over the handling of the North Korean nuclear challenge and other issues of political and security significance, the dispute between these two pairs of states now was interpreted through the symbols of national identity: the Yasukuni Shrine and territorial disputes over Dokdo/Takeshima Island and the Senkaku/Diaoyu Islands. The shrine and islands symbolized Japan's history—to many Japanese, overly criticized; and to many in Asia, insufficiently apologetic.

With unprecedented post–Cold War fervor, charges of sovereignty at risk and unrepentant victimization captured the spotlight in relations between these three states. And in addition to these old problems now revived, new issues had arisen with powerful implications for national identity. Chinese–South Korean relations stumbled over newly asserted claims that Koguryo, a state that had existed 1,300 to 2,000 years ago straddling the borders of today's Korean Peninsula and Northeast China, was in fact a part of Chinese history. At the same time, the Japanese were obsessed with the abductions of thirteen or more citizens 25 to 30 years ago by North Korean agents, treating the abductions as at least equal to the North's nuclear weapons and missiles in deciding how to respond to the Six-Party Talks taking place in Beijing. Explanations of international relations could not account for the impact of such issues without tying them to national identities. In comparison with the period from the 1970s to the 1990s, they galvanized far more people and had far greater effect on bilateral ties, even if they did not block all efforts toward reconciliation over identity differences.

In April 2008, the world's gaze was fixed on China's pre-Olympics "sacred torch relay," for its hubris in rallying citizens of China around the world to defend the nation's honor. Whether they were opposing Tibetan demonstrators for religious/cultural rights or the international community's criticisms of China's recent human rights abuses, an honor guard attending to the flame buttressed by an aroused nation hijacked the Olympic spirit as testimony to China's rise in a world perceived as still bent on humiliating it. In May and June, while China refocused its nationalism on a massive disaster relief effort after the Sichuan earthquake, South Koreans revived their "candlelight vigils" to humble their new president, Lee Myung-bak, especially for his audacity in agreeing to allow U.S. beef to reenter the national market. The government was temporarily paralyzed; public support fell precipitously for a man recently elected by a record margin due to an obscure issue that resonated as failure to listen to the national will and symbol of renewed shameful dependence on another country. Although visits by Lee and China's president, Hu Jintao, to Japan during this same period ameliorated the national outrage of recent years to that country in response to provocative historical revisionism, Japan's seasonal pilgrimage of political leaders visiting Yasukuni with considerable public backing stands as the ultimate symbol of defiance in support of historical honor. The sacred torch relays, candlelight vigils, and Yasukuni pilgrimages each reflect a distinct national identity, but one also finds signs of a shared syndrome that operates in all three of the core countries of East Asia.

In 2009, the U.S. Obama presidency posed a new test for national identities in various states. Despite the global financial crisis, which further emboldened China, Obama rekindled U.S. idealism in a manner that made clear its centrality as a marker against which other national identities are set. China's handling of Uighur-Han violence in Xinjiang Province, for which it blamed foreign provocations and foreign press coverage, clashed with U.S. respect for minority rights. Japan's first electoral transfer of power in more than half a century raised questions about how closely it would continue to profess support for U.S. alliance ties at the cost of Asianism. Meanwhile, a divided South Korea searched for a new consensus, including on U.S. ties, in the shadow of a renewed threat from North Korea, which was now in possession of nuclear weapons and missiles that threatened regional stability. As Obama asserted leadership, based not only on a preponderance of power but also on new appeals for trust in U.S. values, uncertain responses reflected varied national identities.

Although an "Obama craze" swept across some nations, states with strongly fixed identities wary of U.S. values, not just of their one-sided twist under George W. Bush associated with a rise in anti-Americanism, were in no mood to succumb. To assess the response, one needs to take a close look at the national identities of America's two most important allies in East Asia and its most important potential adversary in this region and also the world.

The impact of national identities related to China intensified in 2010. The Chinese framed problems in terms of identity clashes, profusely criticizing Japan, South Korea, and especially the United States in essentialist terms. In turn, criticisms in these states of China pointedly singled out the values reshaping its policies. If national identities figured in earlier discussions of many regional themes, they burst into the limelight in the tense atmosphere of 2010 in unprecedented ways. China put these issues in the forefront, as in diatribes against the Nobel Peace Prize being awarded to Liu Shaobo, the imprisoned advocate of democracy; vitriolic charges against the lingering "Cold War mentality" in the United States and its allies in East Asia as the source of all regional tensions; and an insistence on civilizational dichotomies that starkly contrasted China's virtuous Confucian and Communist legacies with the heinous imperialist and hegemonic traditions of the West. Although extreme, these narratives are embedded in the forces of identity formation intrinsic to East Asia.

Why Do National Identities Matter?

Social science repeatedly returns to the challenge of incorporating culture into discussions of social change and international relations. This is particularly apparent in writings on East Asia, where debates over modernization theory from the 1960s to the 1980s and constructivist approaches to international relations in the 1990s and 2000s have kept the issue of culture in the forefront. Some interpretations have suggested that culture is an immutable force left from the deep recesses of history, but agreement has been hard to reach on the real nature of that force. Other explanations have treated culture as an oft-changing factor, to the dissatisfaction of critics who deny any social science utility from this ad hoc treatment of causality. The national identity literature steers a middle course, pointing to some cultural factors with deep roots but also with the potential for transformation at critical moments. Identities are constructed by state actors drawing on strands of earlier thinking as they make choices that can be viewed through the dimensions that are shared with other states.

National identities may be explicit or implicit and are usually a combination of the two. When explicit, they are constructed as official, self-serving pronouncements of what entitles one's state to positive evaluations and contested benefits. When implicit, they can be used by elite groups to put pressure on their leadership or to mobilize a mass following. Policy choices are made against the background of how leaders will be judged by those who claim the mantle of the national identity. This is especially true in matters of international relations that bear on sovereign rights and the relative power of states. In the historical context of East Asia, sensitivity remains high toward policies that might be perceived to be contradicting the claims and symbols of one's national identity. In East Asian states, implicit identities also derive from hesitation to alarm the United States or other partners about long-term aspirations, masking ambitions in a reassuring rhetoric.

Whether in a strictly top-down process or in contentious politics, states construct an identity meant to legitimize their existence and orient the aspirations of ruling elites. These ideas about a state's past, present, and future are meant to instruct people, both at home and abroad, on why they should accept this state as the primary institution for controlling the use of power and deciding the rules of operation for important institutions. Given the potential for rival interpretations, the main concept of national identity may spur clashing claims for transforming the state. To preempt such claims, authorities endow their official version of national identity with sacrosanct qualities. In contrast, those who insist that they have a more correct understanding of national identity are likely to embellish their struggle against the status quo with references to alternative sources of political and/or cultural authority. Assertions of national identity often serve the foreign policy objectives of strengthening sovereignty, maximizing claims to territory, and gaining an advantage in bilateral relations by staking out the moral high ground. One purpose typically is to isolate potential or actual political rivals by coalescing opinion around the notion that compromise on issues deserving great symbolism is anathema for the nation's "face."

In each country, one can observe an ongoing debate about the national identity. Some variant is invoked to appeal to values as important in making policy choices. By doing so, proponents of one choice or another seek to gain an edge. Others may frame the choices in terms of national interests and seek debate among various alternatives, but a group whose arguments are steeped in national identity rhetoric lays claim to a deeper justification that allows little room for compromise. Long-term calculations backed by reasoned analysis may be lost in the furor over how much appears to be at stake that is vital to the essential values for which the country stands. Indeed, values are often raised in ways that do not lead to weighing priorities. The fact that a state has multiple values and that they produce contradictory policy choices may be lost in the heated environment of arguing over potential disregard for the national identity. Although typically interests are pursued by diplomats and other specialists, who may proceed behind closed doors to achieve incremental results, values episodically rise to the surface, advanced by politicians alert to symbols with popular appeal. They lend themselves to easy manipulation by those who would twist them, perhaps misleading the public in pursuit of ulterior ends. Boisterous claims to be proceeding in accord with a deep national purpose often leave little room for patient deliberation with specialists or attentive assessment of possible reactions abroad.

In East Asia, there is no sign of states growing weaker or national identities that even imply that the importance of the state, especially in competition with other states, should be lessened. One observes China's focus on boosting comprehensive national power through the state; Japan's appeal for a "normal state" no longer impaired by constitutional limits imposed during the U.S. Occupation or the self-restraint of a chastened, defeated power in dealing with its Asian neighbors; and South Korea's strong presidency able to exercise great prerogatives in international relations and under pressure from the public to be more assertive. At a time of Bush's "imperial presidency" in the United States, even more evident in international than national affairs, East Asian national identities were no less oriented toward assertive manifestations of power and more steeped in historical thinking that puts a premium on strong, hypersensitive, leadership on behalf of identity. In China especially, the impact of national identity was peaking in 2010 with no signs of any abatement ahead, while the impact in Japan and South Korea was finally receding somewhat.

The Six-Dimensional Framework

For comparisons of national identities, I utilize six dimensions of analysis. First are the *ideological* radiants, revealing contestation between the right, the left, and centrist advocates. Everywhere national identity is the subject of political debates and moves to co-opt them. Second is the *temporal* dimension, in three stages: prewar, postwar, and post–Cold War. Comparisons treat how identities are viewed from the present and how the current stage reflects the balance of memories. Third is the *sectoral* dimension, whereby cultural, economic, and political identities each rise to the forefront, even as the balance shifts. Fourth is the *vertical* dimension, reflecting three levels: a family-community micro level; middle-level administrative, electoral, or abstract identities such as social class, ethnicity, religious affiliation, gender, and social movements; and a macro level, state identity. The fifth dimension is *horizontal,* where a three-way division captures the main variations: the critical inner circle is the U.S. dyad, next are regional relations apart from the United States, last is the international community inclusive of the United States. The sixth dimension focuses on the *depth* of national identity, a factor that is stressed in the discussion of EANIS and how it can reflect the intense emotionalism over identity.

There are other ways to approach national identity. In part II, the book concentrates on how national identities evolved, treating history not from today's perspective but as it shaped thinking. There the contributors also take a historical approach to the horizontal dimension, examining the way diplomatic choices were deemed important for reshaping national identities. The above-described six dimensions cover a broad range of disciplinary interests, demonstrating that this concept is unlikely to be adequately appreciated from one or another angle. Juxtaposing the six dimensions shows more clearly what national identities are and how they lead to EANIS.

The East Asian National Identity Syndrome

In particular periods of world and national history, the thinking in certain states about some other states is heavily influenced by perceptions of the unique character of one's own nation and the distinct nature of past associations with the others. In the post–Cold War era, we argue that such a syndrome with distinct features operated for all three of the main countries of East Asia, especially in their relations with each other and with the United States. Bilateral issues become emotionally charged, sensitivity is high toward images of one's state in the other states, and instability exists as seemingly minor events arouse intense reactions. The regional presence of this syndrome requires explanation.

China, Japan, and South Korea have strong national identity components in their foreign policy, we argue. Although each was regarded as pragmatic over long periods, we find acute latent emotionalism that can result in a loss of perspective and deep sensitivity linked to supposed tests of respect for one's country. The Japanese were apt to stress "shocks" that leave them feeling abandoned. The South Koreans were left in an inflammatory state after the roller coaster ride of the inter-Korean summit of 2000 and the ensuing dashed hopes in the Sunshine Policy. The Chinese rested their dreams so fully on the Olympics that they were left on edge as its preparations proceeded unevenly. Each response demonstrates the intensity of national identities in this region, suggesting the need for a regional, historical explanation and an interactive one as spikes in identity sensitivity reinforced each other.

The national identity syndrome of East Asia blends a minimum of five ingredients: (1) a premodern legacy mixing a Confucian civilization of historical honor with an incipient inward-oriented, closed national pride; (2) a desperate catch-up mentality for modern reform with uncommon ambivalence about management of the historical legacy as top-down transformation and international borrowing occur at breakneck speed; (3) an era of extremist claims isolated from international currents that face sudden rejection but lie in the background as potent factors in limiting convergence with outside thinking; (4) pride in an economic miracle accompanied by a strong sense of entitlement that cannot easily be satisfied, as expectations and frustrations both mount; and (5) sudden spikes in optimism that a desired breakthrough is within reach, accompanied by sharp letdowns in which other countries are blamed for frustrating these hopes. In each of these respects, we find far-reaching differences with other nations as well as regional similarities. We also trace a cumulative process of national identity formation with enduring consequences.

Contemporary national identities are a product of the sequential development of self-images stressing honor, historical relevance, uniqueness, urgent competitiveness, extreme claims of merit, great pride in modern achievements, exaggerated claims to entitlement, deep frustration over unrealized aspirations, and cycles of hope and disappointment over perceived breakthrough opportunities. No single period of history or cultural orientation by itself explains the nature and intensity of East Asian national identities. After forming in the environment of a particular regional civilization, they acquired new form under the impact of a particular stage of world integration, they were refined and further embedded in eras of national challenges to the existing order, and in recent decades they adjusted to a more complex world and regional order in which opportunities are growing even if the forces of globalization and rival nationalisms increase the chances for frustration. These are national identities of states accustomed to success and optimistic that more lies ahead, but they are also signs of resentful states concerned that their ambitions may be denied.

East Asia is known for its Confucian traditions, which emphasize state leadership in setting a moral compass through writing histories and instructing the public on what constitutes virtuous conduct by themselves, but also by a properly functioning state. This legacy lays the foundation for exceptional attentiveness to national identities in modern times. We explain below that this legacy was twisted in late premodern times in a kind of xenophobic manner. Also, this region later passed through Japanese colonialism and the reactive nationalism nurtured by both what Japan did and how it sought to rationalize its conduct. National identities became entwined in constructed memories of this experience. Saving face, being treated with respect, and behaving in accord with relative status are regional orientations that put a premium on national identities driving dyadic relations.

Another shared experience in Japan and then China was a period of mobilization behind claims of moral superiority that accompanied insistence that an exemplary model of modernization had been established and efforts to export their model. In each case, this extremism followed desperate borrowing in order to catch up: Japan's Meiji Era borrowing draws interest as the foremost case of rapid, top-down, autonomous copying of capitalist institutions; and learning from the Soviet Union in China stands as the primary example of similar copying of socialist institutions. Following a rupture with the state that had served as its model, Japan in the 1930s and 1940s experienced about a decade as the self-professed champion of a uniquely harmonious model that it sought to spread through the "East Asian Co-Prosperity Sphere."

And China in the 1960s and 1970s heralded its "Cultural Revolution" as the non-"revisionist" socialism for the rest of the world.

Although for a time Japan's surrender and Deng Xiaoping's repudiation of Mao Zedong's "continuous revolution" narrowed the horizons of each nation, continuities in leadership in each state and newfound confidence with its "economic miracle" rekindled pride in the society and in state-society relations. Each country emerged with high expectations for equality with the United States in some aspects of global power and regional leadership independent of this superpower. With national identity leading both to unrealistic optimism about potential breakthroughs within reach and undue pessimism about other great powers reluctant to grant a rising superpower the status it sought, frustrations kept redirecting attention to what stood in the way of its aspirations. Instead of national identities gradually giving way to realist calculations and convergence with liberal values, they remained powerful prisms for viewing the world.

As the Japanese, the South Koreans, and then the Chinese enjoyed some of the world's most spectacular rates of economic growth, there was a curious lack of satisfaction at the level of individuals and in policy assessments of state success in the international arena. Rather, attention turned to the unfairness of others being denied the anticipated fruits of economic success. This indicates the importance of unrealized goals. The catch-up process could concentrate attention on material and career goals, whose realization provided a certain amount of satisfaction. As attention turned instead to other goals, especially state-centered ones, we find evidence of greater dissatisfaction, especially with the outside world. There was talk of the Japanese shifting from a community-orientation to individualism in the 1970s and 1980s, of the South Koreans seizing on democratization in the late 1980s and 1990s to turn away from values focused on the state, and of the Chinese revealing their fragmented nature as the state receded from their lives in the 1990s and 2000s—yet value convergence with the outside occurred only haltingly. Dissatisfaction intensified and, to a noted degree, was redirected outward. Materialism lost some of its appeal, but liberal values, including "postmodern" ones, were slow to emerge as nationalism fixated on symbols to steer values differently.

Early in its modern national development, Japan and then China laid out a blueprint for a utopian society and world putting their country at the center. Japan did this in the 1930s, with its multilayered community solidarity that made strong demands on all citizens as subjects of the emperor, as members of tightly organized communities, and also as members of families idealized for the collective control they could provide. As the nucleus of the East Asian Co-Prosperity Sphere, Japan was intent on spreading its model, even if other societies were regarded as inferior. China made its grandiose claims during the various peaks of Mao's radicalism, notably the Great Leap Forward and the Cultural Revolution. Deemphasizing its use of coercive methods such as those many found in the forefront in Stalin's Soviet Union, China followed Japan in showcasing the thorough inculcation of social values. It also sponsored revolutionary movements to spread its Communist model with claims to surpass the Soviet Union as the rightful center of this emerging order. In both Japan and China during these spikes of utopianism, Western values were rejected along with the idea that their state's modernization would converge with that of earlier modernizers. The moral superiority of their states under essentially infallible rulers and their more harmonious model combined with fierce opposition to those excluded from it promised to accelerate catching up along some dimensions of development while taking the lead along others. Later, when these models had obviously failed, there was almost no reassessment of the real reasons for their emergence. Perhaps, the inclination to arrogance a half century later in Japan in the 1980s and China in the 2000s stemmed from similar roots and proceeded more easily in the absence of serious reflection on earlier utopianism. It was also accompanied by confidence in top-down centralized politics, a society seen as more harmonious than contentious, and belief that superior economic results followed.

Comparisons shed light on the spikes in national confidence: Japan in 1987–88, when it appeared to be the big winner in the dénouement to the Cold War; South Korea in 2000–2001, when the Sunshine Policy offered hope that it could occupy the driver's seat in the reorganization of Northeast Asia; and China as anticipation of the Beijing Olympics in 2007–8 led to expectations of a triumphal coming-out party for the next superpower. In each case, a long-cherished goal seemed to be within reach, the future after an "economic miracle" and diplomatic diversification in Asia and beyond looked bright, and admiration was coming from many directions. The people of each country basked in this global limelight, embracing nationalism to the degree that they were more willing to challenge the United States and others who might be seen as pressuring their country. Long-term objectives may still not have been close at hand—equality with the United States and regional leadership for Japan, an end to one-sided dependence on the United States and reunification for South Korea, and an end to deference to the United States and recognition as the center of East Asia for China— but hopes had risen fast that a giant step toward them was being taken. All three states measured their success through transforming bilateral relations with the United States and achieving upgraded status while steering surrounding countries toward some sort of regionalism that gave them a central role. For all, it was also a matter of national identity vindication, allowing their past to be reinterpreted more positively.

Each of the three emerging East Asian states faced a shock just after its hopes reached a high point. Japan's confidence in the late 1980s was at its peak, but in a short period of time it became obsessed with what had gone wrong: the world order changed in unfavorable ways where anticipated breakthroughs failed to materialize; the United States was blocking Japan's path and "bashing" or "passing" it without appreciating its true contribution; and Japan's own system let it down as the bubble economy collapsed, the harmonious society lost its luster, and the political system fell into discord. Soon, many were obsessed with symbols of what was frustrating them while doing relatively little to address the real causes. South Korea's confidence in the mid-1990s was also at a high. If the shadow of the first nuclear crisis with North Korea dulled the satisfaction and then the Asian financial crisis caused a letdown, the Sunshine Policy lifted hopes to a new peak. As in the case of Japan, much of the blame was put on the United States for "causing" the nuclear crisis and then not responding well, but there was also recognition of a precarious regional order that could be troubling for the country's future and of problems in the society and its values. Unlike Japan in 1993, where only a makeshift coalition took power temporarily, South Korea saw a transfer of power to political forces with clashing views on national identity. Finally, in China after confidence appeared to be building to a peak in 2008, the world financial crisis stimulated even more intense Chinese arrogance by 2010. Acting in accord with rising confidence, China alienated other states and aroused a backlash that led Internet nationalists, military spokesmen, and others to grow even more vociferous.

Spikes in national identity are prone to turn into troughs of disappointment linked to resentment of other countries. Rather than calling into question the inflated objectives that had contributed to excess hopes or soberly analyzing the conditions that kept their hopes from being realized, a tendency exists to blame others, especially the United States, for spoiling one's chances. In the period 1989–92, Japan hesitated to give its ally credit for ending the Cold War, while criticizing Washington for "Japan passing" by ignoring the issue of four islands instead of pressuring Moscow to yield to Tokyo's demands and also for "Japan bashing" by blaming it for economic protectionism and a "free-rider" approach to international security, including not sending troops to the Persian Gulf War despite large cash contributions. In 2002–4, South Korea turned even more strongly against the United States after national emotions had been aroused during the World Cup and then a divisive presidential election campaign. The Bush "axis of evil" approach to North Korea was a form of "Korea passing," while repeated criticism of Seoul's posture toward Pyongyang could be construed as "Korea bashing." With China unable to realize world approbation from the Olympics, as it relied on censorship and crackdowns on possible dissent, its leaders found it convenient to channel nationalism toward the recurrent message of the world, led by the United States, trying to slow China's rise through accusations to deny it the fruits of its success. Talk of "China bashing" has accompanied the letdown from 2010.

Each East Asian state harbors resentment over an unjust international order and is still struggling to adjust the current order without having a clear blueprint of what may be sought. In the 1890s and 1900s, Japan resented unequal treaties and insisted on changing the regional order. In the 1920s and 1930s, it repudiated unjust imperialism and racism as if it could liberate Asia without intensifying these evils. Recent resentment centered on unjust use of the "history card" to bash it, but that is being superseded by other concerns over China.

China has cultivated a worldview based on humiliation due to imperialism, hegemonism, and now supposed containment. It justifies the 1949 Revolution and most Maoist foreign policy as a response to provocations, and the 1989 brutal suppression of demonstrators is also explained in this enduring context. Two decades later, this mindset remains strongly embedded as the Chinese charge that other states oppose their country's rise. Even in South Korea, there is ample evidence of resentment that the world gave its approval to Japan's annexation of their country, then to the division of the country, and recently to balance-of-power maneuvering that holds the peninsula hostage.

Many do not perceive a supportive regional order for reunification or even for avoidance of another state seeking regional dominance. Exaggerated charges of an unjust past are fueling fears of an unjust future.

The East Asian nations have a sense of entitlement and of history being interrupted with expectations that things will change. In this process, their state will regain a morally superior status, independent in important respects from the international system. These unrealistic expectations leave national identities skewed. Although room exists for pragmatic diplomacy setting aside identity concerns for a time, the intensity of identity ensures that it will reassert its impact. China's history was interrupted in the mid–nineteenth century, Japan's in 1945, and Korea's in 1945, and each nation is still recovering. This reasoning undermines reassessment of national identity on the basis of existing conditions. It leads to a misplaced dichotomy between national and Western ways of thinking, obscures the need to look objectively at the nature of past identity, and delays readjusting the identity to reflect the transformation of Asia and the world. Approaching it without a comparative, regional analysis contributes to misjudgments about identity, delaying any sense that a "normal" state has been reached—or even a strategy to move in that direction.

In this book, we concentrate on top-down identities constructed with state input and reflected in publications. This can obstruct awareness of alternative views, such as those emerging in South Korea before democratization and, especially, in China, where tight censorship keeps a lid on open expression of views inconsistent with the official line. Despite these limitations, we still find merit in focusing on East Asian state-centered narratives. Such narratives predominate in the media and provide insight into policy decisions. National identities are contested in ongoing political struggles, but they are also constructed with intensive input by current political leaders, especially in China.

Chapter 1

Japanese National Identity: A Six-Dimensional Analysis

Gilbert Rozman

Japan's much-discussed but still narrowly understood national identity underlies deep-seated problems between Japan and its various neighbors, casts a shadow on U.S.-Japanese trust, and leaves Japan adrift in forging a consensus on foreign policy and even domestic reform. Labeling the culprit "historical memory" begs the question of how that fits into the broader matter of identity. Approaching the matter narrowly in terms of one or another visible identity strand threatens to lead one back to the unsatisfactory, simplistic explanations of Japan that long were popular. Instead, a concentrated examination of how multiple dimensions combine in shaping identity reveals Japan at an identity crossroads.

Observers have long been confident that they know what Japan's national identity is. Because it is an unusually homogeneous nation that for more than half a century was under the dominance of one political party and that is dependent on a superpower ally that would not betray its trust, the image prevailed that its national identity was secure.

Compared with its neighbors China and South Korea, it loomed as a bastion of stability. A stable democracy, it was inured to political shocks. It was resistant to large-scale immigration or company take-overs, and its vulnerability to cultural or economic shocks was limited. Tethered to the U.S. alliance, Japan was also deemed immune to foreign policy shocks, apart from bouts of seeing itself as being bashed or passed over by the United States. Yet such assumptions failed to antici-pate challenges to what its identity really is. Recent debates inside Japan reveal signs of deeper change.

Treatment of the current transfiguration of Japan's identity centers on an ideological clash in late 2008, the election impact of late 2009, the external shocks in 2010, and the March 11 earthquake–tsunami–nuclear radiation catastrophe of 2011. Having been stunned by the triple shock of President George W. Bush's decision to remove North Korea from the list of terror-sponsoring states, the United States–originated global financial meltdown, and Barack Obama's victory, the forces in Japan pressing for a stronger national identity had to regroup. They had no choice but to stress political identity after cultural and economic iden-tity lost vitality. Moreover, they aimed to boost macro-level state iden-tity, given the reduced visibility of other levels of identity on the domestic ladder. In the face of new currents in support of Asianism and interna-tionalism, many were more prepared to cast doubt on U.S. ties even as they withdrew into an insular worldview. The victory of the Democratic Party of Japan (DPJ) over the Liberal Democratic Party (LDP) in September 2009 challenged Japan's association with the United States in three respects. First, the DPJ leaders criticized the U.S. model of capital-ism both as the cause of the global financial crisis starting in 2008 and as unsuitable to the traditions of community and harmony in Japan (with its paternalistic firms and state policies standing against mass lay-offs and cutthroat competition). Second, these leaders pressed for more equal alliance relations, reflected in resistance to U.S. calls for military base realignment and maritime logistical support and insistence on more independent foreign policies. Third, they gave priority to Asian region-alism, breathing new life into efforts to forge an East Asian Community exclusive of the United States and tamping down revisionist challenges to Asian neighbors. Yet, as much as these moves reasserted some long-standing national identity ideals left in the shadows since Koizumi's leadership, they showed little regard for finding workable solutions to many urgent problems Japan faced at home and abroad.

In 2010 the DPJ leaders Prime Minister Hatoyama Yukio and "shadow shogun" Ozawa Ichiro were replaced. The former challenged the United States on the Futenma base relocation, casting doubt on the alliance at a time Japanese were growing more anxious about China's assertiveness. The latter fell over corruption charges, but his focus on achieving a breakthrough with China following his earlier championing of a "normal" Japan reflected idealism about an East Asian community too. Though the LDP had failed to provide clarity about national identity—wavering from Abe Shinzo's "beautiful Japan" as a revisionist blueprint focused on history and the Constitution to Fukuda Yasuo's quiet effort to sustain both alliance and Asianist tendencies— the DPJ effort hit an impasse. The national identity exploration of the past quarter century, reflecting a spike in pride and then a loss of confidence, appeared to be subsiding in favor of awareness of China's challenge and the importance of the U.S. alliance and association with universal values.

In the spring of 2011, in the aftermath of the 3/11 disaster, Japan was reeling from the most serious blow to its well-being and pride suffered since 1945. Parts of the Tohoku region were left in shambles, as the country fell back into recession and shattered families struggled to regroup. A further blow was struck against the political system, which was exposed as culpable, and the waning identity of a nation proud of its administrative efficiency. Although outside support, led by the United States with its military assistance, reassured the Japanese that they were not alone, their growing sense of vulnerability, both internally and externally, cast a shadow on hopes for a heavily indebted state to regain its momentum.

The six-dimensional approach enables one to delve more deeply into this identity crossroads, by explaining the context of how these dimensions have evolved and showing their current situation. Ideology is not absent, despite postwar revulsion against its impact. The temporal dimension remains a strong preoccupation, although school curricula hint at historical amnesia for the critical prewar and war years. The three types of sectoral identity have alternated in intriguing fashion—with political identity increasingly superseding cultural and economic identity as the focus. If both the vertical and horizontal dimensions attract keen attention, due to uncertainty over Japan's domestic restructuring and international relations, they still require greater clarification. Shifts in the intensity of Japanese national identity must also be assessed to complete the application of this six-dimensional framework to circumstances that have changed greatly during the past two decades.

The Ideological Dimension

Modern nationalism arose in the nineteenth century, but its premodern roots were unusual, as were the speed and character of its intensification at the end of the century. If many analysts have identified the distinctive features of Tokugawa society whereas others have clarified the buildup of national identity in the Meiji Era, the connections between the two warrant special attention in accord with a clear framework of analysis. Assessing the ideological dimension, one can observe that the thrust of competition among lords and the samurai retainer bands left no opening for serious challenges to rightist thought focused on strict hierarchy, unlimited authority as long as it accepted the collective rules of a fixed order, and statist assumptions of collective sacrifice for the common good. After decades of alarm and then reform, a new ideology gained dominance in the Meiji Era, resisting the spread of socialism as its looming rival after Western centrist ideas had also won support. The conservative side proved unable to resist militaristic expansionism and suppression, making centrist opposition more difficult in the 1930s and 1940s. Defeat in 1945 and the U.S. occupation opened the door to it, but sudden progressive empowerment coupled with persistent conservative nostalgia left centrist thinking without sufficient momentum.

Throughout the Cold War, conservatives in power and progressives dominant in the media, cultural circles, and academia stood in uneasy equilibrium. The former repulsed the naive idealism of a foreign policy that broke with the U.S. alliance, while the latter was able to block revisionist ambitions that would have shocked Asians and Westerners alike. Centrist thinking did not make much headway from either side, although realism on the right accepted U.S. leadership as a stabilizing force and idealism on the left lent some support to the United States–led international community and to ways to build on normalization of relations with China. The persistence of this odd balancing act gave the Japanese the impression that no ideological choice was necessary, postponing consideration of centrist thinking.

Under the umbrella of the Yoshida Doctrine, with its pragmatic economic priorities, patriotic symbols were eschewed. But two conflicting ideologies loomed in the background, vetoing political consensus on a centrist worldview. The right looked ahead to the left's weakening and to rising Japanese economic power in order to bring into the open its true, revisionist agenda, while the left stuck to its ideology rather than seek more support by moving to the center. After the Cold War, the right was emboldened as the left, after a brief respite in 1993–95, lost ground without giving way to a centrist ideology in an opposition party that papered over wide differences through vague slogans.

Japan lacks an explicit ideology. It has incompletely embraced universal values despite being wedded to democracy. It had found Asian values appealing until China was seen to be hijacking them on behalf of an agenda that would marginalize Japan. The right and left wings have kept tugging in opposite directions; the former wielding veto power in the LDP, and the latter relying on a residue of pacifist idealism that was difficult to dislodge. Each side keeps failing to inspire support as prime ministers see their popularity plummet soon after taking office. Without a renewed centrist ideology, Japan faces a lingering vacuum.

The ideological dimension could be better balanced by marginalizing the extreme right and left through a political realignment. Centrist thinking lacks symbols to rally support, but the dual security and economic challenges facing the DPJ, along with the long-term demographic alarm of a shrinking, aging population, may finally galvanize public opinion behind support for U.S. leadership in a closer alliance and a common agenda of universal values. After sixty-five years of ideological lethargy, as advocates waited in vain for favorable conditions to materialize, today's sobering realities offer the best chance for a centrist consensus. Many acknowledge the urgency, warning that the fate of the nation is at stake. A sense of crisis has aroused Japanese to concerted action before. The situation in the 2010s is also dire.[1] In comparing China's new arrogance with Japan's past arrogance, the Japanese are focusing on an identity challenge in a more mature manner with fewer of the previous illusions.[2] Yet ideological change is not easy, and neither the DPJ nor LDP is leading the way.

The 3/11 cataclysm showed the irrelevance of the ideological stands of both the right, which had glorified an irresponsible state with historical revisionism in mind, and the left, which looked helpless in leading the response after long being sidetracked by its own history narrative. If the discipline and determination of the Japanese people kept order and reconstruction going well, political leaders offered no vision to rekindle confidence. There was a vacuum that previous ideological thinking could not fill, raising the prospect that a more centrist leader might arise.

The Temporal Dimension

Comparing crises of identity in Germany after 1945, Japan after 1945, and Russia after 1991, former UN ambassador Owada Hisashi argues that the trauma was greatest in Japan because its past identity was most negated. If Nazism was deemed an aberration of barely one decade in Germany and Communism might have represented a failure of seven decades if many Russians had not continued to find merit in at least portions of their history, Owada argues that the Japanese were different because they could not separate the perpetrators of the wars from the people as a whole and the war period from the eighty years of modern history—including the achievements of modernization—that form the core of their history. Coupled with the "mini cold war" that followed within Japan between progressives and conservatives and the slow reconciliation with its Asian neighbors, finding a national consensus was impossible. Forthright national debate and textbook accounts were set aside in what Owada calls this "virtual reality" and "self-contained "psychological cocoon." A mercantilist state encouraged "townsmen" values rather than the "samurai" values that had been renounced, reversing the imbalance in the Tokugawa era. This narrow approach to values left little room for embracing a broad internationalist identity, not focused on the "cult of pacifism," which was little more than a rejection of responsible thinking about the conditions of the world. Thus, Owada treats the end of the Cold War as a shock, due to new security threats, new foreign pressures, and, not least of all, a prevailing mindset woefully unprepared for the openness of globalization.[3]

Views of Japanese history through the Meiji period shifted from one extreme to the other. Led by progressives, writers during the early postwar era traced the blame for militarism back through history, uncovering a negative dynamic that was ameliorated only by popular culture, suggesting *minzoku* (ethnic nationalism). As this negativism lost force, conservatives responded with an opposite take on history: redeeming pride in the samurai ethic of "bushido," glorifying the Meiji Era for both its modernizing reforms and its foreign policy successes including victory in two wars, and conjuring up Nihonjinron (belief in an exceptional Japanese cultural identity) as a tribute to the Japanese people that stressed loyalty, harmony, and community (sharing glorification of *minzoku* but rejecting the progressive *minshu,* or mass theme centered on resistance and rebellion). Both sides found cause for cultural pride, but the conservatives linked it more persuasively to new economic success and gained an edge.

At the core of national identity confusion is the virtual silence for half a century about the most important decisions affecting Japan's fate: the attack on Pearl Harbor, the dropping of atomic bombs and decision to surrender, the Tokyo Tribunal, and the San Francisco Peace Treaty.[4] Leftists did not provide a convincing narrative, ignoring realist arguments rather than refuting them. Rightists hesitated to raise such issues, biding their time until the nation became more receptive and the international environment grew more favorable. Even as many on the right are growing bolder, others fear that the effect of this debate will be divisive at home and provocative abroad. An inability to reach a consensus on the period up to 1945 casts a dark shadow on efforts to clarify Japan's national identity. The rightist push for historical vindication hangs as a millstone around Japan's neck, and stands in the way of a centrist national identity and of trust in the United States and South Korea.

Instead of taking pride in the postwar era, both conservatives and progressives see it as a transitional period toward something much more desirable. Today, some even see it as an unfortunate blot on Japan's past, starting with criticism of the way Japan's defeat was handled. Ito Kenichi, president of the Japan Forum on International Relations, argues that "straight acceptance of decisions of the Tokyo War Crime Trials caused the Japanese to lose not only the identity they had embraced but their pride as well," as did the decision to entrust security to a foreign power to concentrate on pursuit of economic prosperity.[5] This sense of shame instead of pride helps to turn the search for political national identity back to the pre-1945 era, adding to pressure to reinterpret it positively as a prerequisite for a "normal" Japan. This pressure became a driving force as the next transition suddenly began in the 1990s, when the Japanese started to reopen sensitive questions about history.

In spite of contradictory opinions from "defeatist progressives" and "romanticist Asianists," statist thinking prevailed and became the rallying cry of those pressing for a "normal Japan." They saw the "postwar system" as enduring after the end of the Cold War and standing squarely in the path of state building. Some sort of "unnatural entity" had emerged, failing to defend sovereignty, acceding to the collapse of the traditional cultural order and a failure to ensure its transmission to future generations, and leaving a vacuum for antistate ideas to spread linked to internationalism.[6] While standing up to China and others who play the "history card" or are mired in territorial disputes with Japan is the usual focus of such complaints, the long-term target for many keen on state building is the United States. Rather than speaking out about key moments in bilateral ties, the Japanese have felt stifled. For some, the list of grievances is irksome, but not serious enough to cast doubt on the important values and interests shared by two long-standing allies. But for any who take the loss of state normalcy seriously, fundamental problems can only be faced by raising their most sensitive concerns with the United States. Compounding the trouble is a spreading impression that U.S. foreign policy takes Japan for granted, whether in dealing with the final years of the Soviet Union, the past two decades of managing China's rise, or the 2006–8 negotiations with North Korea. On the most critical foreign policy matters, the Japanese were distracted by symbolic images of America "passing" Japan and Japan's dependency on America. The crises in 2010, however, decisively turned attention elsewhere, improving trust in Japan's sole ally. So too did the massive U.S. support after the 3/11 disaster.

The post–Cold War era offered tantalizing glimpses of breakthroughs in national identity, but these were increasingly submerged in bitter disappointments. Japan's economic and political identity suffer from unexpected failures, and its cultural identity has lost much of its appeal. The search for new clarity about identity has led to dead ends, as those who favor revisionism centered on the war (*sensoron*) have won a following but no prospect of political consensus and those who favor the idealism of the East Asian community have found a region in turmoil under China's unwelcome quest for leadership. To salvage this era, the Japanese need to avoid extremes in dealing with pre-1868 and pre-1945 history, deny revisionists a chance to damage foreign relations, and upgrade their image of the postwar achievements and the continuities between that period and the post–Cold War decades. Embracing a United

States–led international community more wholeheartedly than was the case during the Cold War, with realistic assessments of threats and opportunities, is critical to centering temporal identity.

The Sectoral Dimension

In the sectoral dimension, one finds deep roots of economic identity in mercantilism at the domain level, bolstered by resistance to foreign economic penetration; of cultural identity in bushido ethics and the townsmen worldview rising in their shadow; and of political identity in the mix of loyalty and honor associated with Japanese feudalism. All these forces that gained ground in the prewar era and reached a new peak in the 1980s were well entrenched on the eve of the country's forced opening. The transformation from Tokugawa to Meiji has long been recognized as one of the remarkable periods in Japanese history.[7] As in the earlier response to China and the later response to the United States starting in 1945, it revealed exceptional adaptability through cultural borrowing. Rather than allow confidence in cultural superiority to block borrowing that elsewhere was deemed threatening to the very core of the value system, the Japanese opened their cultural system as well as their political and social structure. The Meiji slogan of *bunmei kaika* (civilization and enlightenment) parallels the postwar emphasis on "democracy" not just as a political mechanism but also as testament to an engrained identity capable of absorbing a torrent of incoming values. This suggests a duality of a flexible statist identity (*kokutai,* the individual exists for the state/emperor) capable of turning from ultranationalist aims to deep dependency, and an embedded cultural identity insistent on uniqueness amid rapid outside borrowing.

Extreme identity claims prevailed in the years of war and expansionism. Success in economic growth and political power reinforced arrogance about cultural superiority through a unique hierarchy of loyalty to emperor, community, and family. This spike in national identity assertiveness led to a backlash after Japan's unconditional surrender and occupation, but there was a residue of pride invoked in the troubled early postwar period. Japanese culture would lead to economic success and, eventually, to a political comeback.

In the 1950s, identity focused not only on shared themes of a global community, notably democracy, but also on new sources of pride.

Progressives sought a pacifist champion with a nuclear allergy, but they were eclipsed by claims resonant with cultural tenets about the distinct and superior nature of Japan, especially linked to a rejection of the individualism and rampant competition seen in the United States. Given the Yoshida Doctrine's focus on economic growth while relying on the U.S. alliance and keeping a low political profile, new claims centered on economic nationalism. Bai Gao describes how even in 1946–49, when economic survival was the priority, the state assumed leadership over resources with the priority production program, appealed to all to bear up under hardship, and soon was stressing accelerated economic recovery or growth as the key to national security. Gao distinguishes the fragmented nationalism of the 1950s from the unified nationalism that followed. Sharp political divisions and a weak sense of Japan's global role yielded, under conditions of high growth, to a conservative consensus on how to ascend the world order in a United States–dominated system.[8] Progressives, too, came to accept economic nationalism.

National identity was intensifying and reconstituting into a triangular combination. In the 1950s, against the backdrop of a fierce battle over the U.S. security treaty during the peak of the Cold War, the media, academic, and cultural elite leaned to the left and to some variant of Japan's unique role as an opponent of nuclear weapons and a defeated power that had learned the lessons of war. If the political right held power and disagreed, it couched its arguments less on challenging the merits of the Constitution renouncing war or of a passive foreign policy than as a plea to proceed in stages under the protective wing of the United States, with attendant economic benefits and space to boost economic identity. Political identity had slipped sharply after past nationalism was blamed for the unconditional surrender and devastating war. Cultural identity also was subject to intense questioning, in light of leftist narratives tracing the failure far back in history to cultural as well as political causes. Economic identity filled much of the slack, reinvigorating the urgency of sacrifice. The pacifist tendencies that many Japanese blame for the nation's suppressed political identity served to foster a victim consciousness, which was useful even to conservatives to keep some distance from the United States and to assist in rebuilding political identity.[9]

Conservatives eyed a strategy to move gradually toward reconstituting "normal" national identity by first rebuilding confidence in a state able to foster public order and gain trust in new, democratic ways—but, above all, to champion economic growth that would draw on distinct national institutions and attitudes while fending off cultural borrowing that could undercut confidence in Japan's distinctiveness. Only later would political identity emerge as the focus of nationalism, corresponding to changes in the global balance of power as Japan gained more leverage in Asia and on the United States. In the 1970s, such thinking intensified, as foreign policy in Asia revealed economic clout being used for political and cultural objectives. Pacifism dismissive of Japan's pre-1945 history had yielded to a passive façade, behind which the search had begun for an alternative to postwar U.S. modernization thinking and its Asian strategy, and finally to active support of the alliance that was really aimed at gradual Asianism without any open challenge to internationalism. In the late 1980s, Japan's "economic superpower" identity reached its peak and its cultural identity was broadly advertised to the world, and talk turned to boosting its political identity, including a breakthrough in its international relations.[10]

Those Japanese who may be apathetic on matters of state security are inclined to accept assumptions of cultural distinctiveness. Well before the arrival of Perry's black ships, the study of Japan's classical literature had embraced *kokugaku* (a new emphasis on traditional Japanese thinking), with distancing from Chinese culture and mythical assertions having xenophobic features. Starting in the 1890s, this claim to a special morality arose in reference to bushido or to an original spirit (Yamato damashii) that persisted through a millennium of Chinese Confucian thought. Postwar substitutes were found to keep alive cultural separateness, even if their nationalist character may not have been highlighted for a time. In the 1960s and the 1970s, what some viewed as atavistic traits that would fade away with modernization were now widely recognized as vital legacies reinforcing cultural distinctiveness. Indeed, many thinkers searched for new concepts to capture the essence of this cultural uniqueness, always with U.S. society as at least an implicit contrast, treating them not just as inherently different but also as positive features of Japan's distinctive modernization, and thus as fully compatible with the new era and with buttressing an identity capable of warding off Western cultural influences. They noted the rejection of individualism (*amae*, groupism, vertical society, collective decisionmaking), social entities with a powerful hold over the individual and a direct link to the state (enterprise paternalism, school group bonding, *ie*, family solidarity), and appeals to homogeneity (middle mass society; Japan, Inc.). The thrust of cultural identity is exceptionalism.[11]

Although many conservatives such as Kishi Nobosuke found economic identity inadequate in the struggle with progressive views of Japanese history propagated through the schools, and many progressives faulted it for leaving dependency on the United States intact, a consensus formed around the notion of corporatism with lifetime employment, seniority wages, and firm-based unions as the basis for a nonindividualist, community-centered economic system. Economic nationalism tied to pride in a distinct social system gained legitimacy as it stressed bringing management and workers together on a path to relatively equal distribution and symbolic community.[12] In turn, as the emphasis on social uniqueness grew, talk of cultural national identity, or Nihonjinron, also intensified.[13] Nihonjinron is not merely a set of abstract ideas and texts about how Japanese should accord with traditions, but also assertions about how people act in daily life. It holds that Japanese are homogeneous and unique, and that foreigners should be excluded in a variety of ways. Even if many had doubts about this appeal to purity, even at its prime in the 1980s, the lingering suspicions about patriotism left this sort of cultural nationalism as the easiest outlet for national identity.[14]

Some Japanese bemoaned the weakness of political identity, fixating on symbols such as the absence of the national anthem and flag in many school ceremonies and continuing opposition by the teachers' union to them. Although political identity had grown, especially under Nakasone Yasuhiro, it still seemed hamstrung by leftist politicians, media, and cultural figures. Yet economic identity had become intense, driven by the national preoccupation with so-called Japan bashing by America, and the nation's cultural identity was at its postwar peak, contributing to a spike in overall identity.

In the 1990s, the Japanese lost hope of reinforcing cultural superiority as the root of economic success. As late as 1995, former prime minister Takeshita Noboru tried futilely to revive this claim, citing quantitative measures of books published, number of museums and libraries, and educational fever.[15] Even more pervasive had been claims of qualitative superiority, reflected in lower crime rates, less social deviance of other types, greater equality, and pride in the conformity of Japanese citizens to the national ideal. Yet, as Nihonjinron books disappeared, bookstores shifted to volumes of self-criticism for insufficient creativity in education, excessive conformity that hampered entrepreneurship, and bureaucratic mindsets that mired the public in a maze of red tape. In place of claims to inherent superiority from traditional thinking, the family system, and the role of the state in reinforcing group-oriented values, books alluded to defects in character that reduced the nation's prospects. If cultural pride began to emerge from the self-flagellation in the late 1990s, the malaise lingered. Rightists insisted that Japan's civilization is distinct and demanded that morale education become mandatory. Fear of multiculturalism spread as calls rose for an increase in immigrant labor to counter demographic trends. Although further cultural opening was slower than in other highly modernized states, the guardians of the nation's cultural identity continued to bemoan the public's lack of cultural pride. The shift away from *minzoku* focused on homogeneity or uniqueness slowly gained ground.[16]

Economic identity only managed to revive briefly after the letdown in the 1990s. Koizumi's reforms targeted some special arrangements that kept Japan relatively closed and allowed vested interests to rely on the state's substantial role in the economy. He was vigorously opposed by conservative politicians, making some progress but unable to create an image of Japan in the age of the World Trade Organization as a country as open as others. This left a residue of the postwar economic identity claims intact even as interdependence with China pointed to its limitations. Similar to culture, it was no longer a driving force. In the downturn of 2009, confidence in Japan's economy suffered a new blow. If anger spread against the U.S. economic model, culminating in moves by the new DPJ administration to reassert a mix of economic and cultural identity, in 2010 attention was turning decisively to the threat to Japan from its economic dependency on China. When China stopped exports of rare earth metals to Japan in the fall of 2010, thoughts of a free trade agreement with that country receded.

Economic identity bolsters national identity when it lauds Japan's exceptional and unique capacity for rapid growth and the extraordinary foundation provided by Japanese society and the state's active guidance. Cultural identity serves political identity through such venerated terms as harmony, consensus, loyalty, and seniority. This occurs when the Japanese people are credited with long-standing traits that are distinctive and superior. By encouraging these value-laden ideals, the state—as it did through an amalgam of feudal and Confucian teachings in the seventeenth century, a mixture of German top-down and nativist appeals in the Meiji Era, and fresh linkage of American democratic and Japanese community-oriented principles in the post-war era—seeks to gain an edge in international competition. Although these three feats of social engineering differed greatly in the extent of ascriptive hierarchy, each minimized the development of autonomous social forces.[17]

In 2011, all three manifestations of sectoral identity are scarred by recent failures. Japan has no prospect of becoming the leader of Asia, as sought in its political identity; the model for a new era, as sought in its economic identity; and the admired champion of an unmatched cultural blend of East and West. It could recover sectoral pride as a partner to the United States in an Asia-Pacific community, a reform leader with an economy for a mature society resilient in the global top ranks, and a champion of universal values that is prepared for long-term competition with China across Asia. Lowering aspirations without undue sectoral claims and ethnic narrowness is the elusive path to balanced identity.[18] This may be easier in the aftermath of the 3/11 devastation because the Japanese people are no longer in doubt that old sectoral identities do not provide answers to urgent questions in an age of globalization.

The Vertical Dimension

Japanese collective identity, S. N. Eisenstadt argues, negates the universal values linked to transcendental visions. This identity is not couched in the framework of a universalistic civilization, but in relation to the unique spirituality of one nation.[19] Even when the old order appeared to collapse in 1945, a new national identity—centered on an autonomous civil society or international integration—arose only haltingly. Reconstructed social networks preempted universalistic principles.[20] This limited support for internationalism and for exploring themes that could expose the discrepancies between *tatemae* (a facade of views displayed in public) and *honne* (true beliefs often left unstated). Little room existed for intermediate levels to express themselves when mutual responsibility served as the method for maintaining order, while the shogunate repulsed linkages that might allow domains to form coalitions or townsmen or religious groups to pool their strength. Later, community controls were reinforced as Japan limited social instability from modern-ization. Hierarchical forms of social control found further vitality in the postwar era without stress on values separate from group identities.

Japanese elites responded to fear of the prolongation of the Warring States period in the late fifteenth century, the danger of social break-down and imperialist colonization of the 1850s to 1880s, and the shock of military defeat and occupation of the 1940s and 1950s with a re-newed emphasis on order. This included explicit attention to forging a moral blueprint centered on group solidarity, respect for hierarchy, and reliance on the state's authority in opposition to ideas deemed threaten-ing to national identity. If after 1945 no equivalent to existed to lord-vassal or emperor-subject relations that had made loyalty the first calling, adaptation of cultural identity filled the void. In place of bushi-do or *kokutai,* there were multiple themes of service and sacrifice in ways that buttressed the state and minimized the impact of civil society. Such themes as administrative guidance, paternalism, moral guidance, loyalty to one's organization, and collective solidarity served the iden-tity-forging crucible. The intensity of personalized loyalty—to the lord, the emperor, or a dominant group in one's life—eclipsed identity formed on the basis of alternative principles. This eased the way to borrow heavily from abroad, as it narrowed the prospects for forging identity with far different meaning centering on intermediate levels in society or on abstract principles. After the confusion of defeat and occupation, the search turned to restoring order through hierarchies centered on the state, bolstered by national identity in line with past verticality.

Eiko Ikegami identifies "honorific individualism" as the creed of the samurai, with lasting significance for national identity. Although "indi-vidualism" may not be the right term, the honor culture that she de-scribes, imbued with devotion to public concerns, fused with nationalism in an atmosphere of crisis. She sees restructured middle-range organi-zations as serving the needs of the state.[21] Preserving a culture of honor eased control refocused on collective identity in the service of the state. Values drawn from the samurai class were critical to modern identity. When a fierce catch-up orientation under a centralized state was added to this mix, the Japanese proved receptive to demands for highly intense cultural, economic, and political identity, reinforcing hierarchies linked to the past.

The culture conflict between the legacy of traditional Japan and Western imports was resolved in the 1870s in a manner that would not be sustainable.[22] Carol Gluck points to a mix of Confucianism and Shintoism aimed at national unity around *kokutai,* backed by the ideals of harmony, benevolence, loyalty, and mystical appeal to Yamato-dam-ashii, a supposed ancient spirit.[23] Obsessed with building state strength, leaders inculcated an intense national identity through the cult of the emperor. Identities, which had narrowly centered on loyalty to lords in the face of intense rivalry with other samurai bands, now focused on loyalty to the emperor to build a nation-state endangered by imperial-ism. A sense of urgency led to tilting the search for national identity along a narrow vector. Political identity was recast through the trium-phal response to the victory over Russia in 1905, skewing perceptions of Asianism in ways that led to imperialist views.[24] Cultural identity buttressed political identity and intensified along with it, especially in the 1930s, as strong economic identity was also boosted. As an imperi-alist power, Japan propagated its own particularist identity, despite claims to be acting in the interest of all Asians. It missed the growth of internationalism in parts of the West, for example, obsessing on the racist nature of U.S. immigration policies. This legacy did not disap-pear even with the shock of defeat in 1945.

Despite occupation reforms aimed at decentralization and individu-alism, postwar Japan fostered an identity of *uchi-soto* (in-groups vs. out-groups), emphasis on seniority, and a highly vertical organization of organizations and society. If tempered by group solidarity and con-sultation that restricted autocratic options, the result was still heavy bureaucratization, a preference for formal organizations, and limited room for individual and alternative group identities. The vertical di-mension was slow to change in the postwar period after taking shape with emphasis on company paternalism and school collectivities, but the end of the Cold War period exposed its shortcomings. Its impor-tance for identity was declining, but the void was not filled by interme-diate associations or international networks with strong potential for serving as a focus of identity.

Minzoku identity had been twisted to support a vertical set of com-munities, but Nihonjinron was accepted by only half the population in the late 1990s, while insistence on Japan as a separate civilization was giving ground to globalization.[25] Reconciliation with South Korea was important in this transformation. It was jump-started in 2010 with the joint shift away from illusions of Asianism and emphasis on shared challenges and values bolstered by the way the centennial of annexation was handled.[26] Right-wing opposition to Kan Naoto's apology, as if South Koreans still hated Japan, was now discounted.[27]

A mainstream view of national identity is reflected in a mid-2004 *Yomiuri shimbun* editorial. Noting that there would likely be no general elections in Japan during the next three years, it held that along with demonstrating how Japan pursues active membership in international society and uses its Self-Defense Forces for increased security, the biggest challenge it faces is to firm up the state with priority to drafting a new Constitution and forging a new national image (*kokkazo*).[28] The focus is on strengthening the state as vital to national identity. This remains the main theme of the vertical dimension, even as the DPJ leadership targets some negative state symbols and promises new power as well as benefits for the people and the localities. Only pursuing this rebalancing offers promise for bolstering the intermediate level, bringing much-needed change to vertical identity.

Clinging to vertical notions of identity won approval at a time when convergence with the United States was of concern, but in the post–Cold War era, China emerged as the most-feared competitor. As tensions mounted, some took comfort in predicting that China's disorderly society would descend into turmoil, slowing China's rise. Yet, as this theme survived, a new preoccupation was of a dangerous competitor organized in a threatening manner. Instead of highlighting Japan's vertical advantages over the United States, the Japanese were pointing to their horizontal differences with authoritarian China.[29] Given the weakness of prime ministers and the rapidity of their turnover, some saw a need to make Japan more vertical. But the lack of vigor in society was of greater concern. The transfer of power to the DPJ intensified criticism of bureaucratism. The Japanese paid more attention to perfecting democracy, searching for ways to overcome stultifying verticality for the sake of economic vitality and social vigor as well as for renewed pride in the face of an existential challenge, especially in the dire days of 2011.

The Horizontal Dimension

Resisting the arrival of the West, persecuting Christians, and censoring heterodox thought, Japan showed no interest in internationalism. There was little reflection on its defeat after aggression in Korea at the end of the sixteenth century or on the rising sense of rivalry with China during the next centuries, despite the absence of reasons for offense from that country. Asianism did not develop—unless one includes dreams to try again in Korea or to replace China at the regional helm. If, in the seventh century, a fledging state became embroiled in the jockeying for control among the three kingdoms sharing the peninsula and then was ejected when China intervened and Korea began a process of unification, the situation was very different in the 1590s, when Japan's unifier sent forces back to the continent for the first time in 900 years in a mission to displace China as the regional hegemon.

During the next 270 years, there was no repeat of this aggression, nor any threat from Korea or China; yet the legacy of defeat would, as in the case 350 years later, leave Japan to ponder how it might reassert itself on the Asian mainland if circumstances changed. It denied China's authority through its tributary system or the Sinocentric order. Separating itself by a self-imposed sentence of solitary confinement, Japan was alerted by the receding Dutch through a designated window to the outside world to the imperialism of Europe and was directly alarmed by the advancing Russians.[30] Xenophobia spread with no countervailing internationalism. When it could not be sustained in the 1860s and 1870s, an intense instrumental approach to borrowing, however rapid, did not really displace it.

After 1868, Japan debated Asianism with increasing expectations of leadership after accepting entrance into the international community with growing distortion of what this means for responsibility, especially in the struggle to avoid a repetition of World War I. Neither Asianism, which allowed room for Japanese colonialism, nor internationalism, which was treated as license for imperialism and war, eclipsed the 1930s and 1940s claims to uniqueness in opposition to the West. This distorted horizontal identity collapsed with Japan's unconditional surrender ending World War II, but the expedient acceptance of U.S. leadership and membership in a West struggling against Communism did not eliminate Japan's aspirations for Asianism.

In the 1960s, the accumulated success of Japan's economic miracle along with the more complex Cold War environment emboldened Japanese on both sides to envision a unique postwar Japanese model, not converging with the United States but gradually gaining an independent leadership position in Asia. War responsibility faded as a theme. Conservatives dropped it as soon as they could, and progressives were mired in abstract class history; preferring to focus on the peace movement that saw the Japanese as victims, helping to raise the issue of victimization that conservatives also embraced and twisted into a foreign policy instrument that targeted first of all the Soviet Union. The driving force in national identity debates had shifted from the left to the right, even as both sides remained capable of blocking the other's ambitions. With the United States mired down in Vietnam and more dependent on Japan, a broader identity at last seemed to be in reach.

With its entry into the United Nations and resumption of active diplomacy in Asia, Japan's postwar orientation settled on three circles: the U.S. dyad, an Asian community; and the international community, at times idealized as UN centered. For a time, all three seemed to be desirable choices, but former UN ambassador Kitaoka Shinkichi argues that in the 1960s a growing sense of Japan as an economic power accounts for the loss of interest in Asian commonalities.[31] Likewise, the UN novelty wore off amid increasing awareness that Japan could shape the international community in cooperation with the United States. Yet, even when Japan affirmed U.S. leadership as if no alternative Asian or international identity existed, it was looking beyond its ally for a fuller national identity. In retrospect, the Confucianization of the Tokugawa Era lacked a China-centered regional orientation, Meiji Westernization proved deficient in "revolutionary" ideals common in comparable social upheavals, and postwar Americanization did not lead to the idealization of important international values found elsewhere. The search continued for alternate identities.

The three decades since the 1980s offer proof of the continued rise in political national identity with emphasis on foreign policy. In the 1980s, Nakasone refocused Japan on historical pride, equality with the United States, and leadership in Asia. As the Cold War ended, this legacy left Japan's leaders awaiting a breakthrough as a political great power and one of the three poles of capitalism secure in its socioeconomic order and able to shape Asianism and a new internationalism—notions left vague. After stumbling through the first half of the 1990s, Japan edged toward a new vision, no longer hopeful about equality with the United States but ready to boost Asian regionalism at the same time as it reached an accommodation allowing room for Japanese revisionism in an era of globalization. In the Koizumi era, reinforced later by Abe Shinzo, defiant revisionism gained ground at the expense of Asian regionalism and with narrow support for U.S. unilateralism without approval for U.S. liberalism. Comparing these three decades to the preceding ones, one observes ambivalent alliance relations, intensified moves on Asianism, and the rising impact of revisionism. Along with the United States, China has become a force against which Japan defines itself. If, in the postwar era, gradually growing activism reflected the fact that Japan's prospects were continually rising, in the post–Cold War era, increased assertiveness has reflected worsening prospects and deepening frustration. Yet the drift toward revisionism was leading to a dead end, and the DPJ was inclined to drop it from the mix while proceeding more vigorously on the other fronts. That, too, failed.

Japan's national identity has been under siege. Instead of a breakthrough in political identity toward a "normal country," apologies became more frequent and options narrowed.[32] Prolonged stagnation confounded claims to a special economic identity. Yet, resistance to these trends intensified. Blaming shortcomings in political identity on the *Asahi shimbun,* teachers, and many academics was combined with accusations against the Foreign Ministry, compromising politicians, and foreign countries. Insisting on more positive media coverage and targeting those guilty of weakness paralleled harsh positions toward the countries seen as standing in Japan's way. Boosting political identity were such symbols as the Northern Territories in dispute with Russia, official development assistance to China, the island in dispute with South Korea, and the abductions issue with North Korea. One symbol was the Yasukuni Shrine, which Koizumi visited annually, despite the anger aroused in China and South Korea. However, strong advocates of political identity remained frustrated as symbols exceeded substance with no real achievements to cite and with public attention easily distracted by economic woes and political scandals. Not only had Abe fallen in unpopularity, Aso, who was inclined to revive revisionism after the bland interlude of Fukuda's tentative moves toward more Asianism, was humiliated in the 2009 elections. Conservative national identity lost ground, but the DPJ made little headway with a different orientation as it was soon obliged to adopt a centrist foreign policy.

Almost the entire burden of intensifying national identity rested with political identity refocused in one of three directions: (1) gaining permanent member status in the United Nations Security Council, as was energetically pursued in 2005; (2) promoting Asianism through the East Asian Community, which was given institutional status in 2005 by establishment of the annual East Asian Summit;[33] and (3) challenging the United States directly over history and values, which for the first time since 1945 were under serious discussion in conservative circles by 2007. Given the long odds against the UN change and the suspicion on the right against the East Asian Community, mounting frustration was leading toward an identity clash with an ally, even when few contemplated doing anything to undermine this indispensable alliance. The DPJ breathed new life into the pursuit of Asianism, but suspicions of China's rise dimmed its prospects. Within a year, a series of shocks had left China's image tarnished as a threat to international society and to sovereignty. Attention to China's brusque treatment of Liu Shaobo's Nobel Peace Prize reinforced this.[34]

As for the circles of foreign policy, conservatives seek more independence from the United States, but not by finding common ground with China. Because they are suspicious of the ideals of internationalism, they suggest that the time is ripe for Japan's "renaissance."[35] In one formulation, this means nothing less than preparing for danger in nearby areas similar to what was faced in the Meiji Era when Japan awakened to trouble. Such a reawakening is called the "new leave Asia argument" (*shintoaron*). With China arming rapidly, North Korea readying nuclear missiles to target Japan, and even South Korea humiliating Japan with its illegal occupation of an island, they perceive the need for a revival of political identity with parallels to the prewar era.[36] The buildup since the 1980s only whets their appetite for a much greater leap, in which cultural identity would advance as well. Given the weak political center, Japan's conservatives continue to drive the identity debate.

In response to the developments in the fall of 2008, one sees appeals for reducing Japan's dependence. One form this took was a rekindling of interest in Asianism led by Chinese–Japanese–South Korean triangular relations. This could be pursued by reducing the entire region's dependence on exports to the United States, by stepping up cooperation as a first step toward forging an East Asian Community, and by launching an unprecedented three-way strategic dialogue.[37] The "demise of Wall Street" added to the impression that an era was ending. Because the United States' global strategy had rested heavily on a financial system dating back to Reaganomics, its new economic distress along with its supposed inability to extract itself from the quagmire in Iraq and Afghanistan left the country unable to sustain its unipolarity.[38] For the Japanese left wing—much subdued after its decline in the

1990s—this opens the door to Asianism. Instead of past idealism about this, however, the main thrust is to seek it as a secondary circle in diplomacy, providing some balance but not replacing the priority of the U.S. alliance. Many writers suggest that a new age is dawning that is marked by a power shift to Asia, and they advise that Japan should increase its trust with China and welcome closer U.S. ties with the Asia-Pacific region.[39] However, often in this discussion one can detect a lack of internationalism linked to suspicions of U.S. unilateralism.

Asianism without internationalism may not offer the balance needed for an enduring national identity for our times. How could Japan refocus on international responsibility? At least three ideas draw one's attention. The first would be for Japan to use the rare moment of a reassessment of the international financial system to attempt again to become a bridge between the United States and Asia, especially China. A second idea would be for Japan to focus on the United Nations, expecting a revival of the 2005 efforts at Security Council reform and expansion to make its case to become a permanent member. And finally, there was the possibility that U.S. president Obama's vision could show the way to combining strong alliance ties with cooperation in internationalism. All these interpretations start with the calculation that this is a time, perhaps more than the end of the Cold War and any other point since the end of World War II, of a tectonic shift in the world power balance. With China and India rising, Russia reasserting its potential, and, above all, the United States losing some of its power, all these options were on the table. Noting that in 2005 the United States was not favorable to the overall reform plan and that Koizumi's visits to the Yasukuni Shrine led to opposition focused on Japan in Asia, Kitaoka Shinichi argues that these conditions have changed. With new ideas for how UN reform might occur and an appeal to Japanese to overcome their "psychology of a closed country," he makes the case for a stronger internationalist identity.[40]

Japan has found internationalism difficult to define or endorse. Repeatedly, U.S. presidents have refocused this concept after first making a strong pitch for a controversial approach, leaving Japan in the lurch. In the 1960s, the United States' stress was on backing the Vietnam War and Taiwan as the legitimate government of China, as it tried to steer Japan toward international responsibility. Yet the shock in 1971–72 from the sudden reversal on China and the United States' isolation and later defeat in Vietnam revealed this pitch to have led down a dead-end road. Similar to Richard Nixon, Ronald Reagan made a strong appeal to Japan for support on security, in this case in opposition to the Soviet Union, but before long Reagan had embraced Mikhail Gorbachev as his partner and had left Japan adrift. Then, in the period 2002–6, George W. Bush made North Korean and Iraq the primary measure of international responsibility, enlisting Japan in the battle against this "axis of evil" before botching the war in Iraq to the extent it became a symbol of rejection of internationalism and then making an abrupt about-face on North Korea, with Japan left isolated. Trouble in finding a clear focus for internationalism cannot be blamed primarily on U.S. mixed messages, and in 1972 there was good reason for Japan to be urged to normalize ties with China, in the late 1980s to find an accommodation with Moscow, and in 2007–8 to join a multilateral coalition ready to coordinate approaches to Pyongyang. Yet the one-sided U.S. interpretation of internationalism before these changes had wrenching implications.

A U.S. approach to values that redefines internationalism and Asian regionalism, offering leadership in connecting the two, is encouraging the Japanese to debate anew their interpretations of these themes. Instead of giving a green light to some conservatives who have attempted to use the U.S. alliance in opposition to reconciliation in Asia, U.S. officials are making the case for a Trans-Pacific Community. As China increasingly looms as the most important external influence and the international community is redefined as the foundation for regionalism, illusions based on the old horizontal triad are losing their appeal. China's national identity spike in 2010 drove Japan closer to both the United States and South Korea, reaching around Asia to Australia, India, and elsewhere.

The Intensity Dimension

One question that confounds observers is how intensely do the Japanese really care about their national identity. In the 1950s, the answer seemed to be very intensely, as many on the political left searched back in the nation's history for features of identity that set the country on the wrong course. By the 1970s, a different response prevailed, as apathetic and economically obsessed images indicated extraordinary disinterest in national identity. Yet the pattern one observes is gradually building pursuit of satisfaction through pride in identity. Looking back as far as the 1980s, Kitaoka Shinichi argues that the Japanese have become obsessed with defining their nation's identity.[41] Confusion over the degree of interest may be due to the multiple layers present, which require differentiation. If one focuses on *tatemae,* we may miss the force of *honne.* If one concentrates on political identity, one may overlook the impact of economic or cultural identity. Combining all these effects, one can conclude that national identity in the 1950s or 1990s did not sink as low as some contended. An upward trend in identity intensity reached a peak in the 1980s, and after the Cold War the continued rise in political identity may have compensated for the decline in economic and cultural identity that was nowhere as great as some have suggested.

Although many assumed that the United States had transformed Japan during the postwar Occupation in far-reaching ways, some changes remained superficial. Because of the eagerness of Japan's officials to foster an image of *tatemae* in the midst of conflicting efforts by the progressives, it became difficult to discern what Japan's national identity was. Japanese officials appeared positive about the new Constitution, the Tokyo Tribunal, and the San Francisco Peace Treaty, but their response can be understood as a kind of *tatemae,* as many sought solace elsewhere. Although the emperor had been removed from the political arena, preservation of his position made it easier to sustain cultural national identity. Continuity in the bureaucracy and its dominant role in rebuilding the country, as well as the effects of the "reverse course" toward those who had at first been purged by the Occupation, left a basis for political national identity. This was made easier because the Japanese managed to postpone any official debate over history or need to revisit past Asian policies. With economic identity forging ahead, there was no vacuum in identity.

If greater uncertainties spiral around Japanese national identity than at any time since the aftermath of the defeat in 1945, that is not the same as having a shaky belief or low intensity of identity. The Japanese maintain an abiding sense of national identity—cultural, economic, and political. If cultural nationalism fell sharply in the 1870s and again from 1945 through the 1950s, a buildup of *kokugaku* in the late Tokugawa Era and the extravagant claims about Japan's cultural superiority up to 1945 left legacies that could not be eliminated quickly. The fact that from the 1890s there was a big rise in cultural nationalism and then in the 1970s and 1980s Nihonjinron spread widely indicate that only temporary respites occur, as after the end of the Cold War.[42] Yet it is unlikely that this type of identity can regain a leading role in boosting pride. The global financial crisis of late 2008 demonstrates the high levels of interdependence that exist, minimizing the chance that economic pride will again become a driving force. The burden rests more on political identity, focusing on the United States and Asianism, reassessing history and reflecting current vulnerability.

Also, the rigid, orthodox nature of the rules of political life meant that repeating the *tatemae* of adherence could not be avoided, even as divergent *honne* intentions arose, because there were no venues for exploring in any honesty or depth possible linkages in national identity formation. Old habits of concealing *honne* and repeating *tatemae* as if they stand alone are only slowly receding. They have led to rapid changes in identity images in the postwar era as a sign of variability in *tatemae.* Conservatives are only now losing past reticence about raising their grievances toward the United States. Identities can still be flexibly detached from overriding principles because the Japanese are accustomed to accept dualistic combinations such as *uchi-soto* and *honne-tatemae,* which are interdependent and not mutually exclusive. This is influenced by the tendency to blur religious boundaries and to avoid abstract principles.[43] By bringing *honne* more into the open, the Japanese can reshape debates about national identity and make more balanced choices.

Conclusion

There are many signs that Japanese national identity is at a crossroads. The members of the LDP and DPJ have each tried their hand at realizing an ideological goal and have failed, exposing illusions in their thinking. In the temporal dimension, the push to find more merit in the war era by overturning views that were enshrined in findings in the early postwar period is still noteworthy, but the urgency of strengthening the U.S. alliance preempts that. Even if the need to find more pride in the Cold War era is not likely to be addressed soon, there is no serious alternative. Disappointment over the post–Cold War era is bound to intensify. The best prospect in the sectoral dimension is to embrace universal values as part of a shift in cultural orientation and a refocusing of political identity on the Asia-Pacific community, rather than on a narrow Japanese political resurgence. The vertical dimension is vital in the reforms required for making Japan more competitive and politics more stable, but its reorganization may be most difficult, given long-venerated thinking. In contrast, a shift in the horizontal dimension would appear easiest in the shadow of China's assertive rise. If national identity spiked excessively in the 1980s and then became mired in a conflicting tug-of-war in the next two decades without the same intensity, new clarity coupled with a rise in intensity less volatile than in the 1980s could offer reassurance of a "normal Japan."

Reviewing the various dimensions, one finds gaping imbalances in the middle. The political center is weak, a lack of pride in the postwar era skews discussions of identity to the prewar era, economic identity is not checking political and cultural identity, the social ladder is weak at the intermediate level, Asianism has failed to develop as a balance to narrow the manipulation of U.S. ties and a basis for international thinking, and an artificial dichotomy of *honne* and *tatemae* is not tempered by forthright inquiries into the links between them. These imbalances pose problems not only for those Japanese interested in setting a clearer direction for their country but also for Americans and others concerned with closer cooperation and trust between allies in order to advance a regional order favorable to stability and to the values that can promote shared ideals globally.

Identity change is a gradual, complex process. If, in both 1945 and 1990, observers were prone to exaggerate imminent changes in Japan, one should avoid a new round of heady expectations. Yet, in contrast to embracing defeat and anticipating victory, the current mood is less conducive to grasping for illusions. Both vertical and horizontal dimensions are aligned for setting aside recent unrealizable aspirations. With eyes fixed on China forcing Japan's hand and with the intermediate sector struggling against bureaucratic dictates, however, the weight of past national identity thinking will not easily realign the ideological divides, temporal obsessions, and sectoral preferences that remain embedded in Japanese minds.

The 3/11 trauma shattered Japan's illusions about national identity beyond anything seen since 1945. It marked the nadir of a series of shocks over two decades, causing a loss of faith in Japan that neither conservative nor progressive ideologues could obscure. The Japanese were left suspicious of temporal identity claims to pride about the past, unable to focus on horizontal identity bashing by others, and doubtful of the benefits of a vertical identity that did not point the country in a new direction. The intensity of national identity sank to a low likely unseen in many decades.

Sectoral national identity stood in the crosshairs after 3/11. Whereas a decade earlier, the September 11, 2001, terrorist attacks had boosted the United States' sectoral (political and cultural) identity, the chain reaction as Japan's nuclear reactors shut down and electricity shortfalls drove production levels downward resulted in a shock to the nation's economic identity beyond that of losing the number-two global gross national product ranking to China in 2010. The entire edifice of a harmonious society suited to economic efficiency was crumbling. And Japan's cultural identity also suffered. Not only were its people insular and averse to globalization—for example, in study abroad, their culture was blamed for the alienation of young people and a demographic rut. Yet the severest malaise centered on political national identity. The political system was broken.

Notes

1. Yabunaka Mitoji, *Kokka no meiun* (Tokyo: Shinchosha, 2010); Sato Masaru, *Nihon shakai o doo kyokasuru ka?* (Tokyo: NHK Books, 2008).

2. *Nihon keizai shimbun,* October 16, 2010, p. 17.

3. Owada Hisashi, "In Search of a New National Identity: An Analysis of the National Psyche of Post-war Japan," in *A New Japan for the Twenty-First Century: An Inside Overview of Current Fundamental Changes and Problems,* edited by Rien T. Segers (Oxford: Routledge, 2008), 234–49.

4. Kazuhiko Togo, "Japan's Historical Memory toward the United States," and Gilbert Rozman, "U.S. Leadership, History, and Relations with Allies," both in *U.S. Leadership, History and Bilateral Relations in Northeast Asia,* edited by Gilbert Rozman (Cambridge: Cambridge University Press, 2011), 17–44, 72–94.

5. Ito Kenichi, "Examining Japan's Identity Now," *Japan Spotlight,* January–February 2005.

6. *Sankei shimbun,* August 15, 1999.

7. Marius B. Jansen and Gilbert Rozman, eds., *Japan in Transition: From Tokugawa to Meiji* (Princeton, N.J.: Princeton University Press, 1986).

8. Bai Gao, *Economic Ideology and Japanese Industrial Policy: Developmentalism from 1931 to 1965* (Cambridge: Cambridge University Press, 1997).

9. James J. Orr, *The Victim as Hero: Ideologies of Peace and National Identity in Postwar Japan* (Honolulu: University of Hawaii Press, 2001).

10. Gilbert Rozman, *Japan's Response to the Gorbachev Era, 1985–1991: A Rising Superpower Views a Declining One* (Princeton, N.J.: Princeton University Press, 1992).

11. Seymour Martin Lipset, *American Exceptionalism: A Double-Edged Sword* (New York: W. W. Norton, 1996), 211–63.

12. Bai Gao, "The Search for National Identity and Japanese Industrial Policy, 1950–1969," paper for conference on national identities in East Asia, Princeton, N.J., 1994.

13. Harumi Befu, "Nationalism and Nihonjinron," in *Cultural Nationalism in East Asia: Representation and Identity,* edited by Harumi Befu (Berkeley: Institute of East Asian Studies, University of California, 1993), 107–35.

14. Harumi Befu and Kazufumi Manabe, "Japanese Identity Statistically Profiled," *Kwansei gakuin daigaku shakaigakubu kiyo,* no. 79 (March 1998): 133–45.

15. Takeshita Noboru, *Heisei keizai zeminaru: Suji de miru sengo no Nihon* (Tokyo: Nikkei BP shuppan senta, 1995), 122–28.

16. Funabiki Takeo, *"Nihonjinron" saiko* (Tokyo: NHK shuppan, 2003).

17. S. N. Eisenstadt, *Japanese Civilization: A Comparative View* (Chicago: University of Chicago Press, 1995), 25.

18. Brian J. McVeigh, *Nationalisms of Japan: Managing and Mystifying Identity* (Lanham, Md.: Rowman & Littlefield, 2004).

19. Eisenstadt, *Japanese Civilization,* 77, 94.

20. Ibid., 103,

21. Eiko Ikegami, *The Taming of the Samurai: Honorific Individualism and the Making of Modern Japan* (Cambridge, Mass.: Harvard University Press, 1995), 329–69.

22. Owada, "In Search of a New National Identity," 245–46.

23. Carol Gluck, *Japan's Modern Myths: Ideology in the Late Meiji* (Princeton, N.J.: Princeton University Press, 1985), 111–36.

24. Gilbert Rozman, "Internationalism and Asianism in Japanese Strategic Thought from Meiji to Heisei," *Japanese Journal of Political Science* 9, no. 2 (Spring 2008): 209–32.

25. Harumi Befu and Kaufumi Manabe, "Japanese Identity Statistically Profiled," *Kansai gakuin daigaku shakaigakubu kiyo,* no. 79 (March 1998): 76–109; Shimizu Keihachiro, *Nihon bunmei no shinka* (Tokyo: Shodensha, 1999); Mayumi Itoh, *Globalization of Japan: Japanese Sakoku Mentality and U.S. Efforts to Open Japan* (New York: St. Martin's Press, 2000).

26. *Asahi shimbun,* September 11, 2010, p. 17.

27. *Sankei shimbun,* August 11, 2010, p. 2.

28. *Yomiuri shimbun,* July 13, 2004, p. 3.

29. *Yomiuri shimbun,* September 1, 2010, p. 7.

30. Cyril E. Black et al., *The Modernization of Japan and Russia* (New York: Free Press, 1975).

31. Kitaoka Shinichi, "Japan's Identity and What It Means," unpublished paper, Japan Forum on International Relations, Tokyo, n.d.

32. Tsuyoshi Hasegawa and Kazuhiko Togo, eds., *East Asia's Haunted Present: Historical Memories and the Resurgence of Nationalism* (Boulder, Colo.: Praeger, 2008), 42–58.

33. Gilbert Rozman, "Japanese Strategic Thinking on Regionalism," in *Japanese Strategic Thought toward Asia,* edited by Gilbert Rozman, Kazuhiko Togo, and Joseph P. Ferguson (New York: Palgrave, 2006), 243–68.

34. *Yomiuri shimbun,* September 12, 2010; *Nihon keizai shimbun,* October 15, 2010, p. 8.

35. Sakurai Yoshiko, "Nihon renessansu," *Shukan shincho,* October 9, 2008, 146–48.

36. *Sankei shimbun,* October 6, 2008, p. 9.

37. *Asahi shimbun,* October 23, 2008, p. 15.

38. *Asahi shimbun,* October 5, 2008, p. 1.

39. *Asahi shimbun,* October 5, 2008, p. 2.

40. *Asahi shimbun,* October 15, 2008, p. 7.

41. Kitaoka, "Japan's Identity."

42. Harumi Befu, "Nationalism and Nihonjinron," in *Cultural Nationalism in East Asia: Representation and Identity,* edited by Harumi Befu (Berkeley: Institute of East Asian Studies, University of California, 1993), 107–35.

43. Eisenstadt, *Japanese Civilization,* 322–29.

Chapter 2

South Korean National Identity: A Six-Dimensional Analysis

Gilbert Rozman

South Korean national identity bears heavily on the future of Northeast Asia as well as on the prospects of a truncated state struggling to find a direction. The South's approach to reunification with North Korea has the potential to reshape the regional core, even as its management of historical memories with each of the region's great powers can shift the course of regional reconciliation. Floundering over domestic policies long made the salience of identity at home high, too. Views of identity are torn between assumptions of deep-seated roots and continuities, reflecting a homogeneous state that has repeatedly impressed others with its nationalist insularity, and images of rapid transformation, fitting for a state buffeted by abrupt shifts in its objective conditions and relations with the great powers. Writings on identity often capture only part of the picture, drawing on current presidential inclinations or popular mood. Examining multiple dimensions, this chapter takes a broad approach to South Korean identity focused on comparative implications.

In 1998–2011 diverse, clashing images of South Korean national identity drew attention. Its claim to an economic miracle faded with the Asian financial crisis. A decade later during the global financial crisis, it again faced the crashing waves of globalization, but in a stronger position to aspire to leadership as host to a gathering of the Group of Twenty (G-20). Cultural identity also gained prominence as South Korea withstood U.S. efforts to spread universal values and then the sudden opening to Japan's cultural exports, while spreading its own TV dramas and music widely in the "Korean wave." Yet after South Koreans had split over criticizing the North's human rights violations and over the meaning of Koreanness in an era of widespread migration and intensified globalization, cultural identity by 2011 was converging with the United States to a degree few would have anticipated. Progressives intent on transforming historical views and political identity and conservatives insistent on different sources of national pride made Korean political identity the most disputed in East Asia for decades, but the progressives were in retreat. Democratic shifts in power help to account for abrupt changes, reflecting a deeper Korean identity malaise.[1]

Ideological flux has been greatest here, as extremes on the left and right crowded out the center. The temporal dimension demonstrates the dearth of any positive period on which to anchor historical identity. In turn, the sectoral dimension treats the balance of political, cultural, and economic identities, recognizing the political side as the most contentious. On the vertical dimension, a sharp divide is also apparent: for a time after the *chaebol* (privileged corporations) had fallen from favor and trust in most state institutions was sinking, calls for social fairness intensified, but reliance on a strong state led by a powerful president was rarely in doubt. On the horizontal dimension, there was likewise a persistent struggle over balancing alliance, regionalism linked to reunification, and internationalism. In 2011, the alliance was winning as a source of identity and security. Finally, the depth of identity is intense, with less hesitancy than in Japan to speak in favor of deep-seated ideals.

In the years 2009–10, South Korea was tested by both North Korea's increasing belligerence and the global financial crisis that led to the new G-20 meeting in Seoul. Such challenges shared by the international community reverberated against the background of a decade of engagement with North Korea that had come to an abrupt halt and memories of the Asian financial crisis, in which South Korea's response drew praise but not without lingering resentment over pressure from the

International Monetary Fund and the international community. Likewise, in the minds of many South Koreans was a tug-of-war over how to interpret history, whether in contested textbook revisions that provoked an ideological dispute or through control over television that some saw as political payback and others as belated objectivity. After Roh Moo-hyun's stress on identifying collaborators with Japan as a step toward forging a more just social order, Lee Myung-bak appealed for consensus in the face of danger. With foreign ties in flux, boosting the U.S. image and coping with a deteriorating image of China and a shift in thinking about Japan, the horizontal dimension also acquired new meaning. Responses to new global tests could not be divorced from struggles over the entire range of identity issues, putting a premium on overcoming past divides in the face of a troubled region.

The Ideological Dimension

The struggle between conservatives and progressives in South Korea resembles that in Japan, but with a different outcome after the Cold War. In each case, conservatives had deep roots in the pre-1945 era and preferred to conceal such linkages, while their progressive opponents were heavily influenced by Marxist thought and intent on tracing the erroneous path of their country far back in history. The two sides also fundamentally differed on assumptions about the international order and how to conceptualize the major governments with which the state interacts. Throughout the Cold War era, the conservatives maintained power, imposing their outlook but also opposing with limited success the spread of progressive ideas through the educational and cultural elite. In Japan, the result was an increasingly apathetic younger generation in a democratic society where the ideas of the left were losing relevance. But in South Korea, the progressive camp overcame the dictatorial imposition of a conservative worldview as its views gained greater legitimacy.

One observes in South Korea both the bravado of a nation anxious to assert its distinctiveness in the midst of the great powers crowding around it and the anguish of a lack of confidence—politically, economically, culturally, and, most of all, historically. The progressives are most eager to proceed assertively, linking identity to reunification with the North as if this gives them an edge in identity debates. They also are driven by grievances toward the injustice of Korean society, dating from the Japanese annexation and reflecting the distorted policies of dictatorial rule that embraced the collaborators. In contrast, many conservatives yearn for the clarity and order of the Cold War era, when the national interest was vigorously defended while society was mobilized to accomplish enduring feats. Unlike states such as Japan, where the ideological divide narrowed after the Cold War, it only came into the open with democratization in the late 1980s and has remained intense under presidents who have made little effort to find common ground.

After being harshly excluded from what had been structured as a democratic polity in the Cold War era, the progressives insisted on their right to drive the agenda for reconstructing national identity. Compared with the Japanese progressives, who were able to contest for power continuously in this era, the Korean progressives gained more legitimacy. In weighing the balance between North Korean brothers and American allies, they cast human rights and universal values to the side, giving priority to notions of sovereignty. Their values centered on forging a fairer domestic social order while more aggressively reconstructing Cold War history, two divisive goals that were unacceptable to the elite mainstream.

Under progressive presidents, Korean high school textbooks began to undercut some foundations of the postwar order. Books approved in 2003 allegedly distorted how the peninsula was divided by the Soviets and Americans and how much U.S. control persisted over the South Korean side. They blamed the U.S. alliance for imposing dictatorship and anticommunism in the interests only of the superpower. Also, they questioned the emergence of collaborators with the Japanese as the postwar power holders. On October 30, 2008, the new conservative administration demanded deletions and revisions in the textbooks, challenging what were seen as "masochistic" leftist views of Korean history. Roh had said in 2003, "Our modern history is a painful one, in which justice was defeated and opportunism gained the upper hand."[2] The conservatives countered that pride is justified in the postwar era, which accomplished rapid modernization and kept at bay the predatory Communist regime in the North. This divide is not yet bridged. Although Japanese rightists have reservations about the Cold War era and Chinese reformers would prefer a more honest accounting of Maoist extremism, only in South Korea does one see paralysis in moving forward on national identity due to the divisions over this period.

One finds in South Korea pockets of coexisting logic, compartmentalized with no integrating narrative. Intense emotions of national distinctiveness have no ready outlet. Gaps between pretenses about identity and realities leave an opening to progressives with a contradictory, simplistic narrative. They gained by capturing aspirations for democracy and turning conservative ambivalence on U.S. values into broader reservations directed against this ally. Yet the progressive critique, after ten years of support from presidents, appears to be losing support. The challenge for the conservatives is to move to the middle in search of a more comprehensive and realistic identity that can draw increasing popularity.

In 2010, the progressives were in retreat. Blaming Lee Myung-bak for provoking the North Koreans did not resonate well in the face of blatant aggression, even warnings that nuclear weapons would be used against the South. The progressive ideology had little to say about the priorities uppermost in the minds of South Koreans in a more dangerous security and economic environment. Yet the specter of war made Lee's responses risky in a manner that might lead more South Koreans toward appeasement as costs mounted. By 2011, issues of social justice had again gained prominence, leaving conservatives torn between those seeking to preempt the progressive appeal and those, including Lee, claiming a superior strategy for economic growth that leaves no room for concessions on social welfare. A centrist approach remained elusive.

The Temporal Dimension

Three features of national identity formation left distinct marks on Korea in the historical context of East Asia. First, Confucianism was raised to a pedestal that merged ruling and elite versions without reconciling growing cultural and political nationalism with intense dependency on China in both respects.[3] Also, Confucianism succumbed to ritualism that invited factionalism as it lost sight of reform objectives, leaving a rut even deeper than China faced in the new conditions of the late nineteenth century. Second, failure to clarify core symbols of national identity in the face of outside pressure left the national identity deeply vulnerable in the nineteenth century. Finally, Japan's colonial rule proved decidedly pernicious for identity to find balanced expression,[4] bestowing a legacy that would be compounded by the forced division of Korea in 1945 and the anticommunist worldview it aroused. Thus, its national identity formation narrowed South Korea's options and left it holding few positive memories on which to build, apart from artificial cultural constructs conducive to narrowly focused Koreanness. Negativity about its entire history except for rare episodes to 1945 has left a deep hole in Korea's anchoring pride.

Confucianism became more inimical to the emergence of Korean national identity starting in the late nineteenth century than to Chinese or Japanese national identity. After all, Manchu officials and Japanese feudal lords had grasped it as a tool for strengthening both their control and legitimacy. They had stopped scholar-officials from seizing the reigns of cultural authority. Although ritual was highly refined in each country, drawing on the same set of Confucian classics, it was most pervasive in Korea. In the second half of the nineteenth century, officials were slow to latch onto symbols of national identity. They struggled with removing symbols that came to be seen as Chinese without having much success in agreeing on symbols that could become the core of Korean national identity.[5] Conservative nostalgia about elements of Confucianism does not negate the widespread understanding that Korea's Confucian past did not prepare the country for challenges.

Discontinuities in national identity abound in Korea. Japan's imposed colonial identity rejected the preceding premodern identity. Postwar identity began with the complete negation of colonial identity. Democratization came next in condemnation of preceding periods of dictatorial governance and many of its claims to national identity, turning also against anticommunism as the Cold War abruptly ended and *nordpolitik* drew Seoul to Moscow and Beijing as partners. The U.S. occupation had a mixed impact. Compared with the occupation of Japan, it was less planned, a lower priority, and unprepared for managing nationalist resentment against the collaborators with Japan, now needed to keep order. If its main legacy for Japan was democratization and the peace Constitution, the emergence of dictators and the continued threat of war resulted in a different outcome. Memories of how the Korean War unfolded with great brutality in the context of a globe polarized into two clashing camps and worldviews meant that shared Korean history remained only a vague ideal in South Korean national identity. Instead of building a bridge to the past or serving as a source of pride, the Cold War era produced an illusory identity without staying power.

In the postwar era, South Korean identity struggled between contradictory forces, as claims to be part of the "free world" and a close ally of the United States clashed with dictatorial rationalizations. The message from the conservatives became garbled, while the struggling progressives found it hard to reconcile claims to be the genuine champions of democracy with sympathy for antidemocratic North Korea. The conservatives were often on the defensive, undermining U.S. moral authority by insisting that they were in harmony with it in a way that made Syngman Rhee appear to be a puppet of the United States when he was really a troublesome partner and Chun Doo-hwan seem to be a favorite when he was not respected. Because U.S. officials were inclined to turn a blind eye to dictatorship on the front line at one of the critical points in the struggle between two camps, they could do little to clarify universal values. Only after disappointment with a decade of progressive rule has some nostalgia arisen.

Park Chung-hee had some success in rebuilding national identity with economic identity in the foreground along with alliance relations with the United States. Japan's presence complicated these efforts. It was ahead economically, serving as the model and the main source of economic stimulus, even as it was making economic identity the core of its postwar revival. Also, it held the favored position of U.S. ally as well as the more ideologically correct one of democratic member of the "free world." With South Korea resting part of its emerging identity on anti-Japanese views, this posed a dilemma. Park reached back in Korean history for ways to bolster national identity, neglecting to boost identification with the United States. Although anticommunism became the backbone of his message, it was rather undercut by the Sino-U.S. reconciliation in 1971–72. Tensions with Washington mounted when Park cynically supported Lyndon Johnson's war in Vietnam, only to find that Richard Nixon was pulling back in Asia with the Guam Doctrine and later Jimmy Carter was contemplating a withdrawal of U.S. forces that could have left South Korea vulnerable to the North. Disputes with Washington, including pressure to abandon the development of nuclear weapons and long-range missiles, made it harder to focus on shared values. Blaming U.S. policy for Park's excesses and then for

Chun's repression, including the Kwangju massacre, contributed to rising anti-Americanism. This too left memories of the Cold War a shaky foundation for current national identity.

Also present in the Cold War worldview was an exaggerated message of Korea as the perennial victim, as if incursions occurred over and over again, when starting in 1392 it was attacked only over one half century during half a millennium. Whether this aroused a sense of national disgrace or determination to resist any new humiliation, the effect was to dwell on the negative. Conservative dictatorship strove to justify a denial of democracy rather than to take pride in how the country was evolving. For economic national identity, it would have helped to reach beyond crony *chaebol,* for political identity refusal to build toward the rule of law and draw progressives into the polity had lasting negative effects; and for cultural identity the contrast with North Korea might have led to championing universal values if the United States had been embraced. Yet fractious conservatives did not provide the balanced direction or support for the United States as did Japan's Liberal Democratic Party. Attuned to popular leftist views of history and fresh symbols of U.S. hypocrisy, many did not trust their sole ally. Also, arbitrary executive power and widespread patronage did not enable the conservatives to consolidate their rule or put in place a respected bureaucracy. This left a vacuum in the 1980s, which progressives moved quickly to fill. The legacy of the Cold War era was perceived so negatively in the course of democratization that hope turned to finding pride in the following era, but that would prove difficult in the face of divisions within the South and complex relations with the four powers and North Korea.

South Korea has struggled with the shadow of the United States. For more than a half century, the United States dominated the stage as the occupying state that had charted the course for postwar development, the indispensable ally, the principal market, the cultural colossus whose values permeated the globe, and the world's superpower that defined the meaning of internationalism. With North Korea looming as a recurrent threat and no great power offering the South any chance to diversify its foreign policy, external options were not available for rethinking national identity. Thus, when democratization occurred along with pride in the country's economic rise that also fed claims to cultural pride, the search for a fuller, more "normal" national identity turned belatedly to foreign relations. First, conservatives tried their hand: Roh

Tae-woo's *nordpolitik* aimed to widen international ties and forge a favorable environment for dealing with North Korea, and Kim Young-sam's globalization and "diplomatic diversification" sought to build on this foundation in spite of the first nuclear crisis centered on North Korea and the United States.[6] Then the progressives took charge: Kim Dae-jung's Sunshine Policy of engaging North Korea produced full-fledged steps to transform diplomacy and national identity, and Roh Moo-hyun's delinking of relations with the United States and North Korea as well as idea to make his country the regional "balancer" raised the stakes for national identity. However, a return to conservative rule under Lee Myung-bak, with emphasis on U.S. ties, managed to refocus the quest for answers. In 2011, the Cold War does not appear so negative and the post–Cold War era seems troubled more than it had earlier. As myths of the premodern era fade and Japan's colonialism is no longer the obsession it long remained, South Korea's identity is grappling for more balance, covering all periods without any longer idealizing or demonizing any of them to an extreme.

The Sectoral Dimension

South Koreans mix cultural, economic, and political nationalism in their claims to distinctiveness. Cultural national identity has traversed a troubled past. Shame abounded about cultural weakness that yielded to Japan's moves to obliterate much of the national heritage. Then, as Japan strove to undermine Korean cultural identity, a backlash resulted in intense feelings of "Koreanness" with lasting links between culture and bloodlines. Park Chung-hee at times took a nihilist view aimed at remaking the nation's culture in order to build a strong state and economy. Yet cultural identity was not nearly as weak as some had suggested. The potential for strong cultural nationalism has been seen at many turns. National honor has often been pronounced in dealings with each of the great powers, suggesting wounded pride. When U.S. leaders, notably Jimmy Carter, tried to press Park on democratization or human rights, the Koreans defensively evoked cultural distinctiveness.

Japan's colonialism posed shocks to cultural identity along with political identity. Given the Confucian heritage, the former may have been no less important than the latter. Also, reversing the order of Korea as culturally superior to Japan to the point of forcing people to be educated in Japanese and replace their Korean names with Japanese ones damaged the underpinnings of pride that could boost national identity. With no reason to accept Japan's authority after its extreme measures and complete defeat, Koreans had to search anew for a foundation to construct a postwar national identity. A backlash against core elements of Japanese national identity, particularly with North Korea even more negative, could not serve as a basis for agreement on a new identity.[7] Another identity hiatus arose that was not addressed in a manner that could contribute to consolidation of an identity suitable to an era of South Korea rising in the shadow of the United States.

Economic national identity intensified long before South Korea won recognition for its "economic miracle." It did not recede with democratization; in the *shintobuli* (body and soil as one) campaign, mounting pressure by the United States to drop protectionist measures made food products potent symbols of a country under duress. In the Uruguay Round of global trade talks, Washington's priority on agricultural openings led at the end of the 1980s to strong resistance, making rice a symbol, similar to its meaning in Japan. Already Koreans had focused on kimchi as their own ubiquitous food, conveniently unappreciated by most foreigners. Later imports of U.S. beef would be interrupted and manipulated as a symbol of food safety. When world attention had shifted in the 1990s to global economic integration, newly mobilized mass movements were ready to defend the nation, and the notion of eating Korean products or buying Korean cars continued to resonate in the mid-1990s when Kim Young-sam appealed for "globalization," also in the Asian financial crisis, and even in 2008 when the opponents of a negotiated free trade agreement with the United States staged candlelight vigils against resumed beef imports.[8] Yet the heyday of defensiveness of the *chaebol* and the protectionist state has faded. With increased interdependence, especially in ties to China, vested interests may use radical methods but no longer bask in identity.

The AsiaBarometer Survey says South Koreans have a low level of satisfaction, "now struggling in confusion as their traditional Confucian belief system collides and converges with global universalism." They also exhibit low trust in public institutions, especially government, Parliament, political parties, multinational companies, labor unions, and the media.[9] When coupled with confusion over cultural identity, including the meaning of "Koreanness" in an era of diversification linked to migration and other forces, these results testify to a high level of uncertainty about what are pillars of national identity in China and Japan, where the AsiaBarometer found much less confusion.[10] South Korea has long been noted for its insular sense of cultural homogeneity and rabid support for sports teams and national symbols, and South Koreans still have fervor when they can find a new symbol, but challenges to what was seen as essential to Korean cultural identity cloud their overall identity. In the shadow of a strong focus on the homogeneity of Koreanness, uncertainty spread in the aftermath of democracy and the post–Cold War opening to North Korea and intensified as more Koreans moved abroad and found spouses from abroad. Yet cultural identity remains the nucleus of discussions of identity after politics and economics faded as symbols of pride. Even so, as seen in later chapters, cultural identity also has receded.

Korean presidents have found it difficult to establish their legitimacy. Their power has been sharply contested. After each leader leaves office or earlier, his image suffers greatly. Cumulatively, this erodes legitimacy, although institutionalization of democratic elections over the past two decades has had some salutary effect. Instead of a shared narrative, we find a sharply contested one. The Cold War is viewed through this short-term prism, as is the post–Cold War era, limiting construction of a viable political national identity.

Although cultural and economic identity long served to rally South Koreans, political national identity takes precedence. If Korea bashing would be taken very seriously, it is South Korea passing that has proven most irksome of late. Fear persists that other states will decide the fate of the nation's most serious problems without listening to it. Each of the past three presidents has been troubled by this possibility, and Lee also cannot avoid similar concerns. The history issue with Japan signifies indifference to national feelings. The Bush administration's handling of North Korea in 2002–4 had a similar effect, and China's image has fallen fast since 2004 with the charge of arrogant Sinocentrism. Great sensitivity to great powers bypassing Seoul is a powerful driver of political identity. Yet, in 2008–11, trust in U.S. support kept rising, making it possible to link political identity to an ally's leadership and the international community. Similarly, economic identity had refocused on globalization far more than in Japan, while cultural identity was losing its ethnocentric narrowness. In the sectoral dimension more balance is now within reach.

The Vertical Dimension

In the rush to modernize in the postwar era, South Korean leaders strove to create a streamlined society that would follow top-down directives. Having been influenced by the Japanese model of late development spurred by state policies and anxious after the inconclusive Korean War and the following years of chaotic governance and economic growth, Park Chung-hee urgently forged an export-oriented economy well buttressed by certain social underpinnings. At the top, macro level, in a three-step hierarchy, he concentrated power in the presidential office and made administrative guidance central to business activity. In the state-led industrialization that followed, unlike in Japan, bureaucrats were poorly shielded from political influences. The criteria for recruitment were more personalized, depending on interviews more than examinations, and society was left more vulnerable to arbitrary state action, leading to widespread corruption. This contributed to state-centered identity at the expense of other levels in society, even as it encouraged a vertical image of such intensity that it cast a shadow on the other levels, excluding decentralization.

Korean leaders managed in their drive to industrialize to forge a social ladder of unusual characteristics. At the micro level, they stressed traditional values tailored, as in Japan, to a corporate culture. Reviving Confucian virtues, they reinforced patriarchy, the subordination of women to men in dealing with the outside world, and symbols of the past such as a ban on intermarriage between those with the same surname. Such moves served family solidarity at a time of massive rural-urban migration and social mobility, but they were vulnerable to economic distress, demographic transition, and changing social values. Starting in the 1990s, as birthrates fell to some of the lowest in the world and divorce rates skyrocketed, doubts rose about the durability of identity perceptions at this bottom level. South Korea lacked the universal criteria and paternalistic enterprise norms of Japan. Instead, clientelism seeping down from the way the state did business formed networks of a personalized nature. Bureaucracy was more compromised than in Japan, as the arbitrary colonial heritage and favoritism of powerful postwar leaders undercut the rule of law. Individualism did not advance far, but neither did universalism. This led to identity becoming attached to such markers as blood, school, and regional ties, and to abstract political ideals linked to a strong sense of nationalism but not to the Constitution.[11]

In Japan, the bottom step on the social ladder was made up of enterprises with strong autonomous identities—many with long prewar histories and which in the postwar period had been able to solidify themselves through depersonalized management without fear of arbitrary state intervention and with help from a growing national obsession with company paternalism. In contrast, the *chaebol* were dominated by owner-operators, were vulnerable to frequent state demands, and produced only a pale imitation of the Japanese enterprise model.

Confucian assumptions about identity permeated this micro level of society. The conservative ideology of Park may have blamed Korean traditions for millennia of inertia, but it also demanded loyalty and social order in ways that reinforced family controls. As networks became decisive for social mobility, ties of kinship, community, and/or school proved important despite the considerable flux from migration. Individualism did not prosper in such circumstances. The community and *chaebol* under the influence of state preferences in employment, promotion, and loans to favorites did not develop strong horizontal ties. Continued identification with the Confucian values of local life served the interests of a strong state, standing in the way of more balanced identities in a middle-class society.[12]

Many younger Koreans associate Confucianism more with barriers to modernity and globalization than with a renewable vision for today. Koreans retain more ties to the past through functioning lineage groups, regular visits to ancestral graves and consultation of genealogies, and a more enduring role of rituals in interpersonal relations. In China, Communism distanced elites and masses from the past; and in Japan, modernization came earlier and advanced further. That leaves the premodern past more alive in South Korea.

Presidents have failed not only to build broad political consensus but also to raise the state's moral authority and trust in central institutions. When conflicts erupt, they take an exaggerated form, suggesting a lack of respect for the law—a tendency to put moral claims above legal ones. Order is often seen as coercion. An anti-state narrative is not matched by determination to find checks and balances to limit state power. Civic groups grew more active starting in the late 1980s, but they do not serve as real checks on power. They have been co-opted or marginalized. If

presidential power is limited by a lack of moral authority, it is not balanced by strong group orientation at the micro level, as in Japan, or by
strong local power and institutions of civil society. This is a fragile
combination.

The Horizontal Dimension

For South Korea to break free of domination by China, Japan, or the
United States is not simply a matter of achieving a long-sought breakthrough in sovereignty. It also reflects persistent aspirations for release
from a civilizational stranglehold, as each of these powers became the
source of legitimation for what was deemed worthy of proper morality.
In pursuit of a breakaway, Koreans could not easily find an alternative
claim to civilization in their own history or turn to regional or global
models. The regional hegemon left a strong imprint on what was conceivable, even as other options arose for foreign partnerships.

The end of the Cold War, the rise of Asian economic integration and
diplomatic intensification, the shifting balance among the powers in
Northeast Asia, and the emergence of North Korea as a subject of national debate have together created the conditions for changes in national identity, but a consensus is lacking on the direction to be pursued.
Lacking a great power identity with expectations of leadership, South
Koreans must set their sights more modestly and realistically on stick-
ing close to the United States, becoming a leading advocate for globalization, and facilitating regionalism when possible.

More than Japan or China, South Korea's national identity takes
shape against the background of relations with the United States. After
all, China and Japan consider their states to be great powers normally
autonomous in international affairs. Searching for any opportunity to
forge an independent regional strategy in Asia, they keep anticipating a
leadership role. In contrast, South Korea faces the United States as a
country burdened with memory of successive bouts of *sadae* (service to
a great power)—toward China over most of a millennium, toward
Japan in such an extreme form that all sovereignty was lost, and since
1945 toward the United States. Similar to the other two, it aspired first
to confirmation of its status as full member of the international community by the world leader, then to recognition of its values as respected
by that community, later to entry into the club of advanced states based

on economic development, next to approval of its independent foreign policy, and finally to the dual goals of symbolic equality in U.S. ties and self-reliance in ways seen as restoring national dignity.[13] Democratization boosted the stature of the South in international eyes, but it was no panacea for either international or self-respect.[14] The U.S. alliance is also insufficient. Whether South Korea's goal is to be the center, the pivot, or even the balancer, there is no doubt about its desire for leverage in Asia.[15] As a result, opinion on the United States is split, mirroring images of a North Korean threat.[16]

Ambivalence to the United States persists. On the one hand, it long was regarded as the principal barrier to status normalization. Its past actions and brusque handling of sensitive matters produced the pain of dependency. On the other hand, since 1945 it has been the source of legitimation. Regardless of the leader, recognition of his standing—similar to investiture by the Chinese emperor in premodern times—confers an essential status for stabilizing his rule. Not only did the dictators Park Chung-hee and Chun Doo-hwan require this early in their tenures, but democratically elected presidents also have recognized the value of U.S. confirmation of their position in tangible ways. It was not just the status of one individual that mattered; the state sought substantial recognition of its standing as a partner, one marker being its entrance into the Organization for Economic Cooperation and Development (OECD), signifying its acceptance as an advanced industrial state. Yet success with the United States did not suffice. It whetted the appetite for actions that would demonstrate the South's ability to exercise autonomy, which might accompany U.S. actions that called the South's status into doubt. Responses of this sort were less about power balancing than status seeking.

Not only had the predictability of the Cold War ended, but confidence in the United States' ability to manage serious troubles also nosedived, first in the 1993–94 nuclear crisis, then in the Asian financial crisis, and starting in 2001 in U.S. handling of North Korea from how to steer the Sunshine Policy forward to how to respond to missile and nuclear tests. Without seeing another option to the alliance, the South Koreans grew more anxious.

Many South Koreans feel beleaguered. They keep raising their expectations in search of a new president who can relieve their deep anxieties, but before he has been in office long, their disappointment is intense. In the second half of 2007, they had long since turned against

Roh Moo-hyun. As one internal Chinese source described the situation, the people felt squeezed as exports to China were growing more slowly and imports from Japan more rapidly. They felt that their country was losing clout or being squeezed by others, including the United States, not only economically but also diplomatically, militarily, and even in matters linked to cultural superiority.[17] The concept of *sadae* recalls the humiliation of kowtowing to a foreign leader, and it puts a premium on national pride. Many accused the United States of using South Korea without respecting it, leading to wariness of U.S. values, historical memories of U.S. hypocrisy, and distrust of U.S. preference for Japan. Yet the U.S. role remains indispensable, and prospects for finding some balance remain slim. South Koreans reawakened to this reality by 2010.

Many issues of intense concern in South Korea center on sovereignty. For nearly half a century, it was either under U.S. military occupation or did not have peacetime operational control over its own military. Even after regaining such control in 1994, wartime operational control drew national attention, to the point that even after in 2007 the United States agreed to its return, there was much confusion over whether this would serve Korean interests. In the Roh Moo-hyun period, conservatives feared that the progressive drive to realize symbols of sovereignty, including this one, would jeopardize national security. Progressives focus on achieving national defense autonomy, while in the backlash again Roh conservatives sought a stronger alliance, leaving the public polarized.[18] A perceived gap in sovereignty is connected to the widespread view that South Korea has yet to achieve normalcy, not only because reunification still seems far off but also because dependency on the United States continues to be excessive.[19] Officials recognize the importance of avoiding any provocation of the United States. Under Kim Young-sam, an ambassador's remarks in Beijing conveyed the impression of equalizing ties with China and the country's sole ally.[20] Under Kim Dae-jung, a summit with Russian president Vladimir Putin suggested joint opposition to U.S. president George W. Bush's pet missile defense program. The United States' ire toward Roh appeared in repeated warnings over one or another transgression. National identity struggles under the weight of perceived U.S. overdependency.

South Korean internationalization drew on the fact that the United Nations had approved a general election for all Koreans, which the North chose to block, and then had authorized the Korean War in resistance to the North's attack. Yet, when the Soviet Union reasserted its veto role and later China joined the United Nations, there was no prospect of support or even entrance into that body until the Cold War had ended. In the 1990s, debate on this theme paralleled Japan's debate in the 1980s. It was advocated by cosmopolitan diplomats and cultural figures to speed social change and acceptance into the global society led by the United States. Given the large number of Korean academics who had studied in English-speaking countries, support was substantial. They favored dropping trade barriers, improving English proficiency, and encouraging Koreans to welcome foreigners and embrace universal values. Yet, under Kim Young-sam, as in the earlier case of Japan, only limited opening of the country was contemplated under strong central control. This was a time not to fall in line behind the United States but to search for a more independent, active policy toward Asia. Conservatives as well as progressives were reserved about internationalism until Lee Myung-bak made this a priority. With Ban Ki-Moon serving as secretary-general of the United Nations and Lee Myung-bak less idealistic about Northeast Asia and more serious about "global Korea," interest mounted in whether South Korea could be a leader through expanded official development assistance and host to the G-20, a bridge between East and West and North and South too through diplomatic activism in Asia, and a model for its democratization and globalization combined with features of East Asian dynamism. In 2010, this profile was drawing increased attention.

History is invoked for many negative lessons. Many in Korea see the period before 1900 as the cause of victimization in the twentieth century. The lessons they draw center on how to escape from continuing dependency and how to avoid a repetition. This leads especially to assertions of identity and methods for reinforcing it that regard Japan as a threat. Koreans long feared the influx of popular culture from Japan. After Kim Dae-jung promised to lift all barriers at the October 1998 summit in Japan, the debate over the mixing of the two cultures flared again in both South Korea and Japan.[21] How remarkable then that the "Korean wave" should sweep across Japan and that the Koreans would easily accept all manner of Japanese culture, as travel between the two neighbors rose precipitously.

Suspecting that other states are intent on dominating a nation can lead to a feeling of being besieged. To lessen concerns about confinement in the absence of reunification may require refocusing on how much is shared in common. The Barack Obama presidency, with its more multilateral orientation toward all regions of the world, provides a favorable opportunity to strengthen trust with the United States without being pressured to agree to policies likely to prove divisive inside South Korea and across the region. More attention to shared interests and values during the past sixty years could be accompanied by renewed symbols of closeness. The responsibility to do this should be shared by the two sides. The differences in how to deal with the North Korean nuclear question pitted security against sovereignty, still vague global values against sharply disputed national values.[22] In 2010 this gap narrowed, adding to the possibility of a broad consensus on national identity.

South Koreans aspire to a proud national identity based on something more than economic accomplishment, democratic rights, and a well-respected place in international society. Success on those dimensions has not quenched the thirst for deeper appreciation of the South Korean state and for the Korean people for their special significance in the past, present, and future of Northeast Asia. Such aspirations were fueled by optimism when *nordpolitik* and a brief improvement in ties with North Korea offered hope in 1990–91 and when the Sunshine Policy put Seoul at the center of regional diplomacy in 2000. Yet, considering how assertive all four of the great powers are, the South only can serve as a facilitator when an overall consensus has been reached. If it distances itself from its ally the United States, there is no regional community or balance or North Korean partner available to fill the void. Unlike Japan, there was no point in anticipating a special role in the international community. Seeking a breakthrough in the horizontal dimension of ties to the outside world is illusory at present. If it appears possible at some future date, South Korea would be best able to seize the opportunity only after moving forward on the other dimensions of national identity and preparing a firm foundation for international relations.

The Intensity Dimension

At each point when national confidence appears to be on the rise, it suffers a sharp setback. The end of the 1980s witnessed a celebration of democratization, pride in the Seoul Olympics, and the growing success of *nordpolitik* as Moscow and Beijing showed increasing interest in bilateral economic and political ties. Yet anger at the incomplete nature of democratization under a former general handpicked by the last dictator was reflected in the continued struggle by progressives to break away from an order in which they took little pride. The mid-1990s marked the culmination of the "economic miracle" as South Koreans prized their entry into the OECD as one of the world's developed states and there was much talk of combining Asian and universal values as a model that could spread as an inspiration in the coming "Pacific century." Signs of hubris, however, faded fast with the Asian financial crisis, where South Korea had to bow before the International Monetary Fund in not only accepting a financial bailout but also acknowledging that its model of state-*chaebol* crony capitalism brought it to disgrace. A new wave of nationalist pride came quickly, when in 2000 Kim Dae-jung's Sunshine Policy brought a summit with Kim Jong-il, a Nobel Peace Prize, and even the impression that South Korea was now driving improved relations in Asia with its diplomatic activism. The euphoria that gripped many Koreans did not last, as criticism mounted over Kim's domestic leadership and his inability to win reciprocal moves from Kim Jong-il or manage relations with George W. Bush once he took office. Even as election campaign optimism peaked in 2002, in the aftermath of national boosterism in hosting and succeeding beyond expectations in the World Cup, and in 2007, when the Six-Party Talks seemed to be moving forward, there was no comparable jump in confidence to obscure deep underlying public self-doubts. Most recently, when Lee Myung-bak's resounding electoral victory after the shock of North Korea's nuclear test appeared to bring a new consensus, the nation fell into bickering in 2008–9 with Lee's approval ratings low and no impetus to a renewed consensus, and it again was uneasy in 2011 over signs of social injustice.

Koreans view China and Japan more negatively than they are viewed by their neighbors. In 2008, there was a 25 percent rise in the proportion of South Koreans who view Sino-Korean relations as poor, bringing the total to 60 percent. (The Chinese figure rose by 10 points, to 16 percent.) The gap was also high and growing between the 77 percent of Koreans who see Japanese-Korean relations as bad (9 percent more than in 2007) and the 50 percent of Japanese with a similar opinion (down 5 percent in a year, reflecting the end of Roh's tenure).[23] In this same year, the obscure issue of fear of U.S. beef imports became the unexpected rallying cry for candlelight vigils against the Lee Myung-bak administration and the United States. Such volatile responses expose a residue of anger reminiscent of the anti-Americanism in 2002–4. These negative emotions toward all the major powers at the center of Korean consciousness serve as the foundation for sharp responses to symbols that can easily become the center of public attention.

South Koreans often feel stifled—by deference to the United States in official ties; by times such as 1965, when a need for Japan's economic support required swallowing demeaning arrangements; and by awareness that with North Korea, China, and Russia, the habit of self-restraint in order to finally foster ties could never be fully broken. Even as the conservatives became more assertive toward North Korea or the progressives vented their frustrations against the United States, other cautions remained in place. Resort is made to surrogate topics to air deeply held nationalist feelings and anxieties, such as that China's rapid rise and growing economic presence across the Yalu River threatens the South's prospects in inter-Korean affairs. Concern about the Koguryo historical claims of China masked these more up-to-date fears. Despite clashing ideologies in the media and political campaigns, not all issues are treated forthrightly. With growing tension in 2010, views were aired more fully and directly.

Democracy failed to bring cohesion to South Korea. In comparison with China and Japan, it is a deeply divided country on national identity. A higher degree of dependence on the United States with fewer options has not led to greater trust but to excessive blame and expectations. Some hold it responsible for the failure of reconciliation with North Korea, normal postwar development through purging the colonial collaborators, or of timely democratization in the South. These are all matters vital to national identity. Uncertainty about the future of Korea raises anxiety levels, which are reflected in exaggerated views of national identity. Although highly contested democratic elections bring clashing notions of identity to the forefront, they have not resulted in a process for achieving consensus. Democracy is not a panacea for the problems that are ailing South Korea, but it can serve to strengthen those institutions that can rebuild confidence in the state and its constructive policies.

Compounding the division over any effort to provide clear direction for national identity are diverse symbols that direct identity debates in scattered directions. They loom more seriously in South Korea than in most other countries, including even China and Japan, raising the potential for sharp reactions to Japan, the United States, or even China. With such symbols of infringement on Korean sovereignty in the forefront, discussions aimed at weighing strategic options are marginalized. When they are reminded of national humiliation when one or another of these emblems of past victimization is invoked, South Koreans often reveal their deeper anxieties without patiently assessing the full panoply of strategic alternatives and their consequences. Forward-looking leadership would tone down the reaction to these symbols and redirect public attention to a balanced, international role.

Although concepts such as guilt and shame have been overused in discussions, one can contrast the Japanese sense of guilt over history, which many recently have sought to reject in order to normalize the past, to the Korean sense of shame for failing to prevent bad outcomes. Shame is proving more troublesome, producing more of a struggle. Some examples that have aroused it in recent years are exposés of how Korean troops behaved in the Vietnam War and also the Korean War. Confronting painful truths, some seek to hide them and others to obsess over them, with neither side succeeding in getting beyond them. The National Assembly keeps fighting old battles and showing signs of extreme behavior as old grudges endure. Presidents dig up dirt on their predecessors, as courts charge them or their family members with betraying the national trust. The truth about North Korea is, perhaps, the most shameful blemish for the Korean people. To break free of this vicious circle requires respected neutral voices to tone down the volume and focus on reasons for pride that will prove that shame really is not nearly as serious as guilt. Overcoming the one-sided progressive approach makes this possible, and conservatives have made some progress in meeting the challenge of finding common ground.

Conclusion

South Korean national identity is at a crossroads. Looking back, Koreans are divided on how much weight to assign in their identity search to the symbols of Japanese colonialism, which continues to arouse strong reactions, as opposed to the earlier prewar period or the postwar period. As recently as the mid-1990s, economic and cultural identities figured prominently, but the balance has shifted to political national identity to uncertain effect. Koreans are accustomed to attaching importance to regional identity within their country as well as *chaebol* identity, but the strong focus on social movement identity of the late 1980s and 1990s survives, as does the close linkage to macrolevel state identity. Perhaps most confusing are the priorities in reaching out horizontally, as seen in the shaky start of Lee's foreign policy, which was deemed too focused on the United States and even Japan. Finally, if one looks behind statements from the progressives on North Korea, despite its renewed hostility in 2008, and from the conservatives on the United States at the time of the election of Barack Obama, one finds signs of unstated ambitions that reveal the depth of national identity. Given the vulnerability shown in the global financial crisis as well as in great power relations, sensitivity to national identity remains intense.

Applying the six dimensions being used in this book to the analysis of national identity in South Korea, one finds evidence of serious imbalance. On the temporal dimension, there is a vacuum in pride focused on each period of history, with the opportunity cost particularly high in the lack of pride regarding the Cold War era with reverberations for the post–Cold War era. As for the ideological dimension, the sharp divide between conservative and progressive lends itself to extremes, and the center is too underrepresented to bring cohesion focused on liberal values. On the sectoral dimension, there were spikes in economic and even cultural national identity before the Asian financial crisis, but neither of these has shown sustained appeal, while political identity has proven so inconsistent and prone to reversal that it fails to provide the essential foundation for national cohesion. A vertical dimension imbalance favors state identity, despite a loss of trust in state institutions, which has not been compensated for by decentralization or a rise of nongovernmental organizations representing interest groups, which were co-opted under Roh Moo-hyun's progressive presidency. As for the horizontal dimension, South Korea's potential role of bridging the U.S. alliance and emergent regionalism has yet to be realized, given that internationalism lacks any anchor and alliance ties have failed to provide the firm footing needed for realistic regionalism. Finally, with regard to the depth of national identity, there is a serious gap in exposing extreme views and filling in silences in South Korean discourse, despite high-intensity emotions related to national identity themes. Given this range of imbalances, the problems of confidence, clarity, and consistency in national identity have remained serious in South Korea, but the potential for change is still considerable. Under Lee, identity has been clarified with enduring potential.

In 2000, under Kim Dae-jung, South Korea seemed to represent all things to all people. To the United States, it served as the epitome of East Asian modernity: the champion of globalization; the defender of human rights and the democratic transfer of power against "Asian values"; and a model ally, not only guarding the front line against the last holdout of Stalinism but also idealistically trying to win it over. To Japan, it had turned into the regional partner for the future, promising to put history aside and be more cooperative than before on culture, economics, and security.[24] To China, the South also became the regional partner for the future, showing deference, integrating economically more than any other non-Chinese entity, and coordinating closely on the North.[25] Even Russia had framed a new positive image of South Korea superior to that of any other East Asian country, deeming it realistic and unthreatening.[26] Yet all these images proved to be fragile, while the search for a new identity within South Korea itself inextricably drew on changing images of these foreign partners and historical memories, as U.S. power and modernity loomed in the background, overshadowing both South Korea and its region.

Under Lee Myung-bak, a more sober view of national identity prevailed in South Korea. Shared values with the United States and, surprisingly, even with Japan served as a refuge in the face of despair over reunification and regionalism linked to values. As illusions were shattered, Korean exceptionalism was subordinated to universal values in a United States–led coalition identified with the international community. Optimism now centered on a middle power's rising impact on globalization as national identity paid more heed to qualities that lead to economic integration, joint security, and cultural compatibility.

As the ideological, sectoral, and temporal dimensions of national identity lost immediacy, even horizontal identity concerns became secondary to vertical identity. The horizontal side lost its volatility after a brief spike in anti-Americanism, and long-standing anti-Japanese emotions diminished, while North Korea was becoming less an identity concern than a security and economic one. Rising negativity toward China was tempered by practical considerations of how costly tensions could be. Yet despite sustained economic growth and relatively low unemployment in 2011, South Koreans have found little satisfaction in vertical national identity. If radical rhetoric lost its appeal with Roh Moo-hyun's ineffectual policies, the underlying sources of anxiety have kept destabilizing politics. They have been a lingering reflection of un-balanced modernization, leaving a few thriving companies in a low-welfare, high-pressure society. Overworked men, overstressed students, and overwhelmed households struggle with demographic realities and seek an elusive normalcy. Lee could not fulfill his economic campaign promises, and he appeared aloof in not meeting expectations for greater democratization and an improved quality of life. The old answers ob-sessed with state-centered development do not suffice for today's iden-tity aspirations. Voting vents dissatisfaction, but it has yet to bring a consensus on how national identity should evolve.

South Korea's status goals have shifted over time. They have included confirmation of its rise as an ally, an economic model, an advanced in-dustrial society, a political force, and a shaper of international relations in East Asia. Each of its presidents has found reason to resent some lack of recognition. And the balance has gradually shifted from seeking confirmation to showing Korean autonomy—albeit progressives have been keener on doing the latter. Rather than continuing to raise elusive goals, a more modest but well-grounded sense of the nation's identity could lower expectations, overcoming the accumulated sense of disap-pointment. Refocusing national identity in line with today's realities would offer a new start for both deeply discordant domestic politics and increasingly perilous foreign policy choices in the face of ominous threats from North Korea and long-term concerns that China's rise will leave South Korean identity in a perilous state.

Notes

1. Gilbert Rozman, "South Korea's National Identity Sensitivity: Evolution, Manifestations, Prospects," *KEI Academic Paper Series,* March 2009, 1–9.

2. *New York Times,* November 18, 2008, p. A6.

3. On the different types of Confucianism, see Gilbert Rozman, "Comparisons of Modern Confucian Values in China and Japan," in *The East Asian Region: Confucian Heritage and Its Modern Adaptation,* edited by Gilbert Rozman (Princeton, N.J.: Princeton University Press, 1991), 157–203.

4. Michael Robinson, *Cultural Nationalism in Colonial Korea, 1920–1925* (Seattle: University of Washington Press, 1988).

5. Andre Schmid, *Korea between Empires, 1895–1919* (New York: Columbia University Press, 2002), 60–64.

6. Gilbert Rozman, In-Taek Hyun, and Shin-wha Lee, *South Korean Strategic Thought toward Asia* (New York: Palgrave, 2008).

7. Alexis Dudden, *Japan's Colonization of Korea: Discourse and Power* (Honolulu: University of Hawaii Press, 2005).

8. Cho Hong Sik, "Globalization and National Identity: *Shintobul-i,* a Case of Cultural Representation of Economic Nationalism," *Journal of International and Area Studies* 15, no. 1 (June 2008): 17–36.

9. Daesong Hyun, "Korea: A Confucian Society in Culture Shifts," in *Human Beliefs and Values in East and Southeast Asia in Transition: 13 Country Profiles on the Basis of the AsiaBarometer Surveys of 2006 and 2007,* edited by Takashi Inoguchi (Tokyo: Akashi shoten, 2009), 104–9.

10. Kang Won-taek, "Hangukin oe kukka jongchesong goa minjok jongchesong: Taehanminguk minjokjuoe," in *Hangukin oe kukka jongchesong goa Hanguk jongchi,* edited by Kang Won-taek (Seoul: EAI, 2006), 15–38.

11. Yong Chool Ha, "Late Industrialization, the State, and Social Changes: The Emergence of Neofamilism," *Comparative Political Studies* 40, no. 4 (April 2007): 363–81.

12. Gilbert Rozman, "Can Confucianism Survive in an Age of Universalism and Globalization?" *Pacific Affairs* 75, no. 1 (Spring 2002): 11–37.

13. Samuel S. Kim, *Korea's Globalization* (Cambridge: Cambridge University Press, 2000).

14. Samuel S. Kim, *Korea's Democratization* (Cambridge: Cambridge University Press, 2003).

15. Jonathan D. Pollack, ed., *Korea: The East Asian Pivot* (Newport: Naval War College Press, 2006); Charles K. Armstrong, Gilbert Rozman, Samuel S. Kim, and Stephen Kotkin, eds. *Korea at the Center: Dynamics of Regionalism in Northeast Asia* (Armonk, N.Y.: M. E. Sharpe, 2006).

16. Lee Nae-young, "Public Opinion about ROK-U.S. Relations," in *KEI 2006: Joint U.S.-Korea Academic Studies* (Washington, D.C.: Korea Economic Institute, 2006), 1–11.

17. "Hanguoren danxin chengwei sanmingzhi guojia," *Gaige neican,* no. 32 (2007): 49.

18. Lee Nae-young, "Public Opinion about ROK-U.S. Relations," in *KEI 2005: Joint U.S.-Korea Academic Studies* (Washington, D.C.: Korea Economic Institute, 2005).

19. Chae-jin Lee, *A Troubled Peace: U.S. Policy and the Two Koreas* (Baltimore: Johns Hopkins University Press, 2006).

20. Jae Ho Chung, *Between Ally and Partner: Korea-China Relations and the United States* (New York: Columbia University Press, 2007), 90–91.

21. *Ilbon pogoso* (Seoul: Chonghap yonguso, 1999); Ko Bunyu, *Ryu o kidoru Chugoku tora no odoshi o karu Kankoku* (Tokyo: Tokuma, 2000).

22. Gi-Wook Shin, *One Alliance, Two Lenses: U.S.-Korea Relations in a New Era* (Stanford, Calif.: Stanford University Press, 2010).

23. "60 Percent Have Anti-China Sentiment," *Korea Times,* November 28, 2008.

24. Cheol Hee Park, "Japanese Strategic Thinking toward Korea," in *Japanese Strategic Thought toward Asia,* edited by Gilbert Rozman, Kazuhiko Togo, and Joseph P. Ferguson (New York: Palgrave, 2007), 183–200.

25. Cui Zhiying, "'Liangjin' huiwu hou Chaoxian bandao he Dongbeiya jushi zouxiang," *Ouya guancha,* no. 3 (2000): 25–28.

26. Vasily Mikheev, "Russian Strategic Thinking toward North and South Korea," in *Russian Strategic Thought toward Asia,* edited by Gilbert Rozman, Kazuhiko Togo, and Joseph P. Ferguson (New York: Palgrave, 2006), 187–204.

Chapter 3

Chinese National Identity: A Six-Dimensional Analysis

Gilbert Rozman

Although at the time of the May Fourth Movement, the Cultural Revolution, and the "culture fever" of the 1980s, many considered key parts of China's national identity to be vulnerable to abrupt rejection, one should acknowledge the depth and durability of this identity. It is rooted in Confucianism, which remained the core of civilizational identity for roughly two thousand years. It is manifested in the notion of the "middle kingdom," heralding a state not only at the vortex of disparate regions but also at the top of a ritual hierarchy. Although associated with imperial rule and now Communist rule, privileging the state as the embodiment of a unified, centralized system, China's national identity also reflects strong pride in the society and its achievements, including material well-being, with the potential to turn against Communist rule in circumstances different from those of recent days. Even at times when the nation appeared to be in peril, a core of cultural and political identity also remained essentially secure. When confidence was bolstered by an upsurge in economic national identity as well, this core could be expanded into a formidable display of great power pride that would be difficult to match anywhere else in the world. Whether at its apex, as at the Beijing Olympics, or at its nadir, the outward signs of identity need to be peeled away in order to analyze the multiple characteristics at the core of China's identity as a nation.

There has been much talk of a rise of nationalism in China in the 1990s and 2000s. By shifting attention to national identity, here I broaden the perspective, while increasing the potential to move the discussion forward.[1] This opens the way to differentiating many dimensions of identity and to clarifying the process of identity transformation. The same six-dimensional framework used for Japan and South Korea is applied to China. In comparison with the other two, China's identity has changed substantially during a short time. Even in the Cold War era, there was an abrupt shift after Mao Zedong's death. Further rapid change has occurred decade by decade. However, focusing on what has emerged does not suggest an ephemeral phenomenon, because China's rise leads to it reclaiming its status at the center of Asia. In 2010, elements of an increasingly confident identity took a central role in rhetoric.

Reviewing the ideological and temporal dimensions of national identity, I cannot avoid passing judgment on the relevance of two unrivaled driving forces: Confucianism and Communism. The former faded after 1911, and especially 1949, as an organizing principle in Chinese thought. The latter endured after 1978 and, more clearly, 1989 in the form of claims about Chinese socialism, despite losing much of its substance. Yet interest here is much less in what official credence is given to these belief systems than in how they figure, however indirectly, in the way the national identity is conceived. The legacy of Confucianism and the way socialism has become entwined with diverse elements of China's identity are inescapable elements of its recently constructed national identity. Each of the two has meaning for discussion of its sectoral, vertical, and horizontal dimensions and also warrant consideration in efforts to specify the depth of national identity formation in China. Although Communism was submerged at a time when China was emphasizing its pragmatism and the nonchallenging nature of its peaceful development, it blatantly resurfaced in bolder claims about identity accompanying the upsurge of pride with the Beijing Olympics and of contempt toward the United States and Western civilization with the global financial and economic crisis starting in late 2008. This could be seen in the sharp contrasts drawn between these civilizations.

The national identity bursting forth in 2010 glorified China's Confucian history and its premodern view of regional relations, in contrast to the anti-Confucius campaigns of Mao. It selectively embraced the Maoist era, submerging earlier criticisms in favor of a continuous narrative about China's superiority except when it was too weak to withstand the humiliation at the hands of the West. Moreover, it reinterpreted reform and globalization from the 1980s to 2000s as a necessary transition for China to enable it to reach a position where it could affirm its national identity fully and shift its policies to be in accord with these ideals.[2] Whether Hu Jintao, who had started with a cautious approach linked to "new thinking" with Japan and shared international responsibility with the United States, was driving this assertive shift or his assumed heir Xi Jinping had capitalized on support from Jiang Zemin to draw on more intense national identity emotions, the result—endorsed by the Political Standing Committee but attenuated at the end of 2010—far exceeded the earlier spikes in identity that occurred in Japan and South Korea when their dimensions were aligned.

To appreciate Chinese national identity requires attentiveness to how selected concepts are twisted in unambiguous support of a dichotomous worldview. Rhetoric on sensitive themes is orchestrated to convey clear, often simplistic messages. By 2010, the demonization of the United States and its allies had reached a fever pitch, whereas only sanctimonious portrayals appeared of the Chinese Communist Party (CCP) and the state related to matters of identity significance. This contrasts with the Japanese and Korean debates. Chinese sources at odds with this assertive narrative were marginalized—but in 2011, in limited ways, were allowed to appear.

The Ideological Dimension

Ideological diversity has been rare in Chinese history and lacks the impetus seen in Japan and South Korea of incomplete resolution of historical questions involving other states. The state exercises a monopoly in the construction of national identity to suppress opposition movements, whether rooted in Confucian reform thinking or Western values. The exception, from the 1900s to the 1940s, occurred when state authority could not be exercised and China was subject to great foreign pressure. In the 1890s and 1980s, movements arose to extend hesitant reforms into a reconstruction of the foundation of national identity, but they were crushed. In contrast, in the 1940s Communists succeeded in seizing power and implanting their ideology in a manner that allowed Mao Zedong to radicalize it at will and prevented, even at times of reform, serious ideological challenge. It is possible that a crisis mood (due to economic stagnation, social unrest, or a political struggle) could lead the Chinese, on a large scale, to challenge this monopoly and revisit the submerged history of the CCP's rule. This might arouse a sense of unfinished history, such as exists in Japan and South Korea, accompanied by a search for normalcy by acknowledging the past and overcoming it. Yet there is no sign of a serious challenge today in defining the manner in which national identity is presented. The CCP remains dominant, striving to structure an unassailable national identity while controlling any dissenting approaches.

In the 1980s, signals were inconsistent on the ideological dimension of identity. Hu Yaobang and various reform voices were sufficiently critical of past excesses that some saw prospects for rejection of Communism and convergence on universal values. Lingering campaigns, such as the one against spiritual pollution, and purges of leaders such as Hu and Zhao Ziyang, lent support to the possibility that socialist orthodoxy could regain its hold on China. Yet Deng Xiaoping steered the country away from either choice, as he kept the goal of strengthening comprehensive national power in the forefront.[3] By the time of the Fourteenth Party Congress in 1992, Deng's ideological legacy was secure, as an amalgam of the CCP, state, and military were designated guardians of a national identity supportive of economic openness but firmly opposed to the threat of "bourgeois peaceful evolution" linked to appeals for human rights or democracy in China.

Chinese national identity continues to be directed against universal values—the oft-criticized concept of "humanism" and the alien notion of human rights as a cynical tool of foreign enemies. Mao insisted in diatribes against Khrushchev that "humanism" is incompatible with socialism, and into the 1990s authors blamed the collapse of the Soviet Union on the humanistic roots of Gorbachev's "new thinking."[4] It allegedly weakens a country's national identity and its defense against the infiltration of a hostile ideology. In late imperial China, neo-Confucianism prioritized purity of belief and foreign dynasties accentuated ideological intolerance on matters of state. Communism has done the same.

Though cautious, unorganized reformers can still be identified in China, warnings and imprisonment have prevented the rise of a reform party or even a reform movement. The situation is more favorable for the political left, where Maoist nostalgia, assertive repudiation of the United States–led world order, and harsher control measures all win support. As China's power grows, Deng's message for leaders to bide their time may appear outdated. Much of the business community and educated elite may be inclined to trust the world community, but the left-center consensus continues to inveigh against hegemonism and universal values in a manner that could well influence emerging policies. The fact that reform thinking has little impact on national identity with respect to political reform and trust in international values does not bode well for the policy choices of an emboldened China. The ideological balance is skewed in a manner unfavorable to balanced choices.

The Chinese contrast their support for a harmonious world with the Cold War mentality of the United States and its allies. They insist that America, in its advocacy of universal values, is driven by ideology, whereas China is pragmatic and only pursuing its national interests. In contrast to U.S. unilateralism, China is praised as a supporter of multilateralism. Although the United States resorts to pressure and even war, China is peaceful and only seeks friendly ties to its neighbors. Also, China is a champion of globalization versus protectionist, divisive tendencies. Counterterrorism is a U.S. pretext for pursuing further hegemonism. Using the term "new diplomacy" in 2009–10 to distinguish China's approach, they projected a world divided by two types of thinking, even when U.S. president Barack Obama was intent on finding common ground, and they applied the same dichotomy to U.S. allies and partners.[5] When the policy results proved damaging and signals of a shift in direction appeared in December 2010, direct contradictions were not printed.

In the post–Cold War era, the Chinese are insistent that the United States and its allies are under the sway of ideology or the inertia of Cold War thinking, while China's focus is pragmatism and reassurance about its preoccupation with peace and development. Others, unlike China, were programmed to construct security threats and enemies.[6] Thus, the way to resolve the North Korean nuclear crisis is to meet North Korea's demands and to drop Cold War thinking.[7] By 2010, an ideological amalgam was celebrated for its combination of Confucianism and Communism. It viewed China as the champion of a rising Eastern civilization in opposition to Western civilization, which had inflicted great harm as the past source of imperialism and an intensified threat to the survival of other civilizations. Even as some voices continued to advocate pragmatic problem-solving behavior without any ideological framework, the ascendant ideology drives a more assertive agenda.[8] No longer are the Chinese shy about portraying the struggle as an ideological clash, placing on one side both Eastern civilization and socialism and on the other U.S. Cold War inertia.[9] In essence, this is a renewal of the defense of Chinese superiority as a civilization based on principles such as "harmony," in contrast to the negative impact of the West based on a fundamentally incompatible civilization. Class struggle is gone, but ideology survives.

The Temporal Dimension

Much can be said about times of flux in China's national identity, but the task here is to look back from 2010 to discern how history is perceived as a factor in current identity. The struggle over identity has often been intense during the past century, and rejection of once-popular themes has suggested more discontinuity than actually occurred, as seen in a later period. Today's identity may also come under such scrutiny, especially because the claims for socialism seem anachronistic to many who have watched the crumbling of Communist ideology elsewhere. That is no longer the lynchpin for other forms of identity. Yet, in combination with nativist rejection of the West, it continues to play a large role. It is being upgraded along with traditional Chinese identity as a shared identity as the West loses the luster it acquired in the 1980s and retained to some degree thereafter.

Premodern national identity had more continuity in China than in other nations. Confucianism served continuously as the guiding worldview. Conflating state and nation into a single notion of universal civilization never was seriously challenged, even when China split into separate governments or was subject to rule by a conquest dynasty. Although this legacy appeared to succumb to the fall of imperial China—leading to the May Fourth Movement, with its inclination toward Western values, and especially to the founding of the People's

Republic of China, with its rejection of "feudal" as well as capitalist values at a peak in the Cultural Revolution—more continuity could be detected in the cultural opening of the 1980s and, more clearly, in the identity amalgam after the end of the Cold War.[10] In the transition from premodern Confucian identity to pre-1949 turmoil in nation building, China was slow to find clarity in national identity. Then, in the transition to the postwar era, nihilism about the past and utopianism about a new identity brought false clarity that in the 1980s was replaced by a groping search for something very different. Finally, in the transition to the post–Cold War era, elements of the previous eras reemerged as a wide-ranging synthesis focusing on China's future and drawing on its past was taking shape.

"Tianxia" (All-under-Heaven), the premodern ideal for international relations, has gained popularity in two justifications of China's challenge to the existing order. First, it recalls the past order of Sinocentrism as the natural order for emerging regionalism. Bereft of expansionism or a missionary zeal to export religious values, this worldview suits diversity, as in Asia today. Second, authors depict this ideal as bridging differences while maintaining stability and avoiding hegemonism. Thus it offers an alternative to U.S. interference in the internal affairs of other states. Premodern China becomes a model for today, winning adulation for its purported success at home and abroad in overcoming cultural differences. In neither Japan nor South Korea is the premodern era venerated as much or the West viewed so negatively, disparaging even its Enlightenment and humanism. The contrast is based on distorting Confucianism into an identity for state aggrandizement without giving any credit to its humanitarian elements or blame to its ethnocentric ones.

Another concept that has been explicitly revived by Chinese leaders is "harmonious society." Coming from the top, it heralds the image of state management of society to foster order through intense moral suasion and a hierarchical approach to responsibility.[11] Although the Tianxia ideal skews thinking about the horizontal dimension of China's ties to the outside world, a vision of "harmonious society" rooted in the past slants thinking about the vertical dimension of organization within China. After Mao's long obsession with ridding China of Confucianism, the question arose of how far the post-Mao leadership would go in embracing China's traditional values and elements of national identity. In the 1980s, the theme of "harmony" already drew interest because leaders were intent on putting "class struggle" behind. After June 4, 1989, the appeal of Asian values grew as leaders looked more to regional relations and models, invigorating the study of Confucianism as well. Yet it was only under Hu Jintao that appeals to this tradition drew strong support with two initiatives: the establishment of Confucius Institutes around the world, and a decision to make "harmonious society" the primary slogan for China's future development. Whereas in the early 1980s authoritarian elements of China's history linked to Confucianism were blamed for the excesses of past rule in order to deflect criticism from Communism, these same vertical elements now win praise as the key to forging harmony, broadening the mandate of the CCP's intervention in society. Later, the theme of "harmonious world" was also introduced. Recent writings suggest that this concept is fundamentally opposed to efforts in the West to enlist China as a responsible partner. Instead of contributing to the existing international order, this notion steers that order in a different direction.[12]

In the decades at the end of the nineteenth and the beginning of the twentieth century, the Chinese were aroused against creeping imperialism and ineffectual Manchu rule as they also were attracted to new currents of nationalism that called for redefining the state as a force for national development and international competition. Amid wide-ranging debate, rival interpretations of China's national identity drew support. Some were cosmopolitan, accepting integration into the existing global community. Others harked back to China's past, highlighting themes that were distinctive. Before Japan's invasion in the 1930s, the Guomindang government drew on China's past to champion a strong state, while its CCP rivals repudiated the past in favor of a view of national identity rooted in the teachings of Vladimir Lenin and Joseph Stalin, although later they preferred to refer to the ideology simply as Marxism. Having lost support after the end of the examination system and the imperial era, Confucianism only indirectly influenced the struggle over national identity, which was unresolved. Only a century after the fall of imperial China is it again a cornerstone to claims of China's superiority.

One element of transitional identity that survived in later thinking was a narrative of abuse of the Chinese nation at the hands of foreign powers.[13] This gained credibility from Japan's invasions in the 1930s and the protracted war of resistance. In battling for power, the CCP found that anti-imperialist themes resonated better than class struggle appeals. This aspect of historical identity highlighted in the Mao era became a popular theme in the "patriotic education" movement of the 1990s.[14] Downplaying varied reforms that contributed to modernization, the thrust of recent rhetoric is on resistance as the basis for forging a national identity that saved China from losing its civilization.

Looking back from 2010, the Chinese have stopped stressing what must be jettisoned from their traditional beliefs and have switched to seeking value in them. After the harsh Maoist denigration of the past, the Beijing Olympics paid tribute to outstanding achievements. Growing pride in contemporary China reverberates in a renewed appreciation of Chinese culture and learning. Above all, the state is intent on glorifying the territorial expansion of past dynasties, in this way confirming control over ethnic minorities such as the Tibetans and of existing boundaries. Laying claim to the Koguryo state, which is recognized by Koreans as the fountainhead of their history, shows the assertiveness of this emboldened attitude toward China's premodern past. At the same time, continued stress on the many humiliations China has suffered at the hands of foreign powers provides a stark contrast with what happens when China does not have a strong central government to which the people defer. Reconstructing the past in this manner supports authoritarianism and vigilance in the face of foreign states that are supposedly predisposed to imperialism or, lately, hegemonism.

The CCP painted a glorious picture of revolutionary valor to interpret national history leading to 1949, followed by continuity in building a revolutionary society. Until the death of Mao Zedong, this narrative put China in the forefront of world development, initially second only to the Soviet Union and then taking the lead. An artificial periodization in which socialism superseded capitalism and superficial indicators of equality displaced real measures of prosperity propelled China to the front. Comparable to imperial times, Chinese self-perceptions put their country at the center of world civilization, demeaning other states as "imperialist," "revisionist," or "unjust" and still in need of a revolution. Although such claims faded after Mao, they have been revived to a degree, especially in the aftermath of the global financial and economic crisis of 2008–10, when capitalism lost its luster.

Three serious challenges to the Maoist worldview arose in the 1970s. First, the excesses of the Cultural Revolution left in shambles many of the claims for China's superiority. Second, China's rapprochement with the United States and then Japan, along with growing evidence of the dynamism of capitalist countries, cast doubt on the main pillars of the past socialist identity. And third, Deng Xiaoping's reforms repudiated the previous model and left a vacuum in national identity. Yet, China's leaders insisted on assessing Mao and his policies as 70 percent positive and 30 percent negative, clinging to aspects of the identity he left. They prepared for a new era by defining the recent past in order to conceal its essence.

If at the start of the Deng era there was much talk about "twenty lost years," the thrust of discussions about the Mao era eventually turned to success in overcoming humiliation and raising China's international stature. Covering up the worst of China's excesses during the period from the 1950s to the 1970s, writers left something of a vacuum while also conveying a vaguely positive image of an independent foreign policy, capped by the breakthrough in relations with the United States in 1972. China's decision to build socialism is not subject to debate; nor are many of Mao's major decisions, despite their negative consequences.

After the years 1989–91, the collapse of international Communism and the Soviet Union left in doubt China's ability to draw on the three decades after the founding of the PRC as a positive source for national identity. Leaders censored revelations that would expose the most negative features, but this became problematic as the sordid history of Communism elsewhere was revealed. The post–Cold War identity stifled the search for meaning in the comparative study of socialism, even as it focused attention on drawing lessons from the fate of other socialist states to allow China to avoid it. Through a distorted lens, the goal was to convey a positive image to strengthen the legitimacy of CCP rule.[15]

According to one report from late 2008, China leads in the revival of socialism from its nadir. Socialism did not die with the twentieth century but is emerging from the collapse of the American bubble economy and China's three decades of reform and open door policies that have continuously added to its comprehensive power and international status. Commentators appraise the latest crisis of capitalism as if it were unprecedented and note socialism's ascendance on the 160th anniversary of the Communist Manifesto and the 30th anniversary of Deng's reform program, as Hu Jintao pointed to scientific socialism and socialism with Chinese characteristics as markers of China's identity.[16] This hybrid mix of national culture and Marxist teachings, however unreal it seems, is drawing attention after an Olympic year of unrivaled triumphalism about China's prospects.

When one assesses the balance of three periods in China's current process of national identity formation, one finds special stress on the period from the 1980s to the present, the recovery of premodern pride, and the renewed concealment of the excesses of Cold War national identity as if that can result in a positive verdict. Given the fragility of images centered on recent economic national identity and the troubled state of identities steeped in censorship and distortions, a review of China's temporal dimension does not offer reassurance that a stable mix of periods has been realized. Only by viewing the premodern era more critically again, judging the Cold War era more negatively, and recognizing more limitations in the post–Cold War period that require attention would China be likely to achieve a balanced approach in treating its history as part of identity. Recent currents are leading in the opposite direction.

The Sectoral Dimension

China's political and cultural identities intersect in exceptional ways. Historically, not only has there been no separation of religion and state, but the two became intertwined in ways that did not make differentiation of civilization and state authority possible. After many invasions of all or part of what was regarded as Chinese territory, the lesson was drawn that outside power might prevail but that the depth of China's superior civilization would oblige even the most heinous barbarians to yield. Starting in the mid–nineteenth century, however, a different type of challenge tested China's civilizational and political identity. Unable to protect its civilization this time, the state lost authority with the population. Only after a century had passed did a centralized state reemerge that was capable of fusing the two types of identity, but it did so on the basis of an exaggerated notion of political nationalism under the influence of Lenin's Soviet Communist Party structure and Stalin's totalitarian state. China struggled to graft the ideology bequeathed by these Soviet leaders onto a traditional view of civilizational superiority and autonomy. An ideological struggle with the United States, and also starting in 1958 with the Soviet Union, further fused these two strands of China's new identity. Even as much of the Maoist legacy was abandoned in the 1980s, this fusion prevailed. In struggles throughout the decade, such as the brief 1984 "anti–spiritual pollution" campaign and the intense post–June 1989 repudiation of "bourgeois evolution," Chinese officials left no doubt that they were no longer opposing "revisionism" but rather were fighting against Western values that newly threatened to overwhelm their country's very identity.

On the sectoral dimension, the Confucian heritage conflated cultural and political identities. It privileged the state with the moral authority to define and transmit civilization. Its obsession with a unified written language for an array of spoken languages and a rigid, universal examination system requiring the inculcation of cultural and political orthodoxy built the foundation for a modern national identity.[17] Elite practice of the approved rituals disseminated an intensely shared identity. Buttressed by high rates of male literacy, mass and even merchant Confucianism joined elite Confucianism in supporting the imperial Confucianism centered on the throne.[18] Although it took time to make a jolting transition to a modern identity focused on a nation-state competing in a global community centered on another worldview, this foundation continued to inform the responses of the Chinese people. Authoritarian rule finds benefit from the legacy of imperial identity, even as it faces challenges from diversity at home and abroad and also from the legacy of reform Confucianism, which pressed for ideals that limited the state. Carefully shaping history in accord with the demands of today, Chinese leaders are making it a key element in identity.

Political national identity was repeatedly aroused in China in ways not seen in Japan or South Korea after 1945. The CCP lauded it as a force that overthrew China's imperial order and resisted the imperialist powers. Although the Guomindang was less effective in harnessing it, the CCP used it in coming to power and afterward, including in the 1980s and 1990s, when there were pressures to Westernize. Treating resistance to hard power and soft power together while often putting more stress on the latter, writers merge political and cultural identity, achieving effectiveness in producing a backlash after the U.S. bombing of China's Belgrade Embassy. At the Beijing Olympics in 2008, rising national self-confidence was paraded before the world. It was treated as a positive force for China's rise as a political power and for its culture to become more influential around the world.[19] Effusiveness about this fusion kept intensifying.

A mix of cultural and political identity exerts a tight hold on Chinese rhetoric. It is based on the linkage established early in Chinese history between Han ethnic identity and the state's political identity, which operated even when the imperial family was not Han but could embrace the Confucian civilizational themes in a similar manner. Also figuring into this complex was economic identity, focused earlier on satisfying well-being and then on catching up and developing in a competitive world. This premodern legacy predisposed the Chinese to perceive a revival of an identity complex in which all sectors are present. With an emphasis on how well interethnic relations were handled in imperial times, the Chinese now replace "Han" with "China," as if a Chinese nationality has successfully bridged all divisions. Only separatists, such as some Tibetans and Uyghurs, allegedly deny this unifying force.

In the early 1980s, Chinese identity appeared vulnerable. Mao's revolutionary identity and even the broader socialist identity were under attack. Coming to the rescue was Chinese civilizational identity, which Deng pragmatically used as he rebranded it part of "socialist spiritual civilization." Even if the concept remained vague and proved in the 1980s to be vulnerable to imported ideas about culture, after June 4, 1989, there was more success in rallying the Chinese people around the notion of a shared civilization that was under pressure from the West. Later, warnings against the danger of others arousing alarm over a "China threat," as if it were much more serious than it is, served a similar purpose of rallying the Chinese against states striving to suppress their civilization.[20]

Cultural identity lends itself to nationalism, venerating themes deemed traditional and rejecting diversity originating from ethnic minorities or international society. Under Mao, demands for cultural uniformity were linked to his twist on Communist ideology, and after Deng took power there were mixed messages. On some themes diversity was accepted, leading even to "cultural fever" in the mid-1980s, but other issues drew warnings against "spiritual pollution." In the 1990s, a cultural amalgam took shape, exclusive of universal values. Yet only later does one find aggressive nationalism in favor of a narrowly defined "harmonious society." The Falungung sect became the most serious religious target, and starting in 2008 the Dalai Lama and Tibetan religious and cultural claims drew increased attention as a dangerous threat to cultural identity, equated with an attack on sovereignty. As in imperial history, China's leaders accept only localized religious activities but reject challenges to their monopoly on cultural national identity. This acquired urgency because of fear of a link-up between such demands and global pressure for universal values.

Economic national identity became a driving force of pride starting in the 1990s. This paralleled a similar phenomenon in Japan starting in the 1960s and South Korea starting in the 1970s. As world praise resounded, the Chinese became the latest East Asian populace to equate an "economic miracle" with sentiment that their state was especially deserving of acclaim. In the other cases, this pride came in the context of political dependency and hesitancy to challenge the universal values of the United States. In China, the first breakthrough came in 1993–94, as the World Bank recomputed China's economy in terms of purchasing power and double-digit growth became a fixture in its image. Complementing this new economic pride with a "patriotic education" campaign linking past and present political national identity and with an appeal to cultural identity centered on criticism of those who denied China the chance to host the Olympics, China's leaders achieved a tripling effect.

Not only was the compounded sectoral impact realized in the mid-1990s, it persisted during the Beijing Olympics and kept growing more intense. The cultural boost of the Olympic gala ceremonies laced with cultural themes and pride in national performances blended into the political boost from narratives of foreign criticisms of the way China handled the preparations for the Olympics and then into the economic boost from the global financial crisis being blamed on the United States and interpreted as signaling the decline of the old economic order as China emerged stronger from the ordeal. Political identity is kept at a high pitch, cultural identity keeps building, and economic identity is now raised beyond previous levels. This is a formidable combination that is no longer tempered by realism about the balance of power, the role of universal values in stability, or how global economic integration is dependent on other types of globalization. A Communist political identity, Confucian cultural identity, and increasingly state-centered economic identity in 2010 made the Japanese and South Korean spikes in sectoral identity pale in comparison. In 2011, some humility was expressed that more time would be needed for China to catch up, but there was little rethinking of the emergent identity.

The Vertical Dimension

Confucianism simplified the vertical levels of society by concentrating on family/kin groups and country. Modern challenges have drawn attention to the additional levels of the world community, the individual, and the intermediate level between state and community. Mao struggled to overturn the traditional hierarchy, forging people's communes and *danwei* (work units) as bodies that preempted other intermediate-level units, while also striving to nullify tendencies to make the individual and the world community significant reference groups. To a degree, indirect reinforcement of family authority and support for the socialist bloc as an alternative to the world community could have empowered more units, but Mao took decisive action to prevent such results. The socialist bloc faded with the Sino-Soviet split, and despite some revival of family and community with the reforms of the 1980s, the reemphasis on vertical controls and identity intensified after June 1989.

On the vertical dimension, the Chinese authorities have thoroughly denied intermediate-level entities to organize, while usually accepting family and local-level initiatives that allow for considerable competition and decentralization. Initiatives of this sort are confined in scope and in political salience, exhibiting little capacity to make an impact on national identity. The ideal under imperial Confucianism and Communism was to give the center more moral authority to meet pressing problems, and leaders tended to overstate the need to do this even if no obvious justification existed. In the absence of the effects of democratization seen first in Japan and then in South Korea, the center's position is much stronger in China, especially as the focus of national identity. Instead of placing blame on excessive concentration of power, as occurred in Japan after the 1945 defeat and in South Korea with the rejection of military dictatorship in the 1980s, the Chinese historically blamed a loss of state authority or the chaos resulting from divisions at the top. They link sovereignty to territorial integrity, with the added twist that state authority must not be limited in any formal manner. As in the past, state-society relations are viewed hierarchically, as are the state's rights over religious groups, merchant groups, ethnic minorities, and so on. If customarily, the state stopped short of exercising its authority in most situations, ritual acknowledgment of it was never relaxed. When China turned to decentralization for economic dynamism in the 1980s, this was delegated authority through appointed officials under central instructions. No shift to local power on matters deemed vital or linked to national identity was contemplated.

In response to the colored revolutions in states that emerged from the former Soviet Union, Chinese leaders intensified their opposition against moves to promote civil society with international linkages. Having reacted to the Tiananmen Square demonstrations and the collapse of the Soviet Union with more determination to control society, their resolve hardened again in 2003–5 as governments were challenged by groups appealing to democracy and backed in the West. In this context, Hu spoke of forging a harmonious society, legitimating only vertically structured cooperation under state direction.[21] Any intermediate organization capable of winning a large following, such as among ethnic or religious groups, was suspect as a challenge to the approved state-dominated hierarchy. A vitriolic campaign against the awarding of the 2010 Nobel Peace Prize to the democracy advocate Liu Shaobo was further indication of unyielding opposition to interference in the CCP's insistence on authoritarian principles. In 2011, fear of spillover from the Jasmine Revolution in Arab countries contributed to a more intense crackdown on cultural figures, lawyers, and others who were regarded as out of step.

The Horizontal Dimension

In premodern times, the horizontal dimension of China's identity was quite unchanging. The world was viewed through the lens of civilized Confucians and barbarians, varying in the degree to which they were removed from this state and had to be treated with divisive moves to prevent a unified attack. In the interim decades before the 1950s, acceptance of the international system was complicated by China's low standing. It was late to play one power off against another and not very successful. In the 1950s, the Soviet Union was the model and the United States was the villain, leaving a legacy of two states that mattered most.

China's leaders shifted to a three-way classification—for a time dividing the outside world into capitalist, socialist, and developing camps—but their categories became muddled. Socialism was confused by the label "revisionist," capitalism was altered by China's rapprochement with the United States, and with the country's dramatic economic growth, efforts to highlight China as a developing state also loss meaning for specifying national identity. As the focus switched from the Soviet threat to the United States threat in the 1980s, a different outlook emerged. In the inner circle of the world were relations with the United States, in the next circle were other great power ties, and just beyond were ties to neighboring states. Further out were links to developing countries. Despite China's important position in the UN Security Council as a permanent member, the place of international society was weak in its national identity. The United Nations only figured as an arena for great power relations and for ties to developing states.

Chinese identity kept fixating on one great power while keeping an eye on two other important powers in a kind of zero-sum logic that sought space for China's rise. In the course of the twentieth century Japan, the Soviet Union, and the United States each had a turn as the obsession that China had to address. In Chinese reasoning, each has posed a threat to the nation's civilization. Branding the Soviets revisionists, the Japanese revanchists, and the Americans imperialists, China tried to insulate itself from the threat of their ideas. If during the past thirty years the United States has continued to occupy the top spot, the mix of these three countries and what they signify for China's national identity have kept changing. Yet the United States serves as the chief rival, Japan as the gateway to regionalism and the rival in shaping it, and since the 1990s Russia as the key to global great power relations that limit American power.

Three ideological challenges arose in rapid succession in the eyes of the CCP leaders: socialist betrayal by the Soviet Union, historical revisionism by Japan, and U.S. spiritual pollution. The first of these threatened to undermine the legitimacy of the CCP and leave a defenseless opening through which repugnant ideas could spread. The second attacked the core of Chinese nationalism, insisting that Japan's goal had been to liberate China while fostering its modernization and the rise of Asia. Of all the challenges, however, the most serious comes from the U.S. worldview, whose future orientation calls on the Chinese state and all who lead it to cede authority to international humanistic standards and representatives. They see a "new world order," a "civilizational clash," and global morality if not governance as hostile to Chinese sovereignty. Early in the 1990s, some Chinese saw a convergence of these ideological strains putting pressure on their already-isolated country. Even when Deng decided to further open the country economically and to dismiss the argument that the Soviet Union fell due primarily to an ideological assault led by the United States, China proceeded to reconstruct a national identity less vulnerable to these outside forces. As long as images of the outside world are imbued with such negativity, the horizontal dimension is unlikely to be reordered in a manner that balances the United States, regional states, and the international community.

From the 1960s to the 1980s, the Soviet challenge to Chinese national identity was foremost, leading to the most intense debates and coverage of its transformation. After the collapse of the Soviet Union, Deng put a stop to this theme, as the socialist character of Chinese national identity was eclipsed. Even in the 1980s, Chinese national identity remained difficult to separate from that of the Soviet Union. In the first half of the 1950s, the Soviet model had been imported in a wholesale manner; and later, in Mao's final two decades, wrestling with how to separate China from what he criticized as revisionism, distorted images of Soviet reality, and leftist claims to a "revolutionary" identity failed to provide a lasting alternative. With the preservation of socialism in China having become an enduring preoccupation in the 1980s, debates on Soviet socialism were of great significance and sensitivity. Yet it was only in the years 1989–91 in the aftermath of the stunted normalization of relations, overshadowed by the collapse of first international Communism and then the Soviet Union, that China was able to clarify a distinct national identity. Its economic component drew considerable attention, becoming the latest claimant to "miracle modernization." Its cultural component grew increasingly eclectic, filling more of the identity vacuum. Most important for China's leadership was the political identity of a country able to play a balancing role in international relations and to provide order while focusing on increasing its comprehensive national power. In the background, debates on lessons to be drawn from the collapse of the Soviet Union strongly informed the search in China for a clearer, convincing national identity.

One lesson centered on nationality policy. Blaming the Soviet accommodation of national republics with some elements of sovereign status, leaders were even more intent to reinforce unified political identity, with no room even for cultural autonomy that could be converted into political demands. Perceived in identity terms, this approach linked the humiliation of China by imperialist states trying to turn minorities away from the central state with ongoing efforts inside China to expand cultural autonomy. Claiming that the CCP is the indispensable force for protecting sovereignty, leaders fused cultural and political nationalism, taking advantage of the fact that 92 percent of the population was Han Chinese. With the return of Hong Kong and Macao imminent and the issue of Taiwan's separation capable of galvanizing opinion, in the 1970s symbols of a unified state and culture served to rally the people.

Another lesson pointed to resistance to a perceived international threat. When the Soviet Union dropped its guard against the United States, it lost part of its raison d'être. China's leaders would avoid this by intensifying warnings against U.S. hegemonism. In this perspective, human rights and democratization are ideological weapons threatening to national identity and requiring stronger CCP control of certain aspects of political and cultural life. Exercised in ways that do not impede economic reform and the kind of "open door" allowed in the 1980s, the leadership's controls were less stringent than in the years 1989–91. Using terms such as "equality," leaders insist that national pride and justice are at stake.

The main critique is reserved for the U.S. threat to China's rise and its identity. The thrust in coverage of the United States is to present an aggrieved, rising China facing a hegemonic, unjust global power. Hegemony refers to more than a realist concern about an imbalance of power, which China has addressed since the 1980s with its obsession on boosting comprehensive national power as fast as possible. It also signifies plotting to implant alien values, spreading one civilization at the expense of others. Human rights are viewed as a subterfuge in international relations to impose this kind of hegemony.

Although leaders repeatedly offered assurances that China is not challenging the existing international system, domestic messages present a different picture. The system is unjust, rife with hegemonism and plots to contain China's rise, and national policies are directed at constructing a different order. More than Japan in the bubble economy and South Korea in the Sunshine Policy after years of an "economic miracle," China raised expectations sharply for regional influence. The year 2008 exacerbated these expectations with a combination of celebration of the Olympics as a party in honor of China's rise to the center of the world stage and defiance against supposedly mounting outside pressure. This was a sure-fire recipe for provoking dissatisfaction as hopes were inevitably dashed. Compounded by dissatisfaction over the global financial crisis, public opinion was newly aroused as the leadership showed signs of growing more assertive on the world stage. In 2010, notions of multipolarity were obscured by insistence that Western civilization led by the United States was losing power to Eastern civilization best represented by China.

Whereas Japan and South Korea have depended for nearly two-thirds of a century on U.S. power, China has perceived itself as a rival to the United States and a force for realizing a balance of great powers. Moreover, for most of two thousand years China's leaders have seen their country as having no peers and obliged to shape the surrounding region. Although it too struggles with U.S. bilateral relations as the first line of foreign policy, the pull of great power balancing and the neighboring region is stronger than in its neighbors. Until the 2000s, China saw the international community mainly as a tool of imperialist states or the United States, making this a less relevant point of reference, except as a venue for great power struggle. This also contrasts with Japan and South Korea.

In the 1990s, criticism of Japan for failing to learn the lessons of history rallied public opinion.[22] The Chinese warned of the threat of "values diplomacy," pressed not only by the United States but also by Japan in pursuit of an end to the postwar system. They associated this term with an assertive foreign policy driven by Abe Shinzo to make Japan a military great power and undercutting China's efforts to realize a harmonious world. It reflected a values-driven approach comparable to U.S. neoconservatism in contrast to the different type of conservatism of Fukuda Yasuo centered on common interests and eager to establish an East Asian Community in which Japan would not insist on leadership.[23]

China's obsession with Japan in the 1930s and 1940s became a driving force in Mao's successful revolution mobilizing nationalism against imperialism. Its preoccupation with the Soviet Union in the 1950s to 1980s anchored the struggle to focus national identity on socialism. By the 1990s, U.S. hegemonism and values occupied center stage in China's leaders' continued fascination with rival powers limiting their own claims to authority. Whether as antagonists or models, these powers loomed large as leaders constructed a great power identity struggling to gain ascendency in a fiercely competitive world.[24]

In comparison with the Japanese and South Koreans, the Chinese approach their neighbors with a strong sense of cultural superiority. The Japanese long felt the superiority of being much more modernized. The South Koreans took some comfort in the virtue of victimization. Yet both types of arrogance pale before the depth of revitalized Chinese confidence in being (1) the source and authentic bearer of civilization that the others only borrowed; (2) the defining authority and ritual center in a hierarchical regional system; and (3) by virtue of population, area, and great power attributes of various types, the country to which others should pay their respects. For South Koreans, Japan's historical effrontery is linked to the territorial challenge to the Dokdo/Takeshima Island, as if the powerful Japanese state could again encroach on what is their land. In contrast, for the Chinese the territorial issue is separate, despite the fact that Japan actually holds the Diaoyu/Senkaku Islands. At stake in history disputes is a challenge to China's cultural status. Until the Japanese agree to a correct view of history, they are overturning the natural order of the region, similar to failing to kowtow to the emperor in imperial times. Also, after taking office in 2008 Lee Myung-bak paid more attention not only to the United States but also to Japan, posing an affront.

Chinese hard-liners use arguments about the national interest to obscure their value arguments, often amounting to ideology. Slogans of noninterference in internal affairs mask deeper differences in values deemed appropriate: prosovereignty regardless of ruthlessness and anti-interventionism on the basis of any claims of international standards; anticonvergence, linked to symbols of irreconcilable differences.

The march of the Olympic torch did not enhance China's image in the spring of 2008, as Chinese students and other overseas sojourners mobilized in nationalist support, often showing disrespect for local protesters and the various causes they championed. In Seoul, the demonstrators complained about Chinese treatment of North Korean refugees, winning sympathy at home and with foreigners long disturbed by the lack of attention to this problem from the South Korean government. It did China no good that officials in Pyongyang mobilized mass support for the torch parade, showcasing how totalitarianism can be more in synch with Chinese expectations. In the midst of much discussion about how China's "soft power" is growing,[25] trumpeting nationalist displays did little good.

The Intensity Dimension

Attentive not to rattle nerves in countries that have been debating a China threat, Chinese spokespersons obscured the nature and depth of critical national identity themes. They were adept at utilizing stock phrases with an upbeat message to cover up problems or attitudes that could provoke negative reactions. The Chinese went the furthest in doctoring their desired message in order to shape perceptions of their country. Yet it was possible to peer behind this facade to see the ardor of the political elite's drive for an autonomous leadership status in the region and the world backed by a national identity orchestrated in the most comprehensive fashion to explain why this is just and necessary. From 2008 to 2010, the need to conceal China's national identity challenge seemed to be fading. In the process, leaders were intent on raising the intensity of this identity, by charging that the United States and Japan, above all, were repeatedly provoking China.

Imperial China placed values in the forefront, claiming a universal civilization that contrasted with the greatly inferior local identities of mere barbarian nations. Yet without concern about serious challenges, emotionalism came from the depth of support for assumptions about identity not from specific arousal. Maoist China insisted that its Communist values made it superior to capitalist states and, after only a decade of alliance ties, to the revisionist states led by the Soviet Union. Although through the first half of the twentieth century and again in the 1980s the Chinese were divided in their search for clarity about values, various forces were driving the pursuit of a values consensus that could reassert the superiority of China's claims. Thus, in the 1990s a postsocialist synthesis found wide backing. After the June 1989 backlash against "bourgeois evolution," Deng Xiaoping's concept of "socialist spiritual civilization" turned sharply against universal human values, and after 2000 gave some signs of tolerance of a duality accepting a place for global principles and insisting on the unique presence of Chinese values. Chinese leaders belatedly showed interest in Asian values during their heyday before the Asian financial crisis, by 2005, as the Association of Southeast Asian Nations + 3 was charged with developing an East Asian Community and in 2007–8, when Japan's Fukuda Yasuo and Hu Jintao praised elements of the historical culture of the other country during an exchange of visits. Yet China's renewed insistence on the distinctiveness of its third claim to superiority over the values of other states became unmistakable by 2010 with new means to utilize the Internet to boost allegiance.

One means of strengthening national identity as undivided and impregnable is to assert it most intensely in dealing with potential challenges such as peripheral areas of the country with separatist elements. In each corner of China, attention has turned to one real or anticipated area of contention. Of course, in the southeast Taiwan stands as a persistent symbol of the greatest significance for national identity, serving as the foremost national symbol. Other areas have drawn more attention of late. If in the 1990s emphasis was given to the positive theme of the recovery of Hong Kong and Macao, in the 2000s more negative images appear of the danger afoot for national sovereignty from ethnoreligious forces in Tibet in the southwest or Xinjiang in the northwest. At the urging of officials in Northeast China, as ties to North and South Korea have shifted somewhat unpredictably, a new focus of concern has become the ancient state of Koguryo. Insisting on China's past sovereignty over it builds a case for future territorial integrity and, possibly, for China's special rights on the Korean Peninsula. In 2010, the focus shifted to maritime territorial disputes, showcasing supposedly aggressive behavior against China. The appeal of sovereignty themes persists as a powerful way to put national identity in the forefront.

The depth of national identity is greatest in China. If Japan has never recovered from the blow of defeat and rejection of wartime hypernationalism and South Korea must calibrate nationalism in the shadow of its exaggerated expression in North Korea, China has no such qualms. The leadership has skewed debate over the symbols of sovereignty and national identity in ways that continue to fuel intense reactions among a vocal part of the population. Treating the temporal dimension as a mix of unvarnished pride in the fruits of Sinocentrism and exaggerated humiliation at the price of weakness, they have produced a narrative relatively unmitigated by conflicting themes. A single approved ideology has stifled exploration of alternative identity foci. Alone among East Asian "economic miracles," China has fully harnessed its political and cultural national identity into sectoral overlap. The vertical dimension boosts the state beyond what is seen elsewhere, as the horizontal dimension demonizes the United States in ways unparalleled apart from Communist states. By combining all these forces, China has constructed a national identity complex of formidable intensity, and it was activating it without restraint in 2010 and with only minor qualifications in 2011.

Conclusion

China's identity has changed more rapidly than that of other states, usually in response to exogenous shocks. The time interval keeps growing shorter between a shock and its powerful impact on national identity. The shock of the Opium War from 1838 took at least to the 1870s to

awaken Chinese officials to the necessity of reforms with potential to alter the country's venerable Confucian identity. Defeat in the war with
Japan in 1895 resonated in 1904 in the elimination of the examination
system as some pillars of the old system were falling. The shock of
Japan's victory over Russia in 1905 and the deal that carved spheres of
influence for both countries was important in producing the Revolution
of 1911 that overthrew the imperial system. In these three successive
blows to China's self-contained worldview, old identities were left indefensible, as seen in the May Fourth Movement and the rise of new political forces after World War I.

Four additional shocks, arguably, followed. The Japanese invasion
shock spurred nationalism that after Japan's defeat in 1945 could be
utilized by the CCP to take power and proclaim a new national identity
in 1949. The Khrushchev shock in 1956–60 gave rise to the Sino-Soviet
split and a more radical revolutionary identity that reached full force in
the Cultural Revolution. The capitalist dynamism shock, in which East
Asian little tigers played a critical role, occurred in the late 1970s as the
Chinese opened their eyes to the world around them, producing a far-
reaching identity shift starting in 1978. Finally, one should add to this
list the collapse of international socialism and the Soviet Union as a
shock from 1989 to 1991 that induced a rapid response, especially in
1992 with the acceptance of economic globalization and political control to shape an identity more resistant to outside influence. In all the
shocks starting in the 1830s one can observe the huge impact of exogenous forces on Chinese national identity.

The three themes of sovereignty, Sinocentrism, and historical justice
all figure into the way national identity influences foreign relations.
Where these themes are invoked, a realist foreign policy is shadowed by
concerns about face or respect. Sovereignty is at stake. The impact on
views of dealing with Taiwan, as with Tibet and Xinjiang, is most intense. Inner Mongolia and the Mongolian state could be added to this
list. For the Korean Peninsula, including not only the past Communist
ally North Korea but also South Korea, Sinocentric assumptions are
brought to bear. They may apply to Vietnam to a lesser extent and may
not be altogether missing in views of other Southeast Asia states and
Central Asia. Unlike balance-of-power considerations, these identity
themes refer to loss of face if other states do not behave in a manner
suitable to rising China's power. All the identity themes operate at the
leadership level and through public opinion. At times they have flared

toward Russia after decades of arousal during the Sino-Soviet split, but leaders have insisted on a realist approach and stifled public doubts. More readily in the past two decades, they have been turned against the United States, even if the case for realism instead of emotionalism for a time received strong official endorsement. Of all countries, Japan has posed the biggest challenge due to the depth of its national identity significance for leaders and the public and the inconsistency in how it has been treated. By 2010, it could be lambasted without reserve, as the United States was also becoming a target of similar accusation.

Leaders take pains to distance their country from others that may impinge on China's national identity. The United States with its calls for universal values and even Japan with some intimation of shared values in an East Asian Community could appear as a threat, but the Soviet Union for half a century posed the most serious challenge. In Mao's split with the Soviet Union, he may have been more aroused by China's identity uncertainty than by its strategic vulnerability. Through the 1980s, after the "revisionist" label had been dropped for Soviet socialism, China no longer positioned itself to the left of the state that showed it the path to socialism as it kept struggling with how much the two states shared a common identity. Then, as the sole major socialist state left from the 1990s onward, it still wrestled with what makes it different from the Soviet Union and would prevent it from collapsing too. No longer claiming to represent a global ideology, Deng broke with socialism elsewhere, drawing on five themes: (1) developmental society, (2) independence from imperialism/hegemonism, (3) Chinese characteristics, (4) CCP control as key to social order, and (5) Han Chinese tutelage of other nationalities. The first refers to economic national identity, the second to political identify facing outward, and the others to inner political as well as cultural national identity. Together, the themes invoke a combination of unity, order, sovereignty, and strength through economic growth. In the early 1990s, this combination found expression in resistance to outside pressure or unfair treatment, as when the vote for the 2000 Olympics went against Beijing and the historic injustice of Hong Kong colonization was approaching an end in 1997. The 1980s themes of developing the economy, opposing hegemonism, and achieving unification gained new support in these circumstances of China under duress. They also were refocused in the wake of the collapse of international socialism and the Soviet Union, China's mentor.

After the spike in national identity peaked in 2010, China's leaders somewhat lowered the intensity through adjustments in the temporal, sectoral, and horizontal dimensions—but notably not in the ideological or vertical ones. The post–Cold War period again appeared as an extended process of biding time, lowering expectations for an early realization of the implied goals of national identity and for confrontation with other countries for standing in the way. Critics of overoptimism were allowed to make their case as long as they avoided the periods up to the 1990s and other dimensions of identity. Economic national identity was likewise subject to warnings that China's ranking on various indicators is not so high and that it has serious problems that must be overcome. Criticisms of the United States and other rivals proceeded with less conviction that the balance had already shifted.

There was no reassessment, however, of cultural or political national identity. If Hu's January 2011 summit with Obama was seen as reinvigorating ties and reducing the need for alarm about international conflicts, the new mood did not explain how critical tensions raised in the literature on national identity could be ameliorated. On the contrary, the stepped-up crackdown on advocates of universal values kept the intensity high in an identity discourse centered on ideological orthodoxy and China's superior domestic order. There was little reason to conclude that the national identity spike had subsided as China's leaders were preparing for the transition in 2012–13 and leadership changes elsewhere in the world.

Notes

1. Allen Carlson, "A Flawed Perspective: The Limitations Inherent within the Study of Chinese Nationalism," *Nations and Nationalism* 15, no. 1 (2009): 20–35.

2. Gilbert Rozman, "Chinese Strategic Thinking on Multilateral Regional Security in Northeast Asia," *Orbis,* Spring 2011, 296–311; Gilbert Rozman, "Chinese National Identity and Its Implications for International Relations in East Asia," *Asia-Pacific Review* 18, no. 1 (2011): 84–97.

3. Mark Leonard, *What Does China Think?* (New York: PublicAffairs, 2008), 84–104.

4. Gilbert Rozman, *The Chinese Debate about Soviet Socialism, 1978–1985* (Princeton, N.J.: Princeton University Press, 1987); *Heilongjiang ribao,* January 2, 1993, p. 3.

5. Xu Bu, "Achievements and Experience of New China's Diplomacy," *Foreign Affairs Journal,* Autumn 2009, 1–7.

6. Liu Yongtao, "Jiangou anquan 'weixie': Meiguo zhanlue de zhengzhi xuanze," *Shijie jingji yu zhengzhi*, no. 6 (2010): 118–28.

7. Gilbert Rozman, *Strategic Thinking about the Korean Nuclear Crisis: Four Parties Caught between North Korea and the United States*, rev. ed. (New York: Palgrave, 2011).

8. David Shambaugh, "Coping with a Conflicted China," *Washington Quarterly* 34, no. 1 (Winter 2011): 7–27.

9. Liang Yabin, "Cong liyi shouguanfang dao zhanlue caibaozheng: Baquan shuailuoxia de Zhongmei guanxi," *Dangdai Yatai*, 2010, 33–40.

10. Gilbert Rozman, "Can Confucianism Survive in an Age of Universalism and Globalization?" *Pacific Affairs* 75, no. 1 (Spring 2002): 11–37.

11. Gilbert Rozman, "What Chinese Characteristics? Looking to the Past for Clues about the Future," in *Determinants of China's Future: Political, Social, and International Dimensions*, edited by Jae Ho Chung (Lanham, Md.: Rowman & Littlefield, 2006), 191–206.

12. Xue Chen, "Fei quantong anquan wenti yu guoji gonggong chanpin gonggei," *Shijie jingji yu zhengzhi*, no. 3, (2009): 62–69.

13. Suisheng Zhao, *A Nation-State by Construction: Dynamics of Modern Chinese Nationalism* (Stanford, Calif.: Stanford University Press, 2004), 44–78.

14. Peter Hays Gries, *China's New Nationalism: Pride, Politics, and Diplomacy* (Berkeley: University of California Press, 2004).

15. Gilbert Rozman, *The Chinese Debate about Soviet Socialism, 1978-1985* (Princeton, N.J.: Princeton University Press, 1987); Gilbert Rozman, "China's Concurrent Debate about the Gorbachev Era," in *China Learns from the Soviet Union, 1949–1991,* edited by Thomas Bernstein and Li Hua-Yu (Lanham, Md.: Rowman & Littlefield, 2009).

16. "Jingcai Zhongguo," *Xinhua News,* December 16, 2008.

17. Henrietta Harrison, *China: Inventing the Nation* (London: Arnold, 2001), 9–32.

18. Gilbert Rozman, ed., *The East Asian Region: Confucian Heritage and Its Modern Adaptation* (Princeton, N.J.: Princeton University Press, 1991).

19. Chen Yue, "Beijing Aoyunhui yu minzuzhuyi: lixing de huhuan," *Xiandai guoji guanxi,* no. 11 (2008): 1–5.

20. Yong Deng, *China's Struggle for Status: The Realignment of International Relations* (Cambridge: Cambridge University Press, 2008), 97–127.

21. John Delury, "'Harmonious' in China," *Hoover Institution Policy Review,* April–May 2008, 1–8.

22. Gilbert Rozman, "China's Changing Images of Japan, 1989–2001: The Struggle to Balance Partnership and Rivalry," *International Relations of the Asia-Pacific* 2 (2002): 95–129.

23. Lian Degui, "Xin Fukudazhuyi yu Zhongri guanxi," *Xiandai guoji guanxi,* no. 12 (2007): 58–62.

24. Gilbert Rozman, "China's Quest for Great Power Identity," *Orbis,* Summer 1999, 384–85.

25. Young Nam Cho and Jong Ho Jeong, "China's Soft Power: Discussions, Resources, and Prospects," *Asian Survey* 48, no. 3 (May–June 2008): 453–72.

Chapter 4

The East Asian
National Identity Syndrome

Gilbert Rozman

China, Japan, and South Korea share an East Asian National Identity Syndrome (EANIS), which differs from the patterns of national identity found in other regions of the world. Although each displays some characteristics of great power or frontline identities found elsewhere, the building blocks of EANIS share identifiable and distinctive features. Drawing on the six-dimensional approach, I list these building blocks while highlighting what the three East Asian nations, which are also heirs to the three long-standing historical nations in the region, have in common. Besides identifying commonalities in the regional pattern, comparisons also illuminate important differences among these three cases.

The crux of this comparative analysis centers on how national identities become unbalanced. Implicit in this analysis is the presence of an ideal type of balanced identity. This ideal type assumes an ideological spread, where centrist thinking open to diverse evidence is not pressed into silence from one or both sides of the political spectrum. It refers to pride in history without particular defensiveness about past failings. The coexistence of political, cultural, and economic identity has become stabilized. An intermediate level on the vertical ladder and the micro level are adequately developed to check the macro level. No foreign policy obsession focuses on a single state, and internationalism and regionalism do not arouse troubled sensitivities. Emotionalism is restrained about national identity, not interfering with an objective examination of the forces at work. Although the ideal type sets a standard that no country fully achieves, it can be useful in assessing variant patterns.

EANIS presents a picture of one type of unbalanced national identity. In ideological orientation, it signifies an overwhelming conservative or progressive narrative that submerges a centrist worldview. In coverage of stages, this means obsession with the prewar or Cold War era in support of revisionism or the legitimation of a particular political group. In sectoral national identity, assertive political identity bolstered by the power of cultural identity eclipses economic identity supported by acceptance of a society open to the world economy and heterogeneous influences. The vertical ladder, as reflected in identity thinking, is also out of balance, sidestepping the intermediate step as one ascends from the micro level to the macro level without the checks and balances of civil society. As states look beyond their borders, they cling tightly to narrow goals with the world's superpower, while neglecting internationalism and regionalism as a leavening, stabilizing force in their own neighborhood. In doing this, each state interprets identity symbols in a superficial manner while staying adamantly committed to unrealized goals, leaving vague and often contradictory the explanatory analysis for how to achieve its objectives. Such imbalances are revealed below for each dimension of the analysis.

Internationalism failed to gain a substantial foothold, especially in China, and centrism was vulnerable to strong challenges from domestic claims to pride. One reason, rooted in the vertical dimension, is that history is largely a state narrative, not a product of civil society. For a centrist approach to gain secure footing would require respect for multiculturalism (not easy, given the makeup of the vertical dimension), balanced regard for the positive role of the United States (problematic, in the context of the horizontal dimension), lively political debate alert to others' views (difficult, due to the ideological dimension), forthright self-criticism about the past of one's nation (impaired by how the temporal dimension is treated), and respect for the true meaning of economic integration (limited by the way the sectoral dimension is perceived). Centrism has emerged slowly, blocked by political forces with state support.

The Ideological Dimension

Japan, China, and South Korea may have taken different paths toward ideological clarification since the end of the Cold War, but the outcomes bear resemblance. Japan's conservatives reaffirmed the path sought by their predecessors—often the fathers or grandfathers of recent leaders—while lamenting that they had faced difficult conditions that limited the extent to which they could express views on national identity. China's Communists have resumed praising the path charted by Mao Zedong on issues linked to identity, and Deng Xiaoping's revised course draws unqualified praise along with overall approval of the course since 1949 in the face of reputedly difficult conditions. The return to power of conservatives in South Korea also means toning down past criticisms of Cold War leaders in favor of recognition of limiting factors, while acknowledging their accomplishments. Despite periods when the Japanese castigated some leaders as "historical revisionists," the Chinese saw some leaders as "ideological fanatics," and the South Koreans blamed "military dictators" for gross injustices, national identity debates have redressed the balance of pros and cons in favor of pride in the past. If South Korean progressives put up the most resistance to such historical whitewashing as the legacy of the democratic movement in the 1980s and this has stood in the way of the sort of consolidation of thinking that occurred in China and Japan starting in the 1990s, their ideological impact also grew stronger in the post–Cold War era, leaving limited room for centrist thinking and reconciliation.

In Japan under the Yoshida Doctrine, China under Deng Xiaoping's slogans until 1989, and South Korea during the ten-year period of conservative rule after democratization in 1987, ideology appeared to be sidelined. Yet, assumptions of narrow pragmatism were later refuted by an upsurge in ideology of an uncompromising sort. Few anticipated the turn to the anti–"bourgeois peaceful evolution" campaign from 1989 and the subsequent echoes of it. Similarly, few expected the right-wing revisionist direction after the Liberal Democratic Party reestablished itself in power starting in 1996, stressing the reversal of historical verdicts. In South Korea, the ideological drift came from progressives, who gained power in 1998, and it grew more pronounced under Roh Moohyun, targeting postwar injustice. Outside observers had highly praised pragmatism, and they often remained at a loss as to what was driving the new ideological push seen across the East Asian region.

The crux of the ideological challenge in each country was the allure of the universal values embraced by the United States. Although Japan and South Korea claimed to share these values, they were prone to qualifying this support. China was forthright in rejecting the concept as a direct threat to its national identity. Japan accepted the basic notion in the 1980s as part of the "free world" struggle against the Soviet Union and with enthusiasm under Koizumi and Abe as a means to put China on the defensive. Yet past sympathy in both countries with "Asian values" and reservations about associating too closely with U.S. "fundamentalism" in imposing values in Asia reflected a concern that their national identities could be put at risk. If China's leaders see an existential struggle in defending a Communist regime, even the leaders of the other two states, where the impact of the United States has been greater, have been strongly protective of a distinct national identity.

Without clarifying the ideological dimension, there is little prospect of stabilizing national identity. When political power is not seriously contested and economic growth favors the regime, simplistic ideological answers appear to suffice or, at least, not to lead to serious questioning. Yet, when economic pride is in doubt, ideologues also find room to capitalize on anxieties. In Japan since the Cold War ended, strident efforts to reinforce a simplistic approach have had mixed results, failing to work for long. Also, in South Korea after the Asian financial crisis, progressive leaders only briefly succeeded in persuading the public of a simplistic, inherently ideological, worldview. Neither Japan nor South Korea has yet to find a clear ideological answer; yet in 2011 centrist thinking was making some headway in association with a rise in realism. China's response, in contrast, is more extreme in rejecting Western values and centrist thinking, and attempts to challenge it are tightly suppressed.

In each country, textbooks serve as a litmus test. Conservatives in Japan have pressed repeatedly for changes in history coverage in order to present a more positive national identity, eclipsing progressives who had fought hard to maintain earlier self-criticisms or recognition of transgressions. After regaining the presidency, conservatives in South Korea moved to rewrite textbooks in which progressives had imposed their worldview since the 1990s, but they still had to prove their support for a centrist outlook. In China during the 1980s, reformers struggled to alter the Maoist language, but after 1989 and again 2008 Communist Party stalwarts moved assertively to intensify the ideological tone.

EANIS reveals a persistent drive for ideological clarity that leaves little room for centrist thinking. As long as obsessions over history drive ideological debates, centrist thought is marginal. These obsessions are intensifying in Beijing, not in Tokyo or Seoul.

The Temporal Dimension

Evidence abounds for common East Asian historical experiences: Confucianism provided the framework for discussion of the state and its role internally and externally; humiliation and its legacy have had to be addressed in order to assert normalcy; a catch-up psychology justified deference to the state as it steered rapid economic growth; and aspirations are high to escape from the shadow of the United States through a broader, deeper national identity. As political leaders looked back in the period 2008–11 to the premodern and prewar years, the Cold War era, and the still unfolding post–Cold War years, they drew on images of these experiences, trying to reshape national identity with keen attention to the enduring role of history.[1] In each case, we find selective memories and an unbalanced mix of past periods, which lead both to shared features of EANIS and to salient differences in identities. Japan's historical memory remains fixated on the legacy of its war years in the 1930s and 1940s, despite nationwide amnesia in educating about it. South Korea's past is colored by the dual trauma of colonization by Japan and division leading to the devastating Korean War, although a paralyzing divide exists in how to deal with the consequences. In turn, China's hypersensitivity centers on the Communist Party's claims to legitimacy, ranging from its verdicts on historical injustice to its brutalizing campaigns from the 1940s to the 1970s to remake China in accord with an ideological blueprint and its later suppression of related truths.

Distinct roots can be traced back to the civilizational development of the area in question. For any state, a story unfolds about its origin and its founding ideas. In most of the world, states are a product of rather recent times, divorcing the story from the distant past. In contrast, the states of East Asia are the unmistakable heirs to an extended history of Confucian state identities referring to the same dominant ethnic group located on the same territory and exhibiting many of the same cultural traits. Continuity between major aspects of premodern and modern identities reflects Confucianism's lasting impact. The state-building process associated with the consolidation of control over territory occurred gradually and left its imprint on modern national identity. This came from fixing images of perceived external threats, reinforcing state authority, and often borrowing from other states and explaining how this matters for one's own identity. Civilizational development became linked to the narrative of state building, solidifying a premodern foundation by the eighteenth and early nineteenth centuries that would be enduring, shared, and capable of generating combinations of political and cultural identity focused on the nation-state.

This legacy, I argue, is particularly significant for contemporary East Asian identities. In China by the mid-Qing, a Sinocentric, Confucian worldview reigned supreme, with few signs of serious challenge to a civilizational identity that put the Chinese state at the center of a long-standing regional tribute system. This venerable tradition left the Chinese confident of their superiority, of regional ritual subordination to their state's hierarchical precedence, and of an established record of state legitimacy. By the mid-Tokugawa period, Japan's *sakoku* system of self-imposed solitary confinement prevailed, as domains inculcated Confucian thinking while seeing China under Manchu usurpers as losing the legitimacy that had made it the center. In the emergent worldview, newly advanced by rival domains in what had been a stable feudal order, only a more centralized Japanese state could hold off approaching forces from the outside, which would require a laudatory narrative about Japan's distinctive heritage and social system. Korea also explained state legitimacy through a Confucian prism; in the later Yi Dynasty, it saw its own application of this tradition as superior to China's, while keeping its distance from Japan and various Western powers through the convenience of dependency on China. With strong state bureaucracies, intense resistance to outside penetration, and wide inculcation through didactic teachings and high literacy rates focused on a secular, state-centered worldview, the East Asian states reached a peak of Confucianization by the mid–nineteenth century.[2] This became a unique, solid basis for modern national identity with lasting ramifications.

In the final premodern centuries, the three East Asia states twisted Confucianism with paranoia toward the outside world, arbitrary authority over domestic reform thinking, and rigidity in the face of evolving social forces. Given the impact of Mongols and then Manchus in China as well as the narrow thinking of the non-elite, peasant-based Ming Dynasty, China tilted the balance to imperial Confucianism over elite and reform types of Confucianism.[3] Although the impact was to look down on others as barbarians, there is reason to view "insulated Confucianism" as the hypersensitive Manchus' holier-than-thou synthesis operating in China itself. Japan entered the seventeenth century reconstituting Confucianism on the basis of the ethics of samurai bands, competing with each other and never secure in a system of a precariously balanced regional or national power, producing "bushido Confucianism." It was rigidly hierarchical and insistent on sharp "us versus them" distinctions. Last, in Korea, struggling in the shadow of China's insistence on ritual superiority and Japan's legacy of brutal invasion in the 1590s, what might be called "hermit Confucianism" reflected similar rejection of outside influences as well as fierce resistance to reform currents from below.[4] Anxiety in all three states over rising pressure from Western powers as well as emerging domestic commercial forces and elite diversity contributed to the narrowing responses in their evolving national identities. Authoritarian, xenophobic tendencies became enshrined in thinking about the nation and the world. But pragmatic, commercialized, education-oriented societies were amenable to rapid change.[5]

As seen in the practice of labeling nations barbarians, the Chinese treated relations with others as a meeting of civilizations and histories that tests how it measures up to any established standards of an advanced civilization. Not only were customary international relations depicted as relations between unequal states, emphasizing the need to maintain rituals and symbols of hierarchy, but it was also assumed that stability derived from retaining the civilizational distinctions— whatever the power balance might indicate. In Japan, a quasi-multi-state system under the Tokugawa centralized feudal order and weighed honor and ritual distinctions highly in maintaining equilibrium for two and one-half centuries, even as the country opted out of the Chinese order.[6] In Korea, incorporation into China's tributary system kept attention alerted to the primacy of respect in bilateral ties. History, honor, and the hierarchy associated with civilization became embedded in views of foreign relations, setting the foundation for emerging identities as modern nations suddenly took shape.

Premodern pride may have left an enduring legacy for national identity formation, but it is too distant and ended with the countries of the region too far behind the West in modernization to remain a major focus. De-Confucianization was necessary to break free of stultifying constraints and begin a national process of catching up.[7] With the region left in material or spiritual ruins in 1945 and in need of outside assistance, its past again became a subject of derision. During the first postwar decades, negative images of the Confucian and overall premodern legacy prevailed, to the point that even as they were later dropped or even contradicted, there was little sentiment for glorification. Discussions about national identity have overcome some earlier negativity, but, as seen in the spurt of "Asian values" and "Confucian capitalism" pride in the 1980s and 1990s,[8] they have not found a way to balance the positive with the negative and restore the premodern era to a rightful place in national identity. China has veered from Mao's anti-Confucianism toward recent exaggerated pride in the past tinged with Communist reluctance to treat it objectively. In Japan, the legacy of Nihonjinron thinking leaves excessive nostalgia,[9] whereas the failure to hold an objective debate on later history still casts a negative shadow on what preceded. South Koreans also find that taboos about the period of Japanese colonialism reverberate in schematic accounts of the Yi Dynasty and a lack of objectivity about its Chinese-inspired Confucianism. Generalizations on premodern times lead to confusion in national identity

National identity was unclear in premodern times, but other strong identities left a foundation for it. In Japan, identification with the local domain was intense, especially for the samurai and the political and economic officials most associated with them. Nesting this type of group loyalty within national identity was a hallmark of Meiji centralization. In China, the universal civilization centered there also provided an intense identification that could be coupled with intense national identity, especially after its Communist variant was shorn of almost all its earlier ideology. The shock or threat of imperialist states prying one's country open put a premium on forging a strong national identity. The Japanese generally are thankful that they could do so quickly, embracing the emperor and staving off the predations of the imperialists.

In turn, the Chinese and Koreans regret that they failed to do so, having fallen victim to humiliating treatment and invasions. Their memories reinforce their determination in recent times to boost the national identity centered on a strong state.

The troubled history of each country in the decades leading to 1945 colors views of the entire temporal dimension. Japan in the period 1945–64, South Korea in 1945–86, and China in 1979–89 were often consumed with self-critical assessments of past low points. Although China's leaders had earlier focused much of the blame on the decades up to 1949, they came to fear that the three later decades would take the lion's share of blame instead, unable to strive for balance without undermining regime legitimacy. In these periods, leaders had to struggle to find elements of glory in the historical narrative. The prospect of hosting the Olympics in each case served as a rallying point to refocus attention to rising admiration on the world stage. There were also one-sided attempts to reinterpret problematic times: Japanese moves in 2005 to recall the glory of the 1905 victory in the Russo-Japanese War; South Korean adulation for the heroic resistance of 1919 commemorated on March 1 each year; and the Chinese efforts in the mid-1990s to reestablish the Chinese Communist Party (CCP) as the dedicated nationalists who resisted Japan in the Patriotic War of the 1930s and 1940s and presided in 1949 over the rise of a liberated China. Although the South Koreans and Chinese commemorate August 15 as the moment when Japan was defeated, the predominant U.S. role in victory diminishes the chance of finding historical merit there.

Premodern, Confucian-inspired pride and pre-1945 war-induced memories exert a lingering impact on national identities, but discomfort with the Cold War for dependency and abnormality also distorts historical memories. Difficulty in dealing with the image of abnormality for the Cold War period is at the root of unbalanced views of the temporal dimension. In China, tight censorship on assessments of the Mao era after the CCP drew its mostly positive verdict in 1981 lies at the core of the problem. If many are generally aware that the period deserves a negative evaluation, an inability to articulate what went wrong and why stymies treatment of Chinese history as a whole. In Japan, government opposition to education about history along with an upsurge in revisionist writings makes the period of the 1930s and 1940s most sensitive; yet post–Cold War tendencies to view the Cold War era as abnormal leaves unrealized efforts to make this the nucleus of a positive national identity.

In South Korea, the struggle since democratization in 1987 between pro-gressives and conservatives leaves unresolved how to evaluate the pros and cons of the Cold War era. The shadow of a divided nation com-bines with unfavorable memories of dictatorship to obstruct efforts to find sprouts of a positive Korean identity.

In the post cold war era each state failed to find the balance that had previously eluded its national identity. Japan fixated on becoming a "normal" state, an illusive goal when on each of the dimensions of na-tional identity it failed to clarify clear, pragmatic ways to proceed. South Korea sought to convert democratization and *nordpolitik* into national reconciliation, an impossibility in light of the problems in each dimen-sion of its national identity along with the conflicting objectives of North Korea. Finally, after June 4, 1989, China made clear that it would aim toward legitimating the CCP's rule, in spite of the national and in-ternational discrediting of the movement and the negative impact on at-tempts to find balance on each of the dimensions of national identity. Setting goals in contradiction to overcoming existing imbalances in na-tional identity undermined any chance of advancing toward a stable framework for the future. All these states remain haunted by history not only in foreign relations but also in their views of national identity.[10]

The post–Cold War period lacks clarity in each state's national iden-tity because it is viewed as transitional. China takes pride in its rapid rise, while it anticipates a new order when U.S. hegemonism is over-come. Japan claims that at last it can speak out without the restraints of prior decades, but this judgment obscures Japan's falling status. South Korea gained new hope as the initiator of the Sunshine Policy, even to the point that Roh Moo-hyun could contemplate it becoming a balancer, before its inherent weakness was exposed. Insufficient opti-mism about globalization compounds deep dissatisfaction with the sta-tus quo in turning eyes away from the most recent period toward identity issues of the past.

A balanced temporal perspective would recognize the extraordinary achievements of premodern times while noting, in comparative per-spective, some limitations. It would show pride in the Cold War era, notably for Japan and South Korea despite problems, and renew criti-cism in China of more serious failings. Japan and South Korea lack pride in this era, not highlighting what they had achieved at its end. China is inadequately critical of this era, clarifying how much was gained at the end and how much still remained to do.

Finally, it would highlight positive aspects of the post–Cold War period without obscuring continuing shortcomings that need to be addressed. EANIS refers to a skewed view of history, proud but troubled and searching for new verdicts but not for impartial justice.

The Sectoral Dimension

When the Western powers successively forced open the doors of China, Japan, and Korea in the mid–nineteenth century, they found countries vulnerable, as elsewhere, to their superior military and economic might, but relatively immune to some of their cultural blandishments. To be sure, political systems proved indefensible, and the basic edifice of knowledge and civilizational myopia could not endure. Yet core elements in their culture that initially appeared to be no more than anachronistic defensiveness found new life in a cultural national identity with vital staying power. In the 1880s, Japan's new political leadership forged a renewed political-cultural combination on this foundation. If China and South Korea struggled until the 1950s to find a similarly secure base, they had the same type of legacy for cultural national identity, combining openness to modernity with confidence in heritage, even if each at times condemned a good part of it. When each of these countries was tested in the Cold War era—Japan's wartime defeat, South Korea's trauma in the Korean War, and the failure of Mao's Communism—it fell back on cultural identity to fill the vacuum. Japanese progressives vilified samurai bushido as the precursor to militarism, South Koreans blamed a culture of subservience for colonialism, and Maoists lambasted Confucianism. Yet the core cultural identity survived. Flux in political and economic identity has obscured relative durability in cultural identity.

The impact of cultural identity can also be negative in blocking openness to the outside and reform. De-Confucianization was a necessity, especially in the first decades of reform, when the tentacles of presumed civilizational superiority were far-reaching. In the 1980s and 1990s, Japan's Nihonjinron cultural arrogance impeded borrowing. South Korean assumptions of cultural superiority, notably before the Asian financial crisis of 1997–98, echoed this, blending with notions of "Asian values." After approaching the extreme in xenophobia during the Cultural Revolution, China guarded against a repeat for a time, but its economic boom increasingly reverberated in cultural overconfidence in the late 1990s and 2000s. On the one hand, irrepressible cultural national identity compensated when other sectors of national identity lagged. On the other, tendencies toward excessive pride in national culture could, when fueled by inflated political and economic national identity, stimulate a national identity spike harmful to domestic reform and diplomacy alike.

Economic national identity has exerted a powerful impact in two circumstances. First, at times of pervasive public doubt, it has become a rallying cry. Appeals for national cohesion in order to catch up rang across Japan from the middle Meiji Era and again under the Yoshida Doctrine, across South Korea under Park Chung-hee, and across China under Deng Xiaoping and Jiang Zemin. At times of lack of confidence in political leaders and a spiritual vacuum, when aspects of culture have lost their luster, economic national identity has gained center stage with the image that the people are joined together in a national mission. Second, in periods of "economic miracle," when the future appears limitless, a rising level of economic national identity has spilled over in increases in cultural and political identity. In Japan in the 1980s, South Korea in the 1990s, and China in the 2000s, we see this overlap. Economic overconfidence reinforces pride in the social system that lies behind economic growth and in the political order that seemingly fosters it. Although this combination faced the most obstacles in South Korea, it reached its apex in China by the period 2008–11.

Economic national identity can be fickle. A loss of confidence in one's economic future has broad ramifications. The collapse of Japan's bubble economy quickly cast doubt on cultural and political national identity, although leaders struggled to boost both. Conservatives stressed symbols of national culture and sought breakthroughs on matters with high diplomatic symbolism. Yet the power of the Yasukuni Shrine as a distraction faded when Tokyo and Beijing agreed on how to handle it diplomatically. South Koreans also have suffered a letdown from the collapse of economic expectations, first in 1997 and again, along with other states, in 2008–9. This has compounded the graver doubts in that country about national identity than in Japan or China. The potential exists for China to experience a similar bursting of the economic bubble along with its inflated mixture of sectoral identities, weighted heavily with the most pronounced political identity of all.

The weight of political national identity has been growing. With the fading of Nihonjinron after the 1980s and of claims to "homogeneous Korea" a decade later, the balance has shifted toward the political process in each state. The August 2009 success of the Democratic Party of Japan steals some of the thunder from the half-century-long presumption that the Liberal Democratic Party uniquely embodies Japan's political identity. Alternation of conservative and progressive rule in post–Cold War South Korea also strips some of the veneer from those who decorate their side in political national identity. With North Korea's luster damaged and reliance on U.S. power renewed, a populace lacking trust in government is not inclined to view any diplomatic initiative or claim to international clout as persuasive. Only in China, where leaders at times cultivate a mentality of endangerment from hegemonism and outside support for "separatism," can one see little sign that political national identity is losing ground. In Japan, the focus of just political treatment has turned to reform of the United Nations Security Council, whereby it would be given a permanent seat. In South Korea, the creation of the Group of Twenty (G-20) has given it a voice among global leaders, but talk of scaling back this unwieldy body to the G-8 plus a small number of rising states arouses fear that a new line will be drawn to exclude it. China's expectations are highest; although it disavows talk of a new G-2 with the United States, even the G-5 at the Security Council does not seem to suffice. Clinging to hopes of enhanced political status retains popularity in the three states.

Whereas Japan and South Korea have deferred for two-thirds of a century to the United States, China has no similar pattern of restraint on its political national identity. Moreover, unlike Japanese and Korean historical experience living in the shadow of Chinese civilization, Chinese cultural national identity developed with few fetters. Given the fact that Communism gave vent to the most extreme versions of national identity and that in the post–Cold War era China's combination of the three sectoral identities lacks the tempering effects felt in Japan and South Korea at the peak of their own identity pride, one hesitates to extrapolate from the recent history of these two cases to China's future. If there are some signs that EANIS is diminishing in Japan and South Korea, it does not follow that this is the case in China or that it will soon become so.

In contrast to the relatively modest aspirations of Japan and South Korea since 1945, China is playing for higher stakes. China's perspective originates with memories of roughly two millennia at the top of the "world system" in which it participated, and points ahead toward a global system in which it either shares leadership with the United States or stands alone. Fusing confidence in cultural, economic, and political national identities, on a scale exceeded by no country except perhaps the United States, China may be poised to sustain its high level of pride. Yet its loss of exceptional economic vitality, accompanied by renewed doubts about its cultural and political superiority due to social disorder or international isolation, could induce a sharper clash over national identity than what has been seen in Japan or even South Korea. China may be approaching a crossroads in the aftermath of the recent global financial and economic crisis and the increasing signs of an international showdown over North Korea and Iran.

EANIS starts with cultural pride that can sustain wide-ranging reform and a temporary deemphasis on political national identity. Even serious misgivings about some aspects of culture can be counterbalanced by confidence in others. Rising economic pride boosts not only an economic identity mixed with positive views of social identity but also cultural national identity. Only when political national identity becomes intense does the full measure of EANIS appear. Limits on the political and economic sides lately in Japan and South Korea, reflecting public reservations or alliance realities, prevent this sectoral dimension from exerting the kind of impact it is having in China.

The Vertical Dimension

Identities nest together in patterns that accumulate to limit or buttress intense support for the nation. The East Asian countries traditionally did not have strong checks on state authority or state identity. Unlike Catholicism and Islam, which vested in religious leaders authority independent of secular leaders, Confucianism reinforced the position of the emperor in China, the king in Korea, and the daimyo in Japan. There were no transnational institutions to control the behavior of these leaders or even to serve as a basis for judgment. Modern states offer room to diverse institutions, but the state in East Asia was the sole driving force for massive borrowing from the outside and for modernization at a breakneck base. Even as elements of the Confucian empowerment of a supreme leader appeared anarchic, the tradition of reliance on the state and on its moral authority was reinforced. Despite Mao's enthusiasm for social class divisions and Japan's claims to make democracy the basis of its social order, neither country broke the habit of a clear hierarchical order centered on the political leadership. Of course, the unchecked power of Mao and the limited rule of law under his successors contrast to Japan's checks on power.

All three countries have a simplified hierarchy, accentuating family as well as the state. In line with the Confucian suspicion of intermediate levels, they reinforced the macro level of the state in postwar times—as part of a "reverse course" following the decentralizing reforms imposed by the American occupation of Japan, leading to what is often called "administrative guidance" by the bureaucracy; as part of China's "democratic centralism," even if during the Cultural Revolution some Soviet-borrowed centralization was relaxed and Deng's reforms added many market elements; and in the strong South Korean presidency that led to calls in 2010 for constitutional reform. Low autonomy for local government on matters of political significance, weak civil society (even in South Korea, where there was a brief upsurge leading to the election of Roh Moo-hyun), and the limited impact of the global community and individualism all reinforce a streamlined hierarchy. To be sure, there is a fundamental difference between China with its 75-million strong CCP and absence of democracy except in village elections and Japan and South Korea. Yet, even as societies grow more diverse, none of these states offers alternative sources of identity to temper state-centered identity for ethnic, religious, or local groups.

Humiliations are associated with a loss of state authority. Whatever the influence of the West on rising individualism and local interest groups, it is blamed overwhelmingly for its negative impact on the Chinese state for more than a century. Even if its effect in Korea included some degree of individual empowerment, Japan's legacy is remembered primarily as stripping the state of sovereignty. Moreover, when the Japanese stress what was not "normal" in the Cold War era and afterward, they are referring to the weakness of the state and patriotism toward it. Assumptions about national identity privilege the state in a manner that diminishes other levels that could combine into a more balanced hierarchy.

Confucian assumptions about identity permeate the micro level of society, but their emphasis on self-identity in order to serve family or group leaves less room for voluntarist individualism. Mao's harsh

rejection of individualism, Japanese paternalism and group orientation fostered through the school and workplace, and Korean patriarchy all left a legacy in the Cold War that slowed the development of a
more individualist ideal of the self. They serve a strong state and state
identity. However, extremely low birthrates in Japan, South Korea,
and urban China—along with recent rapid changes in family structure, in part driven by rising divorce rates—raise the potential for a
new attitude toward individualism. This is less likely as long as family
efforts to prepare children for highly competitive examinations remain
the ideal pattern.

Nongovernmental organizations (NGOs) operate in Japan and
South Korea differently than in the United States and the European
Union. In Japan, they evolved slowly and have largely concentrated on
a few domestic issues. The ones active in foreign policy are mainly rightist organizations with close ties to official circles. In contrast, Korean
NGOs thrived in the 1980s struggle to democratize and have continued
an active role, including on foreign policy issues. Long associated with
leftist causes, they often take an anti-American stance. If anti-
Americanism has had some appeal in Okinawa, the national movements with that theme faded after the 1960s. Ironically, future pressure
for turning away from the United States is likely to come from those
groups that are most vocal in support of the alliance. Their historical
revisionist agenda has found this pairing convenient, but ultimately remains under the sway of strong, divisive historical memories that make
it difficult to find a broad consensus over values.

Middle-class values are often linked to NGO activism, social movements capable of challenging state authority, and participation in politics through demonstrations and elections. In comparison with China
and even Japan, South Korea has an abundance of such mass involvement in politics. Its student and labor movements against authoritarian
rule presaged the wider democratic movement of the late 1980s and
continued activism over international issues and domestic policies. In
contrast to the other states, such movements, along with parliamentary
challenges and a contentious press, serve to keep alive a vigorous opposition. The movements reflect the progressive side overwhelmingly,
whereas the press disproportionately supports the conservatives. In the
Roh Moo-hyun era, the main television stations favored the progressives, as did new Internet news services, but the close association of the
NGOs with the administration led to declining trust in them as voters

turned to the conservatives.[11] After Lee Myung-bak's election, the situation remained unstable. Yet easy co-optation by Roh of these movements and their lack of influence under Lee, even if they could mount vigils, did not bode well for new limits on state authority.

Given the acceptance of at least the ideal of universal values in Japan and South Korea and their recognition that sovereignty lies in the people as expressed in democratic votes, they contrast with China's unabashed concentration of authority in state leadership. Hu Jintao's "harmonious society" directed from above has no parallel in the two democratic states. Brutal repression of dissent or even of local protests against abuses of power is only found in China. This is one reason that EANIS is most pronounced in China.

Vertical identity faces challenges from ideas about the purity of the masses and the exceptionalism of the once-silent majority. Both these approaches are anti-elitist and are rooted in claims to a more authentic cultural identity linked to aspirations for a significant shift in political identity. Progressives in Japan and especially South Korea reinterpreted history as a struggle by the masses suppressed by domestic elites, at times cooperating with foreigners interfering in their nation's development. This, of course, echoes the Communist class struggle ideology, which was at the core of Chinese identity under Mao. In all three countries, however, a different challenge arose from claims to exceptionalism that focused only indirectly on the masses as a sort of silent majority now awakening to the cultural threat from cosmopolitan elites. They targeted elements of elite society who do not subscribe to what purportedly makes one's nation distinctive. In Japan and South Korea, such claims kept being tempered by support for universal values, but China was fundamentally different in its extravagant notions of uniqueness and the way they buttressed a rigidly vertical society. Although Japan in the 1930s and 1940s and South Korea from the 1960s to the 1980s experienced a spike in verticality, which revealed the inherent risk of a lack of checks and balances and a concentration of authority, China has both a history and a leadership prone to extreme assertions of exceptionalism.

Premodern Japan and Korean bequeathed traditions of lasting horizontal potential, such as the Japanese emphasis on multiple communities (*kyodotai*) and behavior in accord with fixed statuses (*mibunsei*) and the Korean legacy of factionalism. In contrast, late imperial China invigorated claims to vertical ideals under the emperor; Mao Zedong launched a quarter century of class struggle to eradicate vestiges of a horizontal society, especially those that had emerged during the past century; and Jiang Zemin and Hu Jintao outdid Deng Xiaoping in circumscribing the political and ideological impact of emerging elites in an age of economic globalization and market competition. Although in the other two states democratization tightened the limits on vertical control, the increased empowerment of Communist leaders boosted verticality, even in economic national identity, as the earlier decentralization was eroding.

The Horizontal Dimension

When the Western powers forced open East Asian countries in the nineteenth century, the option of autarchy ended. National identities took shape in a global environment that centered on imperialist states but also offered potentially useful international ideals and, by joining with other Asian states, a possibility for regionalism, in part, as a means for resistance. China failed to find balance among these, seeking to reinvigorate its "tribute system" for collective support and, later, turning toward Communism as a variant of internationalism but one that had been stripped of universal ideals and become weighted with nationalism in the Soviet Union and then in China. South Korea also failed, as some naively welcomed Japan's calls for Asianism, only to be betrayed. Only Japan seriously explored a mixture of the three principles, but its leaders set aside international ideals on the premise that they did not matter in a cutthroat struggle of imperialist states and distorted Asianism as if it could rationalize Japanese imperialism.[12] In the Cold War era, Japan would address these themes anew, as would the other states in revisiting national identity.

China from the 1950s to the 1970s, under the sway of Stalinist logic and Maoist revolutionary Communism, dismissed internationalist ideals as irrelevant, while still during the 1980s treating Japanese or U.S. interest in Asian multilateralism as a threat to national identity. China's preoccupation with the U.S.-Soviet standoff narrowed its thinking. South Korea was preoccupied with anticommunism and hostility toward Japan, leaving scant room to consider other aspects of internationalism or regionalism. Ambivalence about the United States as either skewing internationalism to reinforce its dominance in bilateralism or the target of internationalism in a way that could assist North Korea was in the forefront. That left only Japan prepared to consider U.S. relations along with internationalism and Asianism, but twisted logic on universal values and history only left room for illusions about these themes. Japan's repetition of the "three basic principles" starting in 1957, as discussed by Hosoya in chapter 6 of this volume, did not satisfy its quest for a more normal identity, because its antinuclear allergy never had any chance of winning UN Security Council support for its permanent membership and "reentering Asia" without help from China or South Korea never gave Japan a chance to escape from the U.S. shadow.

Japanese conservatives oppose realizing Japan's "renaissance" to embracing the ideals of internationalism. Although they endorse a U.S. alliance rooted in national interests and pay lip service to shared values as long as these contrast to those of China and North Korea, they are adverse to a broader agreement on values with ramifications for thinking about wartime Japanese conduct and a resurgent, distinctive Japanese identity. Even more than conservatives, Korea's progressives object to viewing its past through the lens of the United States. They find some solace in blaming this superpower for its history of sacrificing Korean interests, standing in the way of Korean democratization, and, lately, standing in the way of steps toward reunification. Although two-thirds of a century of close ties have tempered the discomfort in Japan and South Korea with a United States–centered foreign policy, the situation is different in China. There, U.S. imperialism and hegemonism have been mercilessly attacked without the leavening effect of an alliance. China's aspirations are higher, and warnings that U.S. power stands in its way are more pervasive. Yet in all three states, one can observe an obsession with the U.S. impact on the region and a drive, open or at times hidden, to gain a free hand in dealing with critical regional objectives.

The obsession with the United States combines concern with "bashing" and "passing." The very country that squelches desired choices is most responsible for the security that makes many other choices possible. It confers legitimacy that is repeatedly being sought. When U.S. leaders appear to be pressuring, national identity is kindled in opposition. When U.S. attention turns elsewhere and one's country is not being taken as seriously as it expects, this too prompts appeals based on national identity. An inability to find balance in internationalism or regionalism keeps the spotlight on U.S. relations.

All three East Asian states still perceive a deficit in sovereignty. China and South Korea approach the United States as divided nations alert to how U.S. policies affect any prospect for reunification. Japan is the lone great power that rests its security on another state, as recognized in the Yoshida Doctrine. All three look to other states in Asia to help in diminishing reliance on the United States for their sovereignty quest. This supersedes any interest in forging a regional community, although that too is on the agenda, to the extent it can meet other national identity objectives. Regionalism is less a matter of finding a new combination of countries to meet national security needs and more an unrealizable shortcut to a new national identity.

In our era of "globalization" and the regional goal of an "East Asian community," the search has intensified in all three states to incorporate a balance of internationalism, regionalism, and United States–centered views into notions of national identity. None has done a good job of achieving that balance. During the George W. Bush administration, distrust of the United Nations and an unprecedented U.S.-European gap left internationalism in the shadows. Meanwhile, Koizumi's one-sided U.S. orientation and Roh's mishandling of U.S. and North Korean ties complicated the search in their countries for balanced images of the outside. On behalf of a rapidly rising China of increasing importance for U.S. policy objectives, Hu may have had the best opportunity to achieve balance. Yet his "harmonious world" did not embrace universal values and advocacy of multilateralism in the Association of Southeast Asian Nations + 3, and the Shanghai Cooperation Organization failed to reassure neighboring states that China was not seeking a Sinocentric order.[13] When Fukuda revived Japan's Asianist goals and Lee abandoned Roh's audacity in contemplating South Korea becoming the "balancer," Hu's China stood at the extreme in opposing more temperate U.S. policies with tired talk of "hegemonism." In response to U.S. president Barack Obama's rekindled internationalism and the Democratic Party of Japan's resurgent Asianism after leadership changes in 2009, Hu remained too committed to the principle of "noninterference in internal affairs" to allow for serious advances toward either objective.

From 2000 to 2002, optimism for establishing an East Asian Community was at a peak. In the previous decade, Japanese interest had become clear, but the Chinese feared that their national identity would be put at risk. By the time plans were moving forward to form an

East Asian Summit, it was the turn of the Japanese to grow wary of Chinese dominance and the threat that could pose to Japan's national identity. Because the history issue is so central to national identity debates, deferring to the other country in the course of forging regionalism poses an existential threat to some. South Koreans face the same dilemma in falling subordinate to Japan in regionalism. Narrow types of cooperation for economic reasons are much less threatening, avoiding the implications of a new "community."

Many in East Asia have written about the promise of East Asian Community consciousness as a basis for regionalism and a sign of shared values. Yet they differ on how much these values overlap with universal values or represent an updated version of "Asian values" in opposition to professed U.S. values. Chinese thinkers tend to contrast regional and universal values, blaming U.S. influence for slowing a rise in consciousness of an East Asian Community. One can observe two variations on this theme. The first stresses a more state-centered political tradition with noninterference in the affairs of other states, usually accompanied by criticism of Japan in recent years for joining U.S. resistance. The second cites Japan's postwar economic and social values, often pointing to its Confucian traditions of diligence, frugality, filial piety, respect for elders, loyalty, and communalism as examples of shared thinking in support of social responsibility.[14] Either way, support for the establishment of a community with values reflecting East Asian traditions comes with at least a degree of rejection of universal values. China's rise as the center of an alternate approach to values rests on this approach to regionalism. As the frontline states in dealing with China and responding to the idea of the East Asian Community, Japan and South Korea play a critical role in any new struggle over values. Paying lip service to the goal of an Asian community, they leave in confusion efforts to sort out the connections among the three circles along the horizontal dimension.

Globalization centering on economic openness has gradually become popular in the three East Asian states. First Japan, then South Korea, and finally China advanced an export-oriented strategy of development, with reservations about foreign companies gaining a foothold. In the 1990s, all three grasped the advantages of more openness, in spite of serious reservations. They interpreted the new mantra of globalization narrowly, seeking to avoid spillover into broader internationalization. If that term was used, values were often set aside for mechanisms, such as wider study of the English language. Unlike European countries, Japan and South Korea did not stress their support for shared values and urge U.S. leaders to adhere to them more fully. Although, in the 1990s, Japan championed the Kyoto Protocol on responding to climate change and at the end of the decade Kim Dae-jung started his term in office during the financial crisis with reassuring promises to end "crony capitalism," these were rare exceptions to the rule. Protective of their rice farmers and narrow in their response to global challenges, they slighted internationalism. As its clout increased after 2000, China was most resistant to interfering in other states in order to achieve humanitarian objectives or even to prevent threats to global security. It was the most disdainful of such efforts, although at times it quietly cooperated on some measures.

East Asian states were determined to receive the respect they believed that they deserved. This influenced relations with the United States and even more relations among themselves. This proved problematic, however, because they did not share the same views on the regional status hierarchy. On a global scale, the Chinese felt that their national status had been denied when the 2000 Olympic Games were awarded to Sydney rather than Beijing. In 2005, many Japanese also felt that their country had been treated unfairly when it did not succeed in becoming a permanent member of the United Nations Security Council. On a regional level, perceived slights were more common. The Japanese interpreted Chinese and South Korean criticisms related to history as slights against their country's current status, including its peace-loving role in the region. For South Koreans, too, after fleeting hopes that the Sunshine Policy would give them respect as the driving force in both peninsular reunification and regional cooperation necessary to achieve it, the letdown from 2001 offered further proof of their marginal role. Respect through international relations starts with U.S. handling of bilateral relations and extends to regional and international status.

China's obsession with Communist legitimacy, Japan's growing preoccupation with revisionist treatment of the period from the full-scale invasion of China in 1937 to the San Francisco Peace Treaty of 1951, and progressive Koreans' deference to North Korea are matters of national identity that distort thinking about foreign policy. All skew views of the United States and raise the importance of pressing it to change its thinking. All make regionalism more difficult. Also, all interfere with support for internationalist causes. These are not primarily realist concerns. National identity shapes foreign policy.

The horizontal dimension of EANIS leaves little room for an Asian identity with promise for regionalism and places little emphasis on internationalism with trust in universal values, however defined. The overriding focus is bilateral relations with the United States and their impact on national identity. Until this is clarified, there can be no prospect for a balanced identity. Historical and ideological issues loom in the background as states respond attentively to U.S. initiatives, finding it no easier to deal with idealism stressing multilateralism from Barack Obama than with George W. Bush's unilateralism.

The Intensity Dimension

The most fervent expressions of national identity have been consigned to the past. During World War II, Japan saw kamikaze pilots and appeals for mass suicides of civilians on Okinawa. On many occasions since the 1980s, South Koreans have worked themselves into a frenzy over national affronts or causes, leaving images of candlelight vigils. Maoist red guards waving their "little red books" left an indelible impression in the Cultural Revolution. But for today's leaders, all such emotional outbursts are recalled with embarrassment. If the Chinese still take to the streets after one affront or another by a foreign power, the state is quick to rein in such blatant emotionalism, even if it incited and organized it to no small degree. If the Japanese generally eschew mass activism and demonstrations, there does not mean that the political right regrets stirring emotions that can be measured in public opinion polls as a basis for steering policy and pressuring other states. In place of some past flagrant cases of devotion to one's state, one sees of late more controlled expressions of national identity.

In the 1980s, Japanese conservatives complained about apathetic youth who cared little about patriotism, as Chinese Communists railed against a "spiritual crisis" that left young people aloof to the CCP and patriotism. Yet, just as South Korean progressives were finding inspiration in the democracy movement of their college days for decades of activism, Chinese college students in the 1990s imbibed the narrative of the patriotic education movement to turn more critical of rival powers. If Japanese youth still drew more attention for dropping out than joining in, they showed little inclination to reject the conservative leanings of political leaders. The lack of susceptibility to idealism in all three states, despite increasing access to international news on the Internet, is evidence that powerful mechanisms still exist to spread, if not excite, national pride. They serve to inhibit a search for historical truth along with redirecting deep grievances.

The struggle over national identity operates at various levels and through diverse mechanisms that obscure what is occurring. Kiyoteru Tsutsui has proposed five frames (which I have combined into four) for dealing with the collective traumas in a nation's history, each involving selective memories of a difficult past and excluding genuine acceptance of guilt. He sees a sequence of (1) denial, claiming that the charges are erroneous; (2) justification, resisting guilt, not by disputing the veracity of the accusations but by pointing to one's own offsetting activities and motives; (3) projection, shifting the blame from the nation to a small group whose role is regarded as a historical aberration; and (4) displacement (or evasion), shifting the focus to how one's own nation was victimized and how other states committed more egregious transgressions.[15] All these frames are visible in defensive reactions taken in Japan after the trauma of defeat in World War II and in China after the tragedy of Mao's ideological rampage. They obscure an objective public discussion of the historical record.

One factor in emotionalism is how textbooks and the mass media cover sensitive issues. Committees have been formed to prepare shared textbooks across the region. Yet they stand little chance of success, given the priorities of national leaders. Censorship in China, including of access to the Internet, is growing tighter on subjects viewed by leaders as politically sensitive. South Korea has the liveliest exchange of views in the mass media and the most vibrant debates about how to deal with patterns of distortions on television. Yet, even amid its diversity, many are aroused by inflammatory rhetoric, as in the vigils against U.S. beef imports in 2008. A sustained inculcation of a narrow worldview can be seen in the schools of all three states, especially China. If Japan's postwar legacy of avoiding moral education lingers to some degree and South Korea's deep divide between two political camps has an inhibiting effect, China's socialist legacy of tailoring studies to conform to political doctrines has the most impact on views about national identity. If some may react against this, either by turning away to materialism or by seeking truths elsewhere, the emotionalism of those most influenced still sets today's China apart.

Although it is sometimes possible to challenge specific decisions of national leaders, the hegemony of a certain worldview is basically off limits—even in democracies, in their own way. The CCP posits itself as the guarantor of this vital interpretation of foreign relations, past and present. With conflicting views off limits of Japan's aggressive past, Taiwan's illegitimate quest for independence, and China's need to rise against Western humiliations, the CCP builds on this monopoly perspective to cast itself as guardian of national identity. Japanese right wingers lack a comparable apparatus of censorship and control, but they have succeeded since the decline of the left in making national identity into a search for pride in history. In this way, they have gained virtually a veto in the political arena on the agenda dealing with the past. Their textbook changes test the limits of internal and external tolerance. They keep the focus on whether leaders will visit the Yasukuni Shrine or make provocative new assertions about the wartime era. As in China, these guardians of the national identity portray their nation as under siege from forces both inside and outside the country that would undermine its essence. China's rise is perilous in the face of such opponents, and Japan's normalcy is similarly imperiled. If the targets in South Korea are not as clear and the defenders are more split between the two ends of the political spectrum, the same basic mentality exists of a worldview under threat—Japan, the United States, and China are variously blamed—amid appeals for national cohesion. Although in each state academic experts align with international reference groups, they cannot go far in reassuring the outside world when they are exposed as peripheral to the far-reaching debates that keep exploding over national identity.

EANIS is fostered by a Confucian or Communist emphasis on the importance of moral education in the upbringing of persons. Since the end of the Cold War, all three states have become concerned about the effects of education, but this has rarely meant greater commitment to international standards centered on universal values. Politicians in China have been especially interested in arousing greater patriotism centered on a narrow notion of national identity that belittles the rights of minority ethnic groups, political dissenters, and true internationalists. Conservatives in Japan and progressives in South Korea have had some success in highlighting symbols to arouse followers. Emotional intensity has been heightened by discussions of sensitive issues that were previously put aside, such as the new Japanese interest in right-wing views of the war and South Korean investigations into the history of collaborators with the Japanese. Although victories by Korean conservatives and the Democratic Party of Japan attenuate these appeals, we see no evidence of a sustained drop in the intensity of emotions related to national identity. Indeed, in China they may have reached their peak since the Mao era, aroused during the Olympic craze and antiminority railings of 2008–9.

When nations are subdued after a crisis or an abrupt political turnabout, national identity is suppressed. When they are either frustrated or emboldened, however, identity may climb to a feverish pitch. In turn, it is apt to blind policymakers to balanced views on domestic political reconciliation and international crisis resolution.

Efforts to forge networks based on individual identities focused on interests or beliefs stumble before the priority of national identities in the minds of those positioned to make significant decisions. Calls for localism, bypassing the nation-state by forging direct links between resurgent localities directly to the global community, fall on deaf ears. Appeals to international principles have not rallied many supporters due to a dearth of idealism in the face of the prevailing national focus. Of late, images of regionalism associated with the vision of an East Asian Community fail to inspire enthusiasm. What makes possible the great intensity of national identities in East Asia is the absence of alternative identities around which to unite. Where enterprise or community identity gains some traction, it lacks a core of ideals to counterbalance national-level identity, serving instead largely to complement or reinforce it.

The Crux of the East Asian National Identity Syndrome

The six dimensions serve as a framework for identifying the building blocks of EANIS. On each dimension, one finds evidence of strength at one or both extremes and a gap in the center. Where there are contesting groups, one finds them strong at the extremes but weak at the center. There is no active bridge to find a path to common ground or to gradually narrow the sharp differences, especially because the political right did not feel much pressure in elections or international politics to move toward the center.

If one treats the early historical stages up to 1945 as a unit, then one also finds a bifurcation in discussing the temporal dimension, concentrating on this distant period and on the present, but taking scant notice of the intermediate postwar era of more than four decades. It is not valued by the right or the left, as each has conceptualized it as a stepping-stone to a subsequent era that has not arrived. Instead of recognizing the success that Japan achieved as a basis for later approaches, many dismiss this intermediate era as expedient and fleeting while looking further back to resolve debates about national identity. On the vertical dimension, one sees a strong statist identity, if not traditional nationalism, and a strong micro-level identity, but no firm foundation at the middle step of intermediate identities that could link the two. On the horizontal dimension, there is also a gap in the middle. The U.S. alliance assumes such a large role that Japan has found justification in not reaching out to its neighbors. The failure to build a foundation for regionalism dates back to premodern times, and it continues to be reflected in national identity debates that incorporate internationalism as a desired, but poorly defined balance, to the U.S. dyad. Finally, between strong *honne,* which undergirds national identity debates, and persistent *tatemae,* which operates in the forefront even when few regard it as adequate, there is a threadbare second layer of logic about Japan's reasoning concerning national identity. In each case, we observe the middle level squeezed between the two outer levels and failing to provide a balanced sequence.

What prevents the center from developing? Where dictatorship exists, backed by reliance on censorship, contending groups are both denied a platform and suppressed. However, another factor is the moral authority of the state. China, Japan, and South Korea place great emphasis on this, steeped in historical rectitude and bolstered by recent achievement. If current leaders lose popularity, as has occurred repeatedly in Japan and South Korea in the post–Cold War era, this does not reverberate in a broad-scale attack on the way moral and political authority is concentrated in the state. Given an emphasis on state virtues, national identity acquires potency, in contrast to self or civil society, as matters of identity. Assumptions about the state date back to Confucian thinking. Some stress limits on the state from appeals to putting familyism first, losing the Mandate of Heaven if policies are burdensome, governing through benevolence and moral suasion, and trusting in officials educated to defend principles of good governance. All these factors were present, but none denied the enormous authority vested in the state in the Confucian worldview. Over time, top-heavy Confucianism—favoring imperial over elite and reform versions under the impact of foreign-led or peasant-origin dynasties, adding bushido elements, becoming mired in rituals and hermit thinking—tilted the balance away from checks on the state.

An unbalanced national identity derives from an accumulation of institution building and idea shaping. History is viewed from the perspective of both a great threat to survival of the nation and a great humiliation that has yet to be redressed. The state's mission then becomes to save the nation, to catch up economically, to regain all claimed territory, and to stand firm against further humiliation of any sort. This leads to acceptance of ideology that distorts the nature of the global struggle. The Japanese clung to thinking about a global fight to the finish among imperialist states long after it was outdated, as Communism and Nazism made totalitarian conquest the critical question. The Chinese and many South Korean and Japanese progressives after World War II adopted Marxist-Leninist ideology, which belittled capitalist states and the universal values they normally professed. Viewing their own societies and the world through a misleading prism, they placed their confidence in the state, as it was or as it should become. Even as their own state was leading economic growth and a resurgence of international influence, such deeply embedded ideas endured.

Confucian traditions, coupled with the legacy of top-down catch-up modernization in an atmosphere fraught with dangers of being colonized, yield to the state an exceptional degree of political and moral authority without endorsing totalitarianism. Traditions of family solidarity and hierarchical face-to-face relations enmesh the self in interpersonal obligations that deny it the scope idealized in the United States. The state is valued as the guardian of society—the force that drives its development in a world where competition among states reigns. Individualist values have gained some popularity, but they are tempered by state values. If the state is weakened, it is often assumed that the economy will grow more slowly, anarchy might undermine existing social controls, and the country could become vulnerable to the depredations of rapacious international forces threatening a people's culture as well as its sovereignty. State-centered values receive at least some priority and often gain outright ascendancy among those with this worldview.

Variations in National Identity among the East Asian States

The Japanese since the Cold War era show the least public patriotism. The South Koreans in the post–Cold War decades are most openly divided on how to interpret national identity. Because it trails the other two states by decades in modernization, China lacks the leavening effect of a higher percentage of people in the middle class and a more complex society. If theories of postmodern thinking nurturing internationalism in place of nationalism hold, than one could draw a continuum of a path with Japan leading the way and China following, and South Korea in the middle well ahead of China. As China's "economic miracle" finally slows, this logic would surmise a loss of confidence in its superior cultural national identity and then in its unique political mission. Although the above comparisons do not suggest that EANIS is so fragile as merely to reflect some universal patterns of modernization, there is reason to expect gradual socialization of China in the international system and rising pressure from middle-class society to temper the most extreme EANIS manifestations.

Given the importance of revisionism over history, one should consider the degree to which Japan is the outlier in national identity. If some revisionists have their way, an altered understanding of Japan's Asian imperialism, the Tokyo Tribunal, and the San Francisco Peace Treaty would pose a serious affront to all the other states in the region. However much this spurred national identity related emotions in China and South Korea, in particular, it would presumably not be accompanied by actions that exacerbated Japan's EANIS. Continuing its alliance with the United States and its relatively cautious foreign policy without any likelihood of intense patriotic movements, Japan has learned the lesson of its extreme behavior to 1945 in a manner that keeps EANIS in check.

In some respects, South Korea appears to be an outlier. Its middle-power role and elite acceptance of internationalism, including close ties to the United States, contrast to the pretensions of China and Japan. If any of the three countries has political forces and mass media reporting that could undercut EANIS, then this is it. Yet the shadow of North Korea looms large. If it collapsed, a resurgence of intense national identity could accompany reunification. Alternatively, if its threatening behavior raised the specter of war without many in the South feeling satisfied that they could shape the way events unfolded, this could produce an inward-looking backlash. Continued volatility in public responses to government policies does not suggest that EANIS is fading.

The case for China being the outlier is strongest, not because EANIS seems to be in decline but because it is reaching its most extreme form since the 1970s. Maoism capitalized on some of its features, although anti-Confucianism and an unstable mixture of antistatist class-struggle rhetoric and hypertrophied state victimization rhetoric did not conform well to EANIS. In the 1980s, Deng's pragmatism appeared to set aside other features, but for the past two decades since 1989 this syndrome has grown ever stronger. The restraining conditions operating in Japan and South Korea, such as democratization and an alliance with the United States, are absent in China. Japan's peace Constitution and South Korea's contrast to North Korea do not apply to China. Instead, in the search for a post-Mao strategy to maintain the authority of the CCP, China's leaders have reinforced the unbalanced elements found in each dimension of EANIS.

All six dimensions reveal China in 2010 to be most extreme in its symptoms of EANIS. On the temporal dimension, its revived pride in Confucian glories, sustained critique of humiliations by foreign imperialism, enforced silence about the ravages that Communism caused, and one-sided treatment of the costs and benefits of developments since the 1989 Tiananmen Square repression all result in unbalanced thinking. In ideological balancing, China's authoritarian controls contrast sharply with the democratic processes in Japan and South Korea, putting more pressure on centrist thinking. As for the sectoral dimension, there has been nothing to match China's recent overlap of economic national identity forecasting overtaking the United States, cultural national identity assuming the superiority of its heritage and of national character, and political national identity fueled by echoes of Sinocentrism and Communist struggle against capitalism. When one turns to the vertical dimension, one sees recent crackdowns on Tibetan and Uyghur ethnic groups in their traditional homelands and intensified controls on the Internet to shape how young people in particular view the world as interest groups are prevented from organizing. On the horizontal dimension, China's struggle with the United States combines cooperation with competition; however, its national identity at stake is decidedly opposed to that of the United States. China's view of the outside world—critical of internationalism linked to universal values, and distrustful of regionalism that would limit its narrow notion of sovereignty exclusive of outside values—greatly reinforces EANIS. All these differences with Japan and South Korea are intensified by the intensity of emotions found among key groups in Chinese politics and in Internet exchanges. All the conditions observed at this time point to political continuity in China that deepens EANIS, whereas a political transition in Japan and a divided polity in South Korea serve to limit EANIS.

In the first half of 2011, Japan's March 11 disaster shook the nation's identity, exposing an urgent need for its reconstruction; South Korea's political divide gained new traction in bi-elections, revealing the incompleteness of conservative answers to the popular quest for identity balance; and China's spike in national identity attenuated only enough to lower the intensity from levels difficult to manage. Political leaders were still unprepared to pursue a sustainable, balanced identity for their nation. Above all, the CCP clung to its hyperbolic interpretation of national identity, perpetuating the recent spike while suppressing popular longings for a more just society that would alter the vertical dimension. The legacy of EANIS in Japan and South Korea shows the difficulty of dealing with the lingering emotions from a spike.

Limitations of the EANIS Framework

National identities are invoked by leaders and opinion shapers to gain a political advantage or steer decisions and public opinion in a desired direction. They are gradually redefined, adding new elements and refocusing on old ones. As political choices loom, leaders consider the national identity implications as one factor in decisionmaking. They are not a determining factor, although they can have a significant impact either as a way to sell polices that otherwise might be unpopular or in tipping the balance when other options could well be chosen. The fact that a syndrome exists helps to explain what one observes in the development of East Asia without offering a substitute for careful analysis of why particular decisions were made in the circumstances of the time.

Evidence of EANIS conflicts with claims that Japan is not part of the same civilization as China and that democratic values are the driving forces in separating China from Japan and South Korea in discussions related to recent national identity. Arguments for a civilizational or democratic divide across East Asia have some merit, but they give too little credence to common historical experiences, especially the importance of relying on Confucianism to frame discussions about the state. By pointing to a deep-seated syndrome at work, I do not seek to distract attention from the way many try to manipulate it. National identity serves to gain political advantage at home over real or potential rivals. A sweeping advantage might accrue from demonizing the other side. This is the result of Communist class warfare, in which opponents are purged or even killed after being branded enemies of the people and their nation. Orthodoxy about class consciousness makes the national identity card a cudgel to support a narrow elite under dictatorial power. In contrast, in democracies with vibrant civil societies, the various strands of national identity may operate quite separately, making it difficult to narrow the notion of national identity in order to make political rivals pariahs. Yet a balance of identities may not last; political elites may grasp for ways to isolate other elites and prevent outsiders from assisting possible rivals for power.

This volume relies on broad-brush comparisons of three countries to argue for the presence of a shared syndrome. More detailed comparisons would reveal more about the dynamics of the syndrome and the factors that limit its application. Extending the range of comparisons would expand our awareness of what makes national identities in East Asia distinctive. With an understanding of EANIS, we can turn next to its impact on international relations at a time of flux following the transition after the Cold War.

Notes

1. Tsuyoshi Hasegawa and Kazuhiko Togo, eds., *East Asia's Haunted Present: Historical Memories and the Resurgence of Nationalism* (Westport, Conn.: Praeger, 2008).

2. Gilbert Rozman, ed., *The East Asian Region: Confucian Heritage and Its Modern Adaptation* (Princeton, N.J.: Princeton University Press, 1991).

3. F. W. Mote, *Imperial China 900–1800* (Cambridge, Mass.: Harvard University Press, 1999).

4. Andre Schmid, *Korea between Empires, 1895–1919* (New York: Columbia University Press, 2002).

5. Cyril E. Black et al., *The Modernization of Japan and Russia* (New York: Free Press, 1975); Gilbert Rozman, ed., *The Modernization of China* (New York: Free Press, 1981).

6. Eiko Ikegami, *The Taming of the Samurai* (Cambridge, Mass.: Harvard University Press, 1995); Andrew L. Oros, *Normalizing Japan: Politics, Identity, and the Evolution of Security Practice* (Stanford, Calif.: Stanford University Press, 2008).

7. Gilbert Rozman, "Can Confucianism Survive in an Age of Universalism and Globalization?" *Pacific Affairs* 75, no. 1 (Spring 2002): 11–37.

8. Gilbert Rozman, "The Confucian Faces of Capitalism," in *The Emergence of Modern Pacific Asia,* edited by Mark Borthwick (Boulder, Colo.: Westview Press, 1992), 310–22.

9. Harumi Befu, "Nationalism and Nihonjinron," in *Cultural Nationalism in East Asia: Representation and Identity,* edited by Harumi Befu (Berkeley: Institute of East Asian Studies, University of California, 1993), 107–35.

10. Hasegawa and Togo, *East Asia's Haunted Present.*

11. Kim Sonmi, "Shimin undo no kikiron to shimin shakai no kozu henka," in *Kankoku niokeru shimin ishiki no dotai,* edited by Okonogi Masao and Nishino Junya (Tokyo: Keio University Press, 2005), vol. 2, 3–23.

12. Gilbert Rozman, "Internationalism and Asianism in Japanese Strategic Thought from Meiji to Heisei," *Japanese Journal of Political Science* 9, no. 2 (Spring 2008): 209–32.

13. Gilbert Rozman, "Post–Cold War Evolution of Chinese Thinking on Regional Institutions in Northeast Asia," *Journal of Contemporary China* 19, no. 65 (2010): 605–20.

14. Zhou Yuyuan, "Dongya yizhi yu Dongya yanjiu," *Dongnanya yanjiu,* no. 5 (2007): 27–31.

15. Kiyoteru Tsutsui, "The Trajectory of Perpretators' Trauma: Mnemonic Politics around the Asia-Pacific War in Japan," *Social Forces* 87, no. 3 (March 2009): 1389–1422.

Part II

The Evolution of National Identities and the Impact of Diplomatic Challenges

Introduction

Gilbert Rozman

Although the six-dimensional approach applies an external framework to the national identities present in three East Asian states, part II approaches identities from a perspective internal to these countries. It traces how identity evolved, while also focusing on one paramount diplomatic principle or controversy for each state to appreciate its pervasive presence. Thus, it complements the analysis in part I, adding a richer chronological background and highlighting the importance since the Cold War of diplomatic choices as key testing grounds for identity construction.

Each of these states held aloft one ideal that expressed the desired national identity. In Japan, the postwar ideal became the "three basic principles," which are described by Yuichi Hosoya in chapter 6. Even as the Japanese chafed at "taxation without representation" as a would-be permanent member of the UN Security Council, the balance associated with an active role in the United Nations remained an ideal. Despite alienation from key countries in Asia, the allure of "reentering

Asia" in a leadership capacity also was part of the ideal. Finally, the sole principle that was realized—the U.S. alliance—proved to be a fragile reed for national identity because it did not satisfy the quest for equality and for balance among the three. For a more long-term perspective on the vacuum in postwar Japanese national identity and strands of thinking that potentially could be drawn together in meeting the challenge even when new Japanese leadership in 2009 reasserted these three principles, in chapter 5 Kazuhiko Togo offers a broad overview of the way national identity evolved in Japanese history.

In chapter 7, Andrew Kim and I provide parallel chronological coverage of South Korean national identity as well coverage of both diplomatic challenges and the tension between ethnic and civic forms of national identity. These tensions are explored in greater depth with respect to recent times by Chung-in Moon in chapter 8. In both chapters, we consider the way ethnic identity has been losing force, as civic national identity comes more to the fore. Compared with Japan and China, the struggle over Korean identity is not only more intense but also has more elements in the forefront of national debate.

The Chinese government has succeeded in keeping matters of sovereignty in the forefront in discussions of national identity. In chapter 9 Jin Linbo presents an evolutionary approach, whereas in chapter 10 Ming Wan demonstrates the importance of noninterference in internal affairs as the guiding principle in China in recent decades. The notion of sovereignty was further extended over time, both to human rights interference in China's domestic affairs and to "core interests" found in nearby maritime areas. As China turns back to historical notions of identity and reasserts themes associated with Mao Zedong's leadership, it behooves us to look back as well.

The Evolution of National Identity

Japan, South Korea, and China all faced turning points in the second half of the 1940s and the second half of the 1980s, and they were facing another key juncture in 2010 and 2011, at the time of writing. China also faced a turning point at the end of the 1970s. South Korea faced one at the end of the 1990s, and Japan not long afterward. As background for the following six chapters on the evolution of national identities and diplomatic choices, some comments are in order on the turning points each of these countries passed.

In the Cold War era, one can observe a pronounced emphasis on national purity: Japan's rising interest in Nihonjinron ideals of Japanese uniqueness, South Korea's preoccupation with *minjok* ethnic identity centered on the Korean bloodline, and China's pretensions to be the wellspring of world revolution along lines only its leaders had followed after they had broken with the false Soviet Communism. Given the presence of two blocs struggling for global supremacy, there were limitations on how these claims of national purity were expressed. Cut off from its Confucian past and attached to an ideology that claimed universal validity, China faced contortions of a more extreme nature. Yet, all three states separated themselves from the rest of the world, regardless of political relations, by their obsession with cultural identity. China's sponsorship of world revolution was on the surface political identity, but the Cultural Revolution linked the two types of identity in ways that rejected external sources of culture and demanded pure internal ones beyond anything elsewhere.

Having such an extreme approach to national identity, China was the first to experience a turning point. It also confronted the most far-reaching turmoil in its identity during the decade following this turning point starting in 1978. Yet, just as the turning point at the end of the Cold War did not uproot Nihonjinron or *minjok,* the Deng break from Mao's extremism did not dislodge a version of cultural uniqueness. The slogan "socialism with Chinese characteristics" aptly reflects the identity sought by China's leaders. During the 1980s, they groped for a suitable mix of symbols to resist spiritual pollution in the form of national identity themes from the West or the dynamic areas of East Asia. Disavowing the notion of revisionism, they looked to the history of socialism. Rethinking the importance of Confucianism, they revisited Chinese history. Claiming a place in a resurgent East Asia, they even found merit as part of Eastern civilization while putting China as its historical source. Before the end of the Cold War, China had joined Japan and South Korea in a narrow emphasis on cultural uniqueness as the critical foundation for national identity.

Japanese and South Korean national identities were tested anew in the late 1980s, the former by great confidence from a bubble economic and the latter from democratization bolstered by growing economic confidence. The Japanese grew more confident in internationalism, which they could more easily shape, and in Asianism, which they expected to lead. Both made it desirable to cast aside Nihonjinron. More support for universal values would have enhanced Japan's claims to world stature, and less defensiveness about Japanese history would have facilitated ties in Asia. At the zenith of bubble economy arrogance and then the nadir of its collapse, Japan did not break the hold of Nihonjinron, despite its declining popularity. Similarly, Korean democratization and *nordpolitik* success in diplomatic diversification brought signs of important change in national identity. Yet, as in Japan, preoccupation with U.S. pressure to open markets fortified views of cultural uniqueness as civic identity only slowly gained ground over *minjok* identity. The next turning point at the time of the Sunshine Policy rekindled support for *minjok,* now linked to hopes for reunification. To a degree, frustration with China and even South Korea "playing the history card" fueled renewed Japanese attention to historical justifications that proved cultural uniqueness also. The intensity of thinking solidified before the end of the Cold War made possible resilience to new challenges and revival amid new opportunities.

In tracing the evolution of Chinese national identity, special attention should be placed on the identity spike visible in 2010 and how it evolved from the choices made during the earlier history of the People's Republic of China. Although the stark language of 2010 contrasts with the more temperate tone that generally prevailed in the previous three decades, its background is rooted in sixty years of the People's Republic's history. China's claims to cultural superiority are deeply rooted, gaining intensity through Mao's approach to Communism and proving to be once again extreme during the current upsurge of national identity intensity.

The first turning point followed Mao Zedong's declaration of China's rise. By leaning to one side through an alliance with the Soviet Union that erased any doubt over China's Communist identity and entering the Korean War linking it to the fight against a century of imperialism in the region, Mao fixed China's identity against the United States and Western civilization in the shadow of Joseph Stalin's polarization of the world into two irreconcilable camps. The second turning point took shape after Nikita Khrushchev's de-Stalinization speech and shift to peaceful coexistence with the United States, while Mao was quelling domestic discontent over inequities in China's policies of building socialism and then his own Great Leap Forward quick fix. By repudiating Soviet revisionism and pressing for continuous revolution, Mao put China on an unsustainable course of association only with the most radical groups fighting against their own governments and the international order. Bombastic rejection of humanism and Confucianism alienated China from the two sources of identity most likely to temper Communism in its most radical form. Simultaneously, the rejection of convergence through modernization and economic integration into the increasingly dynamic East Asia region left China at a national identity dead end.

The failure of the frenzied peak of the Cultural Revolution and breakthroughs with the United States and Japan took until the end of the 1970s to produce major changes in national identity. New waves of anti-Confucianism in 1973–74 and antirevisionism in 1976–77 accompanied twisted logic and a virtual freeze on writings capable of challenging distortions that sustained a tortured rendition of identity. New China championed class struggle that was destroying its development potential and anti-imperialism with such far-reaching scope that it isolated the Chinese from global currents in all spheres. Its unsustainable, contradictory national identity left China paralyzed without domestic reform, global support for modernization, and especially public debate over past mistakes and future opportunities. Only under Deng was a third turning point realized. From 1978 to 1982, Chinese national identity shed many of its fetters. The process was tightly controlled, allowing for only faint hints of the sort of glasnost that occurred under Gorbachev in the USSR and barely a murmur of dissent against the emerging "Chinese spiritual civilization." Caution, however, about China's weak position led to constraints on how national identity could be constructed. Even after 1989–91, when a succession of shocks led to more assertive identity claims, caution prevailed in how they were packaged.

In 2008–10, we discern another turning point, bringing into the open themes obscured under Deng's warning for China to bide its time. Although the focus on noninterference in China's internal affairs persisted, it was expressed more aggressively as in the blunt warnings to countries that contemplated sending a representative to the Nobel Peace Prize celebration for Liu Shaobo. Sovereignty concerns no longer awaited some future resolution. Instead, China pressed its demands on maritime boundaries with both bolder actions and a more definitive condemnation of the world system that was deemed responsible as well as the dangerous thinking of the states whose claims were disputed. These responses fit into an evolving national identity narrative, which is set forth in the chapters of this volume.

National Identity and Diplomatic Principles

Diplomacy is a venue for the expression of national identity and also an incubator for honing elements of identity that reverberate domestically. The East Asian countries faced the challenge of being overwhelmed by the spread of U.S. national identity with its strong assumptions about universal values and political and cultural convergence accompanying economic and social modernization. Having been occupied by the United States and then become an ally totally dependent on this one superpower, Japan was the first to respond to this challenge as its double-digit annual economic growth fueled predictions that it was following the U.S. or Western development model. Its choice in 1957 of the "three basic principles" to diversify its diplomacy signaled resistance to becoming subsumed under the narrow confines of this model. This marked an important turning point, centered first on economic national identity but also carrying the seeds of resurgent cultural and political national identity. When modernization theory with attendant arguments in favor of far-reaching convergence was introduced into Japan in the first half of the 1960s, there was already a shared consensus on the political right and left with little dissent from the political center that it did not meet Japan's needs, notably for its national identity.

South Korea trailed Japan by two to three decades in squarely confronting the challenge to national identity from an even more overwhelming U.S. presence through diplomacy. In the face of the North Korean threat and with a colonial legacy rather than an imperialist one, it lacked the great power confidence that empowered Japan as early as the 1950s. In the 1980s, however, three forces coincided to enable South Koreans to explore diplomatic outlets to express a distinct national identity: (1) an "economic miracle," which, building on the precedent of Japan's widely heralded economic achievements, served as a vehicle for pride over "Asian values" and provided clout for diplomatic leverage; (2) a democratic revolution interpreted by many Koreans as accomplished in spite of the United States, not as a result of the spread of U.S. values; and (3) the waning of the Cold War, which opened the door to *nordpolitik* in overtures to Moscow, Beijing, and even Pyongyang that gave meaning to diplomatic diversity. By the 1990s, national identity was being explored with renewed enthusiasm as well as with political contestation far beyond that seen in Japan.

China's diplomatic resistance to the West gained traction when it joined the Soviet Bloc, and it acquired broader scope with the slogan "noninterference in internal affairs." In Mao's decision to break with the Soviet Union, China reinforced national identity against all potential challenges. Yet, the problem of U.S. values grew more serious in the 1980s, as China lowered its guard against foreign influences, repudiated much of Mao's legacy, and relaxed controls over airing alternative views on cultural or even certain political themes. The question of Western values spreading in China in place of discredited socialist ones gained urgency, especially with the massive Tiananmen Square demonstrations, the collapse of the socialist bloc, and then the collapse of the Soviet Union. By forcefully reasserting the principle of noninterference in internal affairs, China's leaders in the 1990s sought diplomatic diversity in conjunction with clarity over a national identity at odds with that exported by the United States and its partners.

A diplomatic slogan can serve as a symbol of national identity, even if various foreign policy realities may contradict it. The Japanese took some comfort from the diversity of foreign policy implied in the three basic principles, even if only one of these merited serious consideration. They expressed an aspiration for Japan's ideal ties to the outside. Earlier, the Japanese search to escape the Sinocentric world preceded the miniature arena that Japan envisioned in its place in the Tokugawa Era, and the more ardent search for an alternative universe to the Western-centered world into which they were thrust from 1853 led to many formulations of Asianism led by Japan starting late in the century. South Korea had to wait until the waning of the Cold War to articulate its long-sought vision for diverse diplomacy suitable to its desired national identity. Overoptimism about China and Russia accompanied *nordpolitik,* rose-colored glasses fueled the Sunshine Policy, and the hopes behind Roh Moo-hyun's moves from initiatives to Pyongyang to plans for a Northeast Asian regional community to hints his country would become the "balancer"—all defied realistic possibilities. With the Japanese dependent on an unequal alliance that stifled debate on sensitive historical issues critical to national identity and South Koreans mindful of a history of *sadae* squelching their voices on national identity, proposed diplomatic ideals temporarily offered some a soothing palliative in the absence of genuine diversification.

China was no stranger to aspirational diplomatic claims. In the 1980s, the goal of equidistance between the United States and the Soviet Union hinted at the lofty ambition of becoming the pivot in the strategic triangle. In the 1990s, insistence that multipolarity is in sight put continued deference to the United States in a positive light. On all sides, as diplomatic advances intensified in the 2000s, the Chinese spun them optimistically: the Shanghai Cooperation Organization is a precursor to diplomatic groupings of the new age; the Association of Southeast Asian Nations (ASEAN) + 3 demonstrates how the "harmonious world" is taking shape; the Six-Party Talks show how multilateralism can respect sovereignty. Wishful thinking coincided with harsh criticisms of U.S. diplomacy for following the wrong principles. China's search for national identity found expression in its rhetoric about international relations centered on U.S. and regional ties.

During the previous sixty years, the search for diplomatic breakthroughs of importance for national identity mainly involved normalization, diversification, and the quest for multilateralism. In 2010, the focus shifted to how to respond to rapid transformation in the balance of power between China and the United States. This was no longer a vague process expected at some uncertain time in the future. Rather, it became an open confrontation initiated by China with direct pressure against its neighbors amid accusations that the entire fault lies with U.S. hegemonism aimed at preventing China's rise. This altered environment had serious implications for the identities of the major East Asian states, which had been tempered by regionalism.

Regionalism exerted a temporary restraining influence on national identity assertiveness. Japan's search for Asianism and reentry into Asia intensified from 1997 to 2002 and somewhat revived from 2006 to 2009. Even in the midst of rising alarm about China's leadership quest and increasing embrace of the U.S. alliance, the pull of regionalism satisfied a long-term identity quest. Only in 2010 did a sobered Japan recognize that East Asian regionalism has become a mechanism for China to seek hegemony while excluding the United States. Similarly, South Koreans sought benefits from regionalism as a complement to the Sunshine Policy, as progressives valued it not only for its potential to forge a favorable environment for North-South rapprochement but also as a balance to dependency on the United States. For them it did not so much impose restraint as embolden distancing from an ally, whose call for caution in enabling North Korean assertiveness was unwelcome. The restraint imposed on China was most significant in the period 1997–2007 as it deferred to ASEAN and, for the most part, appealed to Japan and South Korea to quicken integration into a regional community. Obviously, China saw regionalism as a way to weaken the U.S. role in both Southeast and Northeast Asia; its own approach paid lip service to forging an East Asian community without actively venturing beyond economic cooperation.

In 2010, the building of an East Asian community was exposed as an illusion. The impact was clearest in Chinese writings, which targeted states in the region as well as the United States with criticisms more extreme than any that had preceded. Although China pretended that the Asian people were eager for regionalism, tortured arguments left no doubt that China's leaders no longer had the will to find common ground. Regionalism as well as internationalism was marginalized in a unrelenting repudiation of the United States and its alliances. Sovereignty reined supreme, as it drove out other diplomatic themes that had coexisted with it in precarious balance.

Japan's shock exceeded anything experience at least since the breakthrough in U.S.-Chinese ties in 1971. As recently as the fall of 2009, optimism about the East Asian community was at the core of the government's diplomacy. For more than half a century, the idea of Asianism, however distant, had provided comforting balance in an identity obsessed with the United States. Despite an inability to reconcile hopes for vindicating Asianism to 1945 and forging Asianism for the future, the Japanese clung to this idea. Suddenly, they awakened to their misplaced denial of total reliance on the United States not only for security but for a shared identity resistant to China. The shock deepened in 2011, when a traumatized Japan searched anew for pride in the midst of disaster. In South Korea, conservatives and progressives were still struggling over the challenge of transcending *minjok* identity, as the shock from China's foreign policy compounded the shock of the reversion of North Korea into an alien threat. As regionalism faded, the reality became further identification with the United States and even a new closeness with Japan. The diplomatic prospects had narrowed along with the identity ones.

Polarization in the Cold War, replaced with optimism about democratization and globalization as well as regionalism, was reviving in the outlook of China on the United States and Western civilization. Only recently having been idealist, Japan and South Korea were forced to reconsider long-standing national identity illusions. Although in 2010 and 2011 this transition was only beginning, and it would depend heavily on national identity thinking in China in the coming years, the context can be set by looking back to the principles for diplomacy associated with national identity in the East Asian states.

Chapter 5

Japanese National Identity: Evolution and Prospects

Kazuhiko Togo

Japan currently faces an important turning point in searching for its national identity. Although the three factors (Western, Asian, and Japanese) traditionally relevant in determining its identity are all present in this search, their alignment is still in doubt. This chapter analyzes how Japanese identity has formed through the interplay of these factors, pointing to differences at three historical stages: (1) the premodern stage, when identity developed in a Sinocentric setting; (2) the prewar, imperialist stage, as Japan started from *nuo* (entering Europe) and then *datsua* (leaving Asia), before shifting to *koa* (raising Asia), which merged with the pursuit of an inherently Japanese factor; and (3) the stage from the defeat of World War II, when Japan was overwhelmed by an influx of U.S. values and responded with a mixture of antitotalitarian, one-country pacifism, and realist economic centrism based on its alliance with the United States. After the Cold War, we see signs of a turning point in the third stage, including a more realist orientation friendly to the United States and also to Asia, but still leaving Japan at a crossroads without a clear sense of its national identity.

On three occasions, in accord with the conventional interpretation, Japan reacted to powerful inundation by a foreign culture by reasserting its own pathway. It reacted to an influx of Chinese civilization in premodern times, to European civilization during the Meiji Era, and to American values after the end of World War II. In the post–Cold War period, as globalization spreads, it is reacting again with two sharply opposed tendencies for determining "Japaneseness" that are competing to define the thrust of national identity.

Japan's Identity in the Sinocentric World

In the premodern stage, Japan borrowed critical elements of civilization from China, often through the Korean Peninsula. The origin of the Japanese people dates back to the tenth century BC, when Mongolian peoples who had lived in the southern part of China (today's Guangxi Autonomous Area Liujiang xian) founded the Jomon Era, and together with new Mongolian peoples who moved to Japan from Korea around the first century BC eventually formed the Yayoi Era.[1] The fundamental technologies of rice-paddy agriculture and bronze weapons were transmitted from Korea in this period. The state of Yamato was formed in about AD 400 as contacts intensified with the kingdoms in Korea, where power politics led to an alliance between Japan, Baekje, and Kaya against Koguryo. Starting in the early fifth century, five Yamato kings sent tributary letters to the Southern Dynasty in China. When China was unified under the Sui, Onono Imoko was sent as a *kenzuishi* (emissaries to Sui), to be succeeded by the *kentoshi* (emissaries to Tang) to Tang China. Fighting against Koguryo taught Yamato horseback riding. Chinese characters, Confucianism, Buddhism, and knowledge of an advanced political system were transmitted through Korea. National identity took its initial shape in China's shadow.

Yamato developed into the center of a growing state where Asuka culture flourished based on what Japan received from the continent. In the middle of the seventh century, the Fujiwara/Nakatomi family replaced the Soga-led rulers, eventually monopolized the state function, and created the Ritsuryo system based on the Sui-Tang administrative system. For the first time, political governance under the Dajyokan and religious governance based on Shinto under the Jingikan were done often by one family. The imperial tradition was established, becoming a lasting force in Japan's identity.[2]

With the Yamato capital at Heijokyo (Nara) and then Heiankyo (Kyoto), for nearly four centuries Japan under the emperor and the aristocracy conducted exchanges with the Tang dynasty and the united Koryo dynasty. In the Nara period, the concept of unified statehood became rooted in the Japanese mind, but the non-tributary nature of the letter Onono brought to the Sui was considered "rude" by the Chinese emperor.[3] Two classics describing the origin of Japan's statehood, *Kojiki* and *Nihonshoki,* established the emerging Japanese identity. The first collection of Japanese poems, *Manyoshu,* was compiled. Buddhism bolstered state stability, while at the grassroots it began merging with traditional Shinto (Shinbutsu shugo).[4] In 894 the dispatch of the *kentoshi* was suspended, not long before the Tang fell in 907. Partly reflecting this change in international politics, in the latter Heian Period, after absorbing many important fundamentals of cultural life, Japan developed the original *Kokufu bunka.* The development of *hiragana* and *katakana* writing, the startling novel of the *Tale of Genji,* the essay of *Makurano Soshi,* and the poems of *Kokinwakashu* were the highpoints in its original literature at variance with Chinese culture and indicative of a separate identity.

A period of samurai class ascendancy—through the Kamakura, Muromachi, Sengoku, Azuchi Momoyama, and Tokugawa eras—established a new direction for Japanese identity. Bushido warrior ethics centered on a strict hierarchy of power, and loyalty and identity focused on individual warlords created a unique cultural tradition in the last stage of premodern Japan. Each era witnessed an accumulation of original culture directly expressing or closely linked with the ascendancy of the samurai class. The Kamakura Period produced a wave of new literature, rooted in the newly emerged samurai class or its tension with the traditional aristocracy. Buddhism changed in three fundamentally new directions: Jodoshu and Jodoshinshu (Honen and shinran), Zen (Dogen), and Nichirenshu (Nichiren), adjusting to a turbulent era of fighting in the world of warriors. The Muromachi Period is known for a highly refined culture developed as a fusion of samurai simplicity in the countryside and the elaborate aristocracy in Kyoto. When Oda Nobunaga and Toyotomi Hideyoshi united Japan, the rising power of the new lords and a powerful and extravagant culture and lifestyle developed in prominent, newly built castle towns. We do not see many signs of outside influence in cultural life. At the time of the Yuan attacks in 1274 and 1281, Japan was saved by typhoons called *kamikaze*. When Japan attacked Korea from 1592 to 1598, the aim was to create a new international order under Japan's power, which would rival the declining Ming, but due to resolute resistance by the Koreans backed up by the Ming, the operations failed.[5] These wars reinforced a collective Japanese identity at a time when disparate local, feudal identities kept the focus away from a united nation.

Despite some animated relations with the arriving European powers from Portugal, Spain, and the Netherlands, the Tokugawa decided to cut off relations with the outside and introduced *sakoku* (locked country), except for the Netherlands (through Deshima in Nagasaki), the Ming-Qing (through Nagasaki) and Korea (through Tsushima). Relations with the Ryukyus were governed by the Shimazu clan and with Ezo by the Matsumae clan. With the establishment of a strict class hierarchy, Japan created a unique, closed society with strict social order, stern discipline, and variegated spiritual and intellectual life. The identity of most people did not stretch beyond their domain. Bushido ethics were based on a strict personal code of conduct and were close to Confucian morality. The Zhuxi school, which emphasized social order and the unity of moral principles to attain the "supreme Ultimate," fit well with Tokugawa society.[6] The Ming scholarship of Wang Yangming emphasized the unity of thinking and action, influencing scholars and in a later period such revolutionaries as Oshio Heihachiro.[7] Yogaku, based on the Dutch language and science, became a narrow but important thread of new knowledge. Starting in the eighteenth century, positivist study of Japanese classics led to the development of *kokugaku,* a new emphasis on traditional Japanese thinking, which stood above imported Buddhism and Confucianism. Motoori Norinaga argued based on his study of *Kojiki* for going back to the inherent spirit of Japan, and Hirata Atsutane called for reversion to a purist Shinto belief.[8] The break in identity with China was deepening.

Until the mid–nineteenth century, Japan was a self-contained universe. The West still did not exist except within a narrow circle of intellectuals and policymakers familiarizing themselves with the exchanges at Deshima and *yogaku.* Having cut itself off in large measure for two centuries and a half from the Sinocentric world and having created a stable and relatively prosperous society dominated by samurai, Japan was very different from other East Asian countries. The identity of ordinary samurai and peasants did not reach outside the domain to which they belonged. The emperor in Kyoto was treated as a spiritual symbol. His position was underscored by the revived *kokugaku,* enabling him to become probably the only "other" to daimyo-led samurai identity.

Japan in the Western-Dominated World of Modernity

As Japan became encircled by the expanding Euro-American imperial powers, the channels opened to the outside world during the *sakoku* period allowed the leaders of both the Tokugawa Bakufu and major Han to detect what was happening, particularly in China, and based on this knowledge, with pain and turmoil, the country opened to the world and made a transfer of power to the new Meiji government in 1868. This was the time when a new identity as Japanese emerged, where the "other" was, first and foremost, the encircling imperial powers. The fundamental task faced by the new government was to keep Japan independent. Japan needed to pull its resources together, embodied in the spirit of the Charter Oath of 1868, and achieve *fukoku kyohei* (a rich economy and strong military) as the leading political direction of the era. The first characteristic of emerging Japanese identity was that, to catch up and make it comparable to the "other," it was necessary to imitate the "other." The Iwakura Mission sent abroad from December 1871 to September 1873 was the most dramatic action taken for that purpose, and *bunmei kaika* (civilization and enlightenment) became the spiritual motto of the initial years.

Japan's approach to Asia changed drastically. Already in 1871, Foreign Minister Soejima Taneomi took a realist, power balance approach, placing Taiwan and Korea under Japanese influence to contain China and prevent Russian advancement in Asia.[9] Fukuzawa Yukichi first expected to realize modernization together with Korea and China, but eventually concluded that under the absolute imperative to face the Western powers, Japan had to go its own way, abandoning Korea and China. Fukuzawa's *Datsua-ron* of 1885 best represented this thinking, and *datsua nyuo* became another prevailing motto of the era.[10] From the Meiji Restoration, it took twenty-one years to establish the Meiji Constitution and twenty-six years to conclude the first treaty with full legal equality with Great Britain. In the process, the Meiji government incorporated a tradition of samurai ethics underpinned by *kokugaku* inherited from the pre-Restoration period. *Wakon yosai* (Japanese spirit and Western technology) became part of identity, harmonizing tradition and reform. In terms of the governance of Japan, the imperial system, which had been kept as a spiritual authority in Kyoto as opposed to political authority in Edo, was brought to the center. Separation of Shinto from the world of *Shinbutsu shugo* took place, and State Shinto was placed above other religions. Under the Meiji Constitution of 1889, the divine emperor became the source of governance.

In the Meiji Era, the Japanese began to define their nation in relation to the West, the most significant "other," and Asia. Fighting and winning the Sino-Japanese and Russo-Japanese wars offered proof that Japan had achieved its national objective since the Restoration of joining the club of civilized states with national might equivalent to that of Russia and other great powers. From the three perspectives of the West, Asia, and Japaneseness, national identity registered a new sense of confidence based on a realist understanding of power.[11] Japan claimed to be no different from Western nations. Accommodation after the Russo-Japanese War with Russia split Manchuria into respective spheres of influence. In the period of World War I and the Russian Revolution, Japan's presence expanded in China and Russia. The United States, after consolidating its position in the Americas based on the Monroe Doctrine, expanded across the Pacific Ocean under Theodore Roosevelt and championed an idealistic world order after World War I under Woodrow Wilson. Its approach to China took the form of requesting "an open door." Rising Japanese naval power, Japan's indignation at the racist treatment of Japanese emigrants in California, and discord between Japan's expansive policy in China and the U.S. open door policy heightened tension between the two imperialist powers. But in the 1920s, Tokyo acceded to the Washington order, taking into account that U.S. power had begun to create a new order in the Asia-Pacific region and had become Japan's main identity focus in the West.

Asia was not a major factor in identity discussions—with two exceptions. First, when government policy was based on realism, some idealist opposition politicians and opinion leaders expressed dissenting views, maintaining that Japan should stand at the side of Asian nations and explore Asian identity. Asian victims of colonial policies had all hailed Japan's victory against Russia, typically expressed by An Chunggun of Korea and Sun Zhongshan of China, but revolutionaries or reformers who thought that Japan was going to lead the liberation of Asia soon became disappointed because Japan, rather than assisting the independence movement, became another colonial power. Yet, Okakura Tenshin in 1902 argued that Japanese culture is a fusion of all of Asian culture from west to east, maintaining that a civilization distinct from European civilization exists.[12]Second, the Japanese government tried to include a resolution in the League of Nations' Charter about racial equality, but it was rejected by the Western powers.[13]

Some optimistic opinion leaders began to assert that Japan might have unique power to stand between or bridge East and West, which some called *tozai yuwa* (harmony between East and West). Yet more pessimistic intellectuals were not convinced, questioning what Japan is, where does it belong—to the West or the East, to Asia or Europe?—and whether it has really modernized. Natsume Soseki, for one, could not give clear answers, and his anxiety aroused sympathy among other intellectuals.

The history is well known of Japan after the Depression in 1929, when it pursued a policy of autarchy, leading to its establishment of Manchuko in 1932, embarking on war against China in 1937, attacking Pearl Harbor in 1941, entering French Indochina, and eventually resulting in total defeat in 1945. From the point of view of Japanese identity, this period saw a sharp reversal from the path Japan had pursued from the Meiji Restoration, when it saw the West as an object for catching up and then a partner on equal footing. The West or the Euro-American world was transformed into a clear "other" as an object of rivalry and threat, typically expressed by the ABCD encirclement perception[14] and the Hull note ultimatum,[15] finally developing into the image of *kichiku Beiei* (devils and beasts, Americans and British).

When it comes to Japan's approach to Asia, 1930–45 saw a sharp contrast between what really happened and what many had desired. This period was, in reality, characterized by the enhanced colonial policy of Kominka (making imperial citizens) in Korea and Taiwan, military aggression keeping a million soldiers for nearly a decade on Chinese territory, and the occupation of Southeast Asia, where brutalities were undeniably committed. This process proceeded with the systematization of Japanese uniqueness combined with the consolidation of a state-centered absolute power structure. One already sees a landmark in 1925, when the universal suffrage law was approved simultaneously with the peace preservation law. But real tightening of power and monopolization of ideas developed in the 1930s, with the mounting criticism against *Tenno kikansetsu* (emperor organ theory) maintained by Minobe Tatsukichi and the majority of constitutional scholars, resulting in its negation by the Kokutai meicho seimei (Declaration of Clear Evidence of the National Polity) declared by the Okada Cabinet in 1935; the declaration of Kokutai no hongi (Cardinal Principles of the National Polity) by the Ministry of Education and Culture in 1937; and the dissolution of political parties and the establishment of Taisei yokusankai (Imperial Rule Assistance Association) in 1940.[16] Many liberals who did not consent to the government's view were successively purged.[17]

Japan's expansion toward Asia was also underpinned by an element of idealism in continuation of the Meiji *koaron* (revive Asia). The slogan the Greater East Asia Co-Prosperity Sphere developed after the adoption of the Kihon kokusaku yoko (Outline of Basic National Policies) by the Konoe Cabinet in 1940. Although the initial implementation of this concept was done as a justification for Japanese colonial rule in occupied areas, in the latter part of the war in the Pacific, this concept was largely advanced by Foreign Minister Shigemitsu Mamoru with a greater sense of idealism, as in a 1943 treaty with the Wang Qinwei government to achieve full withdrawal from China. Shigemitsu became the architect of the notion of the liberation of Asia, which was proclaimed at the Greater East Asia Co-Prosperity Sphere Conference in 1943.

Among Japanese intellectuals and opinion leaders, there were those who tried to find the causes of war from a Japanese perspective. Nishida Kitaro and his disciple Tanabe Hajime established the Kyoto School, from which emerged a philosophical justification for Japan's war against the West, namely, that Western thinking is facing a dead end and therefore that Eastern thinking, at the center of which lies Japan, must take the lead.[18] In 1943, Kosaka Masaaki concluded that "the strength of the total war reveals Japan's independent identity. For Japan maximizing its power is a historic necessity, but to achieve this objective, a gigantic torrent of world history should underpin Japan's independent identity. This historic torrent must comprise multiple values from the whole world."[19] The purpose of the debate was "to create a plural historical order against the Anglo-Saxon led historical order."[20] Also in 1943, Kawakami Tetsutaro concluded that "we the intellectuals were left ambivalent because of the split between Japanese blood, which worked as the true dynamo of our activities, and Western knowledge, which unseemly systematized it."[21]

All the tracts that argued for the supremacy of Japanese philosophy were practically reduced to naught by Japan's surrender. The West was turned into occupying forces. Japan's Asian policy was tainted by the brutality and arrogance of its soldiers, particularly in China. Shigemitsu's idealism toward Asia, even if supported by some intellectuals and political leaders, materialized too late to leave a trace in history. The defeated leadership tried, with its best efforts, to preserve the imperial household as the core of the national polity, but at the beginning of the occupation it was not entirely clear what would unfold. Thus, Japan ended the war with a sense of total loss, a huge psychological vacuum that all values accepted to that time were being negated.

Japan's Attachment to the West in the Polarized Cold War World

In the Cold War period, Japan was overwhelmed by the influence from America. It created the foundation of Japan's defense security structure as well as that of economic development through the system of multilateral free trade. Not only in these spheres but also in the cultural arena, the American way of life inspired many Japanese. Considering how Japan fought desperately until August 15, 1945, the smooth and quick postwar adoption of a new set of values—democracy, peace, and economic reconstruction—may appear surprising, but both the flexibility and complexity of its identity formation can be well appreciated in this seemingly huge transformation.

The conventional wisdom has been that the first ever national defeat and occupation by foreign troops and the negation of values that accompanied this situation created such a psychological shock that Japan was willing to accept all new values, jumping from a totalitarian, militaristic state to a new world of peace and democracy.[22] In fact, the situation was not that simple. The first postwar identity search—led by intellectuals, opinion leaders, media, and opposition leaders—was uniquely Japanese, seeking a new Japan based on democracy and pacifism but strongly criticizing America, particularly after its shift to combat Communism under rising Cold War tensions. Several questions need to be answered. Who were the opinion leaders who led

Japan toward pacifist and antitotalitarian ideals? There was a basis for democracy in prewar Japan, notably the Charter Oath, the Jiyu minken undo (Freedom and People's Rights Movement), and "Taisho democracy" (political and social movements based on democratic and liberal values—such as seeking universal suffrage, women's equality, and greater freedom of expression—during the Taisho era, 1912–26).[23]

Many liberal scholars who were purged in the 1930s had been nurtured in Taisho democracy and returned to the mainstream of intellectual life. Maruyama Masao became by far the most influential representative of this group. What was the essence of their thought? On the one hand, acceptance of democracy was based on strong criticism of the prior totalitarian system. Oguma Eiji describes in his *Minshuto aikoku* how postwar Japanese intellectuals and people at large, particularly in the first decade after the defeat, desperately questioned why Japan had lost the war. Many shared the view that it was the nationwide totalitarian system that did not allow the manifestation of individual ability and patriotism that had led to this defeat. Contrition for allowing that system to become a monster transformed into determination to seek a new democratic system. "What was the relationship between 'Imperial Japan' and 'subject citizens,' which resulted in irresponsibility accompanied by mass killing and mass destruction? What should be the relationship between 'public' and 'private'? With what new principles can Japan restructure 'human bonding among the people' which was destroyed?"[24] These were the questions it had to face.

Maruyama Masao's May 1946 *Sekai* article, "Chokokkashugi no ronri to shinri" (Theory and psychology of ultrastatism), caused a sensation for a large number of intellectuals and people at large. His famous synthesis of the "system of irresponsibility" caught people's attention.[25] "There is no independent identity consciousness and no one has inner restraint for actions. Everyone's existence is prescribed by the existence of his superior and a new phenomenon of keeping spiritual balance by transfer of oppression from the above capriciously to below."[26] Maruyama's thinking was fresh to many, because his single greatest criticism was directed at the lack of individual thinking and sense of responsibility. This applied to the system of irresponsibility, which not only led to the war but also allowed the Japanese to make an overnight about-face in August 1945.

Article 9 of the Constitution adopted in November 1946 also reflected the views of a large number of Japanese who sought a new national identity for rebuilding a devastated Japan into a "peaceful state" or a "cultural state." Ishihara Kanji argued just after the war that "once we are defeated, we need to put an end to the military in an honorable manner, and face the world's opinion with the pride of being a developed country in peace."[27] "Peace and morality became the last vestige of national identity for Japan, which was defeated militarily and economically. It was connected to the sense of rivalry against U.S. and European military power, symbolized by the atomic bombs."[28] In the initial years after the occupation, Article 9 was a political reality from which Japan could not have escaped, but at the same time, some political forces welcomed it because "pacifism appeared as an extension of a moral state."[29] When the United States changed its policy with the onset of the Cold War, particularly after the outbreak of the Korean War, protest against its pressure for Japan to become a realist power became a manifestation of Japanese nationalism. "Article 9 became the symbol of 'national independence' of Japan, weakened by defeat, in opposition to the U.S."[30]

Another relevant factor is the position of Communists in the immediate postwar period. Among intellectuals, there was a widespread sense of remorse that they did not speak out during the war to object to Japan's totalitarian-militarist drift. Tokuda Kyuichi and Miyamoto Kenji, who had stayed in prison for years and did not collaborate with the regime, were virtually deified in the first decade after the war,[31] but there were few such figures, and the majority of Communists just tried to take the winners' side. Other intellectuals were anticommunists. Some formed the Heiwa mondai kondankai (Peace discussion circle) in 1948, led by Yoshino Genzaburo, which combined nationalism with pacifism. Neither group responded positively to the U.S. plea to fight against Communism in East Asia.[32] Throughout the Cold War period, the search for a unique identity based on one-country pacifism and total negation of pre-1945 statism stayed influential. The teachers' union's complete denial of pre-1945 Japan strongly influenced compulsory education; the national anthem could not be sung, nor could the national flag be hoisted on festive days at many schools. In this vein, Ienaga Saburo filed his first lawsuit in 1965 against the government to accept his textbook, which had more passages on Japan's wrongdoings.

A second stream of identity searching gave all-out priority to the reconstruction of the devastated economy. Economic recovery was a necessity, but it was also a manifestation of a new Japanese identity as a country seeking a "rich nation through peace." But unlike the first stream of thinking, described above, it was also based on realism. It was generally adopted by the conservative government, which accepted American values and U.S. foreign policy guidance without fundamental objections. Called the Yoshida Doctrine, it was based on economic reconstruction first, a minimal self-defense force, a U.S. alliance to fill the security vacuum, and, generally speaking, an Anglo-Saxon-friendly policy in the Cold War period. On the whole, it worked well. Economic recovery proceeded with stunning vigor, achieving 10 percent growth in the 1960s, overcoming the Nixon and oil shocks in the 1970s, and reaching the height of the bubble economy in the 1980s. Japan's economic miracle was credited to cooperation among politicians, bureaucrats, and businesses, the three pillars supporting the system of 1955. Trust in their top-down guidance became an integral part of the national identity.

After revising the security treaty in 1960 to make the Japan–United States relationship more equal, and achieving the reversion of Okinawa in 1972, Japan went through a period of trade conflict with the United States, in which voluntary export restraints and opening the Japanese market succeeded in reducing the trade imbalance. The ruling Liberal Democratic Party (LDP) and government officials further tried to curb one-country pacifism, slowly but steadily strengthening the Self-Defense Forces and enlarging host nation support for U.S. forces. Prime Minister Nakasone's new position that Japan is an inseparable partner marked the height of assertiveness that Japan belongs to the Western camp in the Cold War context.[33] Intellectuals, such as Kosaka Masataka in his 1963 *Chuo koron* article, gave voice to realist thinking that influenced national identity thinking, and some advised prime ministers, including Sato Eisaku and Nakasone.[34]

Regaining Japan's Asian identity was a complex issue during the Cold War. Criticism against the prior system was primarily related to responsibility for losing the war. The issue of responsibility for committing atrocities in Asia came to be generally recognized by the people only gradually, as they did not hide their dismay and shock.[35] Information disclosed at the Tokyo Tribunal on past atrocities, including the Nanjing massacre, was followed by the voices of soldiers returning from the front, particularly from China. About a thousand returned detainees in China who became cognizant of their atrocities formed a union in 1957 explaining what they had done.[36] Honda Katsuichi's *Report on China* (1971) and the *Devil's Gluttony* (1982) left a sense of contrition about the conduct of Japanese soldiers, which was heightened by the Kaikosha Veterans' Association's 1983 expression of deep apology for the massacre committed at Nanjing.[37]

Parallel to this learning process among opinion leaders and the public in general, the normalization of government to government relations in Asia was a gradual process, starting with states in Southeast Asia in the late 1950s and resulting in relations with South Korea in 1965 after fourteen years of negotiations. It took a long time for politicians, opinion leaders, and the public to realize that the total negation of Japanese colonialism had become the foundation of a new Korean identity. In the Cold War context, Japan had no choice but to establish diplomatic relations with the Republic of China (Taiwan) at the expense of the People's Republic of China before 1972. Improved relations with Asia were not a monopoly of the political left. In the 1970s and 1980s, pacifist intellectuals gradually began to merge with Asianists supported by the Japan Socialist Party and able to influence public opinion. Yet, as Japan's economic success spread to a flying-geese formation drawing Asian states along, especially in the 1980s, LDP leaders had the upper hand in shaping thinking about Japan's role in Asia. Building on high hopes that had arisen after the conclusion of a peace and friendship treaty with China in 1978 and China's economic reforms that were presumed to put it at the back of the flying-geese formation, Nakasone succeeded in forging solid ties with Hu Yaobang, the General Secretary of the Chinese Communist Party, as well as with Chun Doohwan, the president of South Korea. Although rethinking was required after both leaders fell, Asianism was beginning to reshape national identity, even as the U.S. alliance remained a greater force.

In terms of continuity from the past, probably the preservation of the imperial household, as Japan insisted at the time of its surrender, was most important in determining Japan's postwar identity. Despite minority views on the left that the imperial system or the emperor himself should bear responsibility for the catastrophic defeat, people in general and opinion leaders were agreeable to preserving the imperial family at the heart of Japan and not to hold the emperor accountable. Article 1 of the Constitution and the decision to leave the emperor outside the Tokyo Tribunal framework corresponded to this general attitude.[38] Yet among leftist intellectuals, centrist conservatives, and newly vocal apologists toward Asia, the contradiction between one-country pacifists and realists split the Japanese intellectual world into two.

In addition, voices emerged that looked back to pre-1945 Japan for pride and national identity—including the publication of Hayashi Fusao's *Daitoa senso koteiron* (1963–65), the transfer of the list of class A war criminals to the Yasukuni Shrine in 1966, Mishima Yukio's seppuku urging people to recapture prewar honor and values (1971), the enshrinement of class A war criminals in Yasukuni in 1978, and the Tokyo Tribunal symposium in 1983. Yet this search for identity proceeded under certain cautions. Emperor Hirohito ceased to visit Yasukuni after the enshrinement of the class A war criminals. Nakasone had long determined to put an end to the controversy by making an official visit to Yasukuni and did so in 1985, but he was confronted by vehement criticism from China and promised to refrain from further visits. In 1986, his understanding of the Korean situation also enabled him to make a bold decision to have a textbook with "insensitive" descriptions rewritten and to sack a minister of education and culture who argued that Koreans were also responsible for the Japanese annexation.

Japan's Post–Cold War Identity Search between the West and a Rising Asia

The year 1989 became an important turning point for Japan and the world. Three major events moved Japan into the next stage in the search for identity: the Malta U.S.-Soviet summit, which declared the end of the Cold War; the establishment of the Asia-Pacific Economic Cooperation forum encompassing the Asia-Pacific nations; and the passing away of Emperor Hirohito, which ended the Showa Era. The end of the Cold War exposed Japan directly to serious security crises in the Middle East and Northeast Asia. One-country passive pacifism was seriously undermined in the first Gulf War. Domestically, the LDP was split, and the system of 1955 ended with the emergence of a series of coalition governments. This resulted in an extraordinary coalition of the Japan Socialist Party and the LDP, and the socialist prime minister had to acknowledge the existence of the Self-Defense Forces and the Security Treaty with the United States. At that point, the Japan Socialist Party even lost its raison d'être as guardian of Article 9 and opponent of the Japan–United States security treaty. Pacifism still remains a powerful Japanese characteristic, but one-country passive pacifism then fundamentally ended.

Three trends can be discerned, each seeking a new image of a Japan that has both global and regional extension and something uniquely Japanese. The first direction is anchored in the Yoshida Doctrine, putting economic power first, and not wavering from the alliance with America. This trend does not have anything anti-Asian, but Asia is not a priority. The second is to consider Japan's reentry into Asia the most important identity agenda. It does not have any anti-American direction, but in some cases it seeks a more independent policy. Finally, a minority with powerful political influence advocates an increasingly fundamentalist position to justify Japan's pride and honor before 1945.

In its relations with the United States, Japan faced a turbulent period immediately after the end of the Cold War. The declining U.S. economic situation and the height of Japan's bubble economy allowed Japan bashing to gain ground. In the first Gulf War of 1990–91, Japan's inability to respond in a timely manner with "boots on the ground" resulted in criticism despite the $13 billion in Japanese assistance. For a while, Japan vied with the Soviet Union for American disfavor, and conversely in 1989 *The Japan That Can Say No* by Ishihara Shintaro and Morita Akio became a best seller in Japan. But Japan swiftly strengthened its alliance with America through a new Joint Declaration in 1996 and defense guidelines in 1997, and after the September, 11, 2001, terrorist attacks, the alliance entered into one of the most solid periods under the Koizumi-Bush friendship. Keeping U.S.-friendly values as fundamental to national identity, thus was confirmed in the post–Cold War era. When alarm about China intensified in 2010, the short-term shift toward Asia of the Democratic Party of Japan (DPJ) was sharply reversed.

From postwar democratic development and a U.S.-friendly policy, there emerged at least three directions for a new identity on a global scale, though without real success. First, during the Cold War there were some efforts to enable Japan to develop a global vision, embracing free and multilateral trade under the General Agreement on Tariffs and Trade and becoming a superpower providing official development assistance (ODA), while enhancing international contributions as a peaceful nation. After the end of the Cold War, Japan became number one in ODA and aspired to become a permanent member of the UN Security Council, so as to expand the sphere of its diplomacy on a global scale. Yet these visions did not amount to the creation of a global Japanese identity. Japan's leadership in rule making under the World

Trade Organization has been hampered by its protectionism toward its agricultural sector; its ODA contribution declined parallel to its failed economic situation; and permanent membership in the Security Council is remote.

Second, starting in the 1980s, some Japanese cultural phenomena—such as sushi, anime, and fashion—attracted worldwide attention. Recently, Japan's soft power and cultural influence have drawn further international attention. As Douglas McGray wrote already in 2002 in his article titled "Japan's Gross National Cool," Japan may be reinventing what it takes to be a superpower; its global cultural influence has quietly grown, from pop music to consumer electronics, architecture to fashion, and animation to cuisine.[39] Yet despite some impact on Japan's recent cultural identity, this attention tends to be transitory.

Third, when an unprecedented tsunami struck the coasts of South and Southeast Asia in January 2005, there emerged efforts to coordinate rescue operations by the United States, Japan, Australia, and India. Some Japanese opinion leaders and politicians began arguing that a "maritime alliance" consisting of these four countries that share common values of democracy should be created. Eventually, this notion developed into a more grandiose concept of regional cooperation, defined as the "arc of freedom and prosperity," as advanced by Foreign Minister Aso Taro under the Cabinet of Abe Shinzo in November 2006. For nearly a year, Japan's diplomacy was suddenly energized toward countries in an arc around China from the west Pacific to Central Asia, and the Caucasus to Eastern Europe. This approach stressed democracy as a lynchpin for cooperation and put Japan without hesitation into the camp of democratic countries capable of values-based leadership, drawing a positive response from opinion leaders who considered that the Japanese government had neglected smaller countries strategically located in Eurasia. But the decision to exclude China and Russia from this cooperative effort made many uncomfortable, and this concept faded from attention under Fukuda. Aso took a low-key approach as prime minister, leaving in doubt the fate of this conceptual effort to establish Japan's international identity. The DPJ did not embrace it either, but in 2010 new alarm about China refocused interest on Japan's ties to its neighbors with implications for identification with a global community led by the United States.

Japan's identity aiming to reenter Asia has also developed in a complex manner in the post–Cold War era. Immediately in the wake of the

Cold War, a more Asia-friendly school within the LDP took office. They were followed by coalition governments with an apologist orientation toward Asia. In 1989, Japan took a position of "not isolating China, while human rights repression is impermissible." Deng Xiaoping's appreciation led to the visit to China of Emperor Hirohito, who expressed his "deep sorrow for the tremendous suffering which Japan had inflicted on the people of China." The Miyazawa Cabinet at the assumed end of the "System of 1955" (the system that was established in 1955 by the creation of the Liberal Democratic Party, which maintained stable conservative rule for four decades) in 1993 adopted an important statement by the Cabinet General Secretary Kono Yohei apologizing over the comfort women issue with a view to healing the wounds with Korea. The subsequent coalition governments all took apologetic positions on history issues, culminating in Prime Minister Murayama's August 15, 1995, clearest apology statement ever.

In the latter part of the 1990s, diverging trends in search of strengthening ties with Asia continued. Hashimoto initiated assistance to Asian countries hit by the financial crisis., while also trying to strengthen relations with Russia to increase Japan's foreign policy leverage in the Asia-Pacific region. Obuchi became one of the most Asia-friendly prime ministers, making Kim Dae-jung's visit a historic breakthrough in 1998 and convening a triple breakfast of Japanese, Chinese, and Korean leaders in 1999 on the fringe of the Association of Southeast Asian Nations (ASEAN) + 3 meetings. Mori adopted a flexible approach on territorial negotiations with Russia from 2000 to 2001. On the whole, relations with China, South Korea, and Russia saw substantial progress during this period. The notion of joining an East Asian community gave new specificity to aspirations for Asianism, but at the same time there was growing nervousness about the rise of China, the key partner in this effort.

Under Koizumi, Japan's position weakened in relation to all major Asian countries. Although Koizumi's own view of history was as apologetic as Murayama's, as shown in his 2005 speech at Bandung, his yearly visits to Yasukuni resulted in a rupture of state visits with China from 2002 to 2006. The pursuit of East Asian regionalism was seen as a split between a China-led ASEAN + 3 and a Japan-led East Asian Summit. Relations with North Korea became fixated on abductions. Russian peace treaty negotiations collapsed because of an ill-conceived policy on the Northern Territories by Koizumi's first foreign minister,

Tanaka Makiko. Tensions exploded with South Korea after the establishment of Takeshima Day by Shimane Prefecture in 2005. Although Koizumi put emphasis on the U.S. alliance, this was not seen as resolving Japan's identity dilemma.

After Koizumi's departure, the overall situation calmed down with Abe's ambivalent policy on visiting Yasukuni and abiding by the Murayama and Kono statements; Fukuda's declared policy of not visiting Yasukuni; and Aso's swift decision to fire an Air Force general who had written an article denying Japan's aggression toward China. China reciprocated, and relations stabilized. Lee Myung-bak's Japan-friendly approach helped to stabilize South Korean ties. In this confused process, the notion of an East Asia community was seriously debated. Some Japanese scholars maintained that certain similarities in urban life, enjoying the same fruits of globalization, might be a source of common identity, and because it was Japan that led the flying geese formation in the 1980s, the emerging identity can be attributed to Japan's quality of life.[40] When Hatoyama Yukio took office with an idealistic but vague notion of "fraternity," there was new hope for a regional identity until tensions with China intensified in 2010.

In the shadows of this majority view, however, a trend in search of more assertive "Japaneseness" could be traced, particularly from the latter part of the 1990s. As if to counterbalance Ienaga's victory in the Supreme Court, Tsukurukai was formed in 1996, leading to approval of its first textbook in 2001. Hashimoto visited the Yasukuni Shrine in 1996 but discontinued doing so in 1997. Obuchi the Asianist adopted a law on the national flag and national anthem in 1999. Then backed up by assertiveness to visit Yasukuni, the Koizumi period is remembered for a spurt in anti-Chinese writings as well as writings hailing Japan's prewar honor and rebuking the Tokyo Tribunal's "self-destructive historical outlook." "The other" was first of all China, and China's incessant rebuke of Japan not to have learned from the history added fuel to people's frustration and right-wing intellectuals' indignation. But the next "other" was America, and the identity formation was equally its rejection. This originated perhaps in rejection of the Tokyo Tribunal as victors' justice. Anger was directed at the sudden postwar transformation in blindly following the American way, forfeiting the Japanese spirit for the sake of material satisfaction. A recent example was shown in the public's anger against Minister of Defense Fumio Kyuma's statement that "the atomic bomb was inevitable," questioning whether "he is a minister of defense of Japan or of the United States." Yet, the growing voices in search of a unique national identity based on prewar honor and values, however loud their presence, are not drawing wide-spread support. An inherently more apologetic DPJ is remote from an assertive Japan that is insistent on challenging Asian states over history, but Hatoyama's initial search for autonomy from the United States and an Asian-centered community got nowhere.

The Way Forward

Conditions may be ripening for the third time in search of an identity that is uniquely Japanese. In the premodern stage, although a part of the Sinocentric world, Japan maintained a sense of independence and detachment from continental culture. During the period of sweeping modernization from Meiji to World War II, modernization for a while put Asia in the position of the "other" to part from, but when the "other" became Euro-American power against which to fight, Asia became the space to anchor Japan's unique identity. This led to total defeat, from which Japan began its recovery sixty-five years ago. Following the American path—in the sense of a way of life, a democratic political system and alliance—and efforts to reenter Asia offer an inclusive type of identity but fall short of the global identity that many appear to be seeking. This historical analysis may suggest that the new Japanese global identity would be based on something uniquely Japanese that the Japanese have yet to find. This unique Japanese identity cannot be based on exclusivity fixating on prewar values and echoing nationalist anti-America and anti-China feelings, but so far neither the search for a global identity nor that for a shared Asian identity satisfies Japanese aspirations.

One may detect some embryonic form of identity search emphasizing traditional culture, a way of life in harmony with nature, technological development, and renewed communal values. Some combination of the above may be perceived as recreating Japan, which is transparent, open, and capable of leadership on a global scale. Governors of some prefectures began to take concrete action to harmonize development policy with nature. Tanaka Yasuo, governor of Nagano Prefecture, in 2001 succeeded in suspending dam construction projects along the Shinano and Tenryu rivers. Nakagawa Hidenao, general secretary of the LDP under Koizumi and Abe, has articulated most vividly the fundamental necessity for Japan to go back to its tradition and nature in order to regain its identity. Before the 2007 election he argued, "Let us build new values, where natural beauty and historical scenery have preference over private rights. In order to make tourism a real strategic industry, private rights have to be constrained."[41]

The DPJ started its reform in 2009 with an indicative slogan of "from concrete to human being," but because it proceeded too abruptly, that direction seems to be waning. The LDP New Development Strategy, adopted in June 2010, has such important factors as "green innovation" and "tourism and local governance" but proceeds only from the point of view of development, not from identity.[42] The directions that have been tried so far do not seem to satisfy the soul searching of the Japanese, leaving us with the conclusion that from the beginning of this century, there has been a rising identity search, seeking something uniquely Japanese that also meets some requirement of becoming a global standard.[43]

The March 11, 2011, tsunami and earthquake disaster, combined with the lingering nuclear catastrophe, give ground for some politicians and intellectuals to argue that this calamity might become a catalyst for the recreation of a totally new Japan in the Tohoku area, with reinvigorated agriculture, fisheries, and industry based on life in harmony with nature and tradition.[44] Such discussions are ongoing at the time of this writing.

Notes

1. Ishii Susumu et al., *Shosetsu Nihonshi* (Tokyo: Yamakawa shuppan, 2008), 6.
2. Ibid., 35; historical analysis of the Ritsuryo system by Mushakoji Atsunobu to the author, February 11, 2009.
3. Ishii, *Shosetsu Nihonshi*, 30.
4. Ibid., 48–49.
5. Ibid., 155–56.
6. Ibid., 93; Marius B. Jansen, *The Making of Modern Japan* (Cambridge, Mass.: Harvard University Press, 2000), 192.
7. Ishii, *Shosetsu Nihonshi*, 209; Marius B. Jansen, *The Making of Modern Japan*, 248.
8. Ishii, *Shosetsu Nihonshi*, 216.
9. Ikei Masaru, *Nihon gaikoshi gaisetsu* (Tokyo: Keio University shuppankai, 1997), 54.

10. See http://www.jca.apc.org/kyokasho_saiban/datsua2.html; in 1885, Tarui Tokichi wrote "Daitogo horon," calling for the creation of an equal union of Korea and Japan. His view represented private-sector opinion leaders who sought an equal Asian partnership, but Fukuzawa's view was by far the more influential in this period. Ikei, *Nihon gaikoshi gaisetsu,* 64.

11. Kazuhiko Togo, *Japan's Foreign Policy 1945–2003: The Quest for a Proactive Policy* (Leiden: Brill, 2005), 9–11.

12. Iriye Akira, *Nihon no gaiko* (Tokyo: Chuokoron, 1966), 43.

13. Ariga Natsuki and Yui Daizaburo, *America no rekishi* (Tokyo: Yuhikaku, 2003), 164.

14. This was a perception in Japan leading to World War II of being encircled by American, British, and Dutch imperial powers aligned with China.

15. Japan-U.S. negotiations under the Tojo Cabinet from early November 1941 developed into a U.S. proposal made by Secretary of State Cordell Hull on November 26, which the Japanese government interpreted as so harsh that it was tantamount to an ultimatum.

16. Ishii, *Shosetsu Nihonshi,* 326–27, 333, 337.

17. Those purged include Takigawa Yukitoki in 1936, Yanaihara Tadao in 1937, and Ouchi Hyoe in 1938. Ishii, *Shosetsu Nihonshi,* 326, 333.

18. See http://homepage3.nifty.com/bunmao/0307.htm.

19. Kosaka Masaki et al., *Sekaishiteki tachibato Nihon* (Tokyo, Chuokoron, 1943), 429.

20. Uchida Keiji, "Mittsu no Zadankai," August 14, 2007, http://www.japancm.com/sekitei/note/2007/note31.html.

21. Kamei Katsuichiro et al., *Kindai no chokoku* (Tokyo: Sogensha, 1943), 182.

22. Togo, *Japan's Foreign Policy 1945–2003;* also see Kazuhiko Togo, "Greater Self Assertion and Nationalism in Japan," *Copenhagen Journal of Asian Studies,* 2005, 5–44; and Kazuhiko Togo, "Japan's Foreign Policy: Achievements and Future Directions," in *Japan Aktuell* (Hamburg: German Institute of Global and Area Studies, 2008), 38–53.

23. Togo, *Japan Aktuell,* 40.

24. Oguma Eiji, *Minshu to aikoku* (Tokyo: Shinyosha, 2002), 65.

25. Ibid., 85.

26. Maruyama Masao, "Chokokkashugi no ronri to shinri," in *Gendai seiji no shiso to kodo* (Tokyo: Miraisha, 1964), 24.

27. Oguma, *Minshu to aikoku,* 154.

28. Ibid., 155.

29. Ibid., 156.

30. Ibid., 465.

31. Ibid., 183.

32. Ibid., 467.

33. In particular, it was clearly expressed at the Williamsburg Summit of 1983.

34. Kosaka's article was titled "Genjitsushugisha no heiwaron." Kamiya Fuji, Nagai Yonosuke, and Nakajima Mineo, among others, joined this group; *Mainichi shimbun,* June 22, 2009.

35. John Dower, *Embracing Defeat* (New York: W. W. Norton, 1999), 504–8.

36. See http://www.ne.jp/asahi/tyuukiren/web-site/other/gaiyou.htm.

37. Kazuhiko Togo, "Japan's Historical Memory: Overcoming Polarization toward Synthesis," in *East Asia's Haunted Present,* edited by Tsuyoshi Hasegawa and Kazuhiko Togo (Westport, Conn.: Praeger Security International, 2008), 66.

38. Oguma describes various postwar reactions to the emperor, but observes that as of August 15, 1948, 90.3 percent of those interviewed supported the imperial system; Oguma, *Minshu to aikoku,* 147. Hosaka Masayasu describes how Emperor Hirohito turned his energy in postwar Japan to travel around Japan and mix with people and how he was accepted by majority of the Japanese people; Hosaka Masayasu, *Showa Teino* (Tokyo: Chuokoron, 2005), 230–35. Herbert Bix describes how, after the war, "most Japanese *politicians* . . . still held the monarchy in reverential awe," and that "at the deepest levels of national identity, emperorism retained its hold over the minds of many Japanese"; Herbert Bix, *Hirohito and the Making of Modern Japan* (New York: HarperPerennial, 2001), 570, 579.

39. Douglas McGray, "Japan's Gross National Cool," *Foreign Policy,* no. 130 (May–June 2002).

40. The Council of the East Asian Community in Tokyo published a report in August 2005, highlighting "similar lifestyles of urban middle class workers." See http://www.ceac.jp/j/pdf/policy_report.pdf

41. Kyodo News Service, April 20, 2007.

42. See http://www.kantei.go.jp/jp/sinseichousenryaku/.

43. See Kazuhiko Togo, *Sengo Nihon ga ushinatta mono: Fukei, ningen and kokka* (Tokyo: Kadokawa shinsho, 2010).

44. See Kazuhiko Togo, *Kyoto shimbun* March 31, 2011; *Mainichi shimbun,* May 5, 2011; and *Asahi shimbun* May 23, 2011.

Chapter 6

Japan's National Identity in Postwar Diplomacy: The Three Basic Principles

Yuichi Hosoya

Setting diplomatic priorities serves the quest for reshaping and clarifying national identity. Forming an alliance with one country may pose a risk to the national identity sought by both political leaders and opinion leaders. Without abandoning the alliance, leaders may seek diplomatic balance not only to pursue national interests but also to assert their preferred national identity. In the Cold War era, U.S. allies faced the challenge of being overwhelmed by a monolithic claim to universal values that subsumed their own nations as little more than similar cogs in a larger machine.

Even as reliable an ally as Great Britain, which was most closely linked with the United States, had reason to seek relief, bringing others into its close circle. Given that Britain was caught between the United States and Europe, Winston Churchill explained in 1948 that it had "three circles," the "British Empire," the "English-speaking World," and "United Europe."[1] Since then, Britain has often faced situations where it has appeared forced to choose between the United States and

Europe. In 1999, Prime Minister Tony Blair said that "for the first time in the last three decades, we have a government that is both pro-Europe and pro-American.[2] A few years later, however, when the Iraq War began, Blair found a sharp divide between the two camps.

Likewise, Japan has often experienced difficulty in presenting its national identity, seemingly obliged to choose either "America" or "Asia." If during the Cold War, Japan, like Britain, could obscure this ambivalence in the shared struggle among partner states against a common enemy, the post–Cold War era has increasingly exposed the difficulty inherent in making this choice as Asia's global importance keeps growing and its search for community lags far behind Europe and proves frustrating.

In this chapter, I look back to the Cold War period to trace how Japanese leaders framed this choice and then reflect on how it was reframed in the post–Cold War period. I argue that the "three basic principles" (sangensoku), which Japan's Ministry of Foreign Affairs enunciated in 1957, have remained at the center of postwar diplomacy for more than half a century. They identify three pillars of diplomacy: membership in the United Nations, maintenance of the U.S.-Japan alliance, and inclusion in Asia.

Tracing how these pillars have been interpreted and transformed opens a window on how Japan's government has constructed national identity. After World War II, its leaders decided that they could not soon turn it into a "normal state"; nor could it return to prewar imperialism. It needed to forge a new identity in the postwar international environment. This was done only in 1957, when Japan's first Diplomatic Bluebook clearly identified the "trichotomy" of three basic principles.[3] Achieving balance proved difficult among the three orientations—an East Asian community seemed to be only a distant ideal, the international community either appeared to duplicate alliance dependence on the United States or to be twisted into Cold War opposition to Japan's ally, and even the alliance did not satisfy Japan's quest for equality with the United States. Yet this set of principles combined to check other orientations, especially by containing extremist nationalism for many decades. Amid doubt that this combination will long survive, here I seek to determine whether Japan's identity has reached a turning point by first looking back to how the diplomatic pursuit of the three principles shaped the national identity as it evolved after the war.

Postwar Japan's National Identity:
Nationalism by Other Means?

During the occupation years, the first task of the Japanese government was to reenter international society as a sovereign state. To accomplish it, Japan needed to reconsider its national identity in two ways. First, it could revive the liberal internationalist tradition that had been robust in the 1920s.[4] Shidehara Kijuro, who exemplified this tradition in the 1920s as foreign minister, seemed appropriate as prime minister in the early postwar years. Likewise, Yoshida Shigeru, another prime minister during the occupation years, represented a prewar liberal tradition because he had advocated close association with the Anglo-Saxon powers.[5] Many leaders thought that Japan could redefine its national identity by reviving the old tradition of liberal internationalism.

Second, Japan was restarted as a new democracy, repudiating its prewar extreme nationalist ideology by embracing both liberalism and democracy in its political system. The Constitution was considered its foundation; however, this did not mean that Japan entirely denied nationalism. Rather, demilitarized Japan tried to accomplish national development mainly through economic means. As Sheldon Garon wrote, "economic nationalism not only continued, but came to define the postwar national mission.[6] In this way, Japan constrained extreme right-wing nationalism.

These two dimensions of postwar national identity were integrated by Yoshida's diplomacy. Yoshida was not only a liberal internationalist; he was also a nationalist who fully understood the importance of economic development for the purpose of strengthening his own country. Kitaoka Shinichi emphasized this point in his study of Yoshida's statecraft, writing that Yoshida firmly believed that "the main aim of states is to promote economic interests based upon trade, and also to deepen association with other developed economic powers."[7] Combining liberal internationalism with economic nationalism became the essence of the Yoshida Doctrine, or postwar Japan's grand strategy. Yet, in the middle of the 1950s, some conservative political leaders criticized Yoshida's statecraft, arguing that he was too dependent upon American power, while neglecting the importance of national independence. At the same time, left-wing intellectuals also denounced Yoshida's foreign policy, insisting that to ally militarily with the United States meant to reverse the postwar democratic course.[8] With the return of Japan's sovereignty in 1952, and also with the return of purged wartime political leaders—such as Hatoyama Ichiro, Shigemitsu Mamoru, and Kishi Nobusuke—the Yoshida Doctrine was modified by right-wing as well as left-wing nationalists, as seen in the transformation of Japan's diplomacy after Yoshida resigned as prime minister in 1954.

The Foundation of Postwar Diplomacy: Kishi's "Three Basic Principles" of 1957

Between 1955 and 1957, there were important developments in Japan's international relations. In 1955, Japan participated in the first Asia-African Conference in Bandung, Indonesia, which signified "Japan's reentry into Asia.[9] It became a member of the General Agreement on Tariffs and Trade in 1955, and it joined the United Nations in 1956. Amid talk that Japan was reconstructing its postwar national identity from a new perspective, Prime Minister Kishi Nobusuke published the first Diplomatic Bluebook reformulating postwar diplomacy.[10] It identified "three basic principles": "United Nations centrism," "cooperation with free countries," and "holding fast to being a member of Asia.[11]Sandwiching the United States–Japan alliance between the United Nations as a symbol of internationalism and Japan's Asian membership as a sign of autonomous aspirations in its own neighborhood was more than a diplomatic agenda. The articulation of these principles in the Foreign Ministry's overarching document was the first occasion for the Japanese government to present its intended national identity to the world.

"UN centrism" reinforced the Constitution of Japan, as the nonmilitary clause of Article 9 presupposes a properly functioning United Nations. Thus the Diplomatic Bluebook mentioned that "while we pursue the ideals of the United Nations, we have enhanced our cooperation with free and democratic states, as a pragmatic measure of contributing to the maintenance of world peace."[12] It was assumed that UN internationalism and alliance cooperation were complementary principles for diplomacy, despite some potential for tension between the two, which gave breathing space to national pride.

The weakest of the three basic principles from the outset was membership in Asia. Japan had difficulty in formulating an Asian policy in the early postwar years. It lacked formal diplomatic relations with the

People's Republic of China and South Korea, leaving Southeast Asian countries as its only conceivable "free and democratic" Asian partners. When Kishi visited the region in late 1957, he sought to show that Japan was intent on strengthening its "membership in Asia."[13] He was not just a nationalist in a narrow sense nor simply an anticommunist cold warrior. He did not aim to revive imperial glory. Instead, pointing toward the defense of regionalism under Japan's leadership, he was a strong proponent of "Asianism,"[14] capitalizing on Japanese sympathy with newly independent countries. This sympathy was shared by conservative leaders, such as Shigemitsu Mamoru, who, as foreign minister, endorsed the Bandung Conference.

At the same time, Kishi fully understood the importance of the United State–Japan alliance from a strategic point of view. He wanted to mitigate aggressive Asian nationalism, because this would be harmful to both Japanese and Asian postwar economic growth. Thus, as the Diplomatic Bluebook clearly stated, Japan as "a member of Asia" should strengthen its association with "free and democratic states" for the purpose of curbing expansive Communist ideology and volatile Asian nationalism.[15] Anti-Western Asianism, as seen in Japan's "Greater East Asian Co-Prosperity Sphere," had been fundamentally transformed into pro-Western Asianism. The harmony of the three basic principles was made the foundation of national identity, while leaving room for interpretations that did not assume complete harmony would last.

Lingering anti-Japanese sentiment caused some difficulty in formulating a postwar Asian policy, despite the fact that Japan's economy was closely tied with the regional economy; postwar official papers noted that Japan's reconstruction could not be attained without that of Asia.[16] The ideologies of Asianism survived, but they had been largely transformed with the Yoshida Doctrine, resulting in important initiatives such as the Economic Commission for Asia and the Far East of 1954. Japan's war reparations to Asian countries were linked to a strategy for "economic cooperation," which benefited Japan's economic growth. The first of these initiatives was Japan's peace treaty with the Philippines. Fully understanding the importance of cooperation with the United States in helping Southeast Asian postwar reconstruction, Yoshida launched a plan of "Southeast Asian development through U.S.-Japanese cooperation."[17] Even before Kishi's three basic principles, Yoshida recognized that Japan needed to join "Asianism" with support for "free countries," as seen in support for the establishment of the Southeast Asian Treaty Organization in 1954.

In January 1955, when Japan was invited to the Bandung Conference, its Asian ambassadors meeting in Karachi insisted that this was "the best opportunity for Japan to restore our position in Asia.[18] Foreign Minister Shigemitsu, who deeply understood the significance of the conference, was a leading advocate of Asian nationalism in the 1930s and 1940s who had launched the Greater East Asian Co-Prosperity Sphere.[19] His Asianism was different from that of the Imperial Army, because as minister of Greater East Asia he had argued in vain for the national self-determination of Asian countries. Likewise, in 1955, he declared that "Asia is a home of Japan, and Japan wishes that Asian nations are liberated and developed themselves on free and independent grounds."[20] He was successful in bringing Japan into the Asia-African Conference, striving as did Kishi against insurmountable odds to insert the theme of "free and democratic countries."[21]

In 1957, one of the biggest problems for Japan with respect to its Asian policy was to reformulate its relationship with the People's Republic of China after having recognized, under U.S guidance, Taipei's Nationalist government as the legitimate Chinese government. Unlike the much more pro-American Yoshida, Kishi sought a proactive Asian policy. Although the Yoshida Doctrine singularly emphasized the importance of Japan's alliance with the United States, Kishi, as a critic of Yoshida's diplomacy, aimed for a broader strategic perspective. In harmonizing his nationalism with his Asian policy, Kishi embraced the idea of "Japan in Asia," which meant "to undertake a mission of developing Asia, with Japan as its leader."[22] In the 1930s, he had been a young economic bureaucrat responsible for the industrialization of Manchuria, and during the war against the United States, he had been a minister associated with the Greater East Asia Co-Prosperity Sphere. As prime minister, he tried to combine a stronger U.S.-Japan alliance with a more ambitious, paternalistic Asian policy, though the two sometimes contradicted each other.[23] Because Tokyo was without normal diplomatic relations with Beijing and Seoul and was unable to change the Cold War realities in Northeast Asia, it turned first to Southeast Asia.

In Northeast Asia, Japan made plans for a positive relationship with the Beijing government. Saito Shizuo, a young official of the Ministry of Foreign Affairs who was responsible for drafting the three basic principles, wrote in his memoirs that he "sought to make both UN centrism and cooperation with the West compatible, in the name of bridging the North and the South."[24] He included Communist China in the latter. By mitigating Sino-American antagonisms and curbing strong anti-Western nationalism in China, he thought Japan could bring stability and order to this region. Along with other Japanese diplomats, he assumed that the Japanese understood the sentiments of Asians much better than the Americans, who relied excessively on military might. Through such assumptions, the Japanese could incubate a postwar national identity that bridged the "free and democratic states" and "membership in Asia," despite a lack of trust from Asians.

Political leaders, as well as many officials of the Ministry of Foreign Affairs, began to feel that Japan could play a larger role in postwar Asia. This feeling was fueled by the Bandung Conference, where, as Kase Toshikazu, a Japanese delegate, noted, "I remember that there were very strong anticolonialist sentiments running through the Bandung Conference, and I was so surprised at that enthusiasm."[25] Miyagi Taizo argued that Japan tried to moderate strong sentiments and ideological confrontations, fearing that it would be stymied in the clash between the "free and democratic states" and aggressive Asian nationalisms. Instead it offered the goal of economic growth and regional stability.[26] Even if Japan's hopes were futile, notably due to China's ideological fervor starting in the late 1950s, whiffs of optimism served to nurture an identity immune to the danger of Americanization.

Although Japan's national identity was largely focused on rapid economic growth, some political leaders argued that it needed to promote national glory in different ways. As the U.S. government observed in April 1955, "The gradual revival of ultra-nationalist forces will continue."[27] Even in the early years of postwar economic growth, politicians began to thirst for national pride. One group of conservative Liberal Democratic Party leaders thought that they had to have a more autonomous policy from the United States, arguing that military dependence could be reduced by *"jishu boei"* (autonomous defense), one necessary step being to increase Japan's defense budget. This movement, in which Shigemitsu and Kishi were central figures, was associated with support for revision of the United States–Japan security treaty and was largely motivated by growing right-wing nationalism, which became conspicuous in the subsequent years.[28]

Between the West and Asia: The 1960s and 1970s

In the 1960s, Japan faced three particularly difficult problems in developing its Asian policy. First, the United States' escalation of the Vietnam War caused severe tensions throughout Southeast Asia. As a U.S. ally, Japan was in the anticommunist camp, which imposed some constraints on Asian economic cooperation. Second, President Sukarno of Indonesia escalated his policy of "*confrontasi*" with Malaysia, while he deepened his association with China. This Beijing-Jakarta axis based upon anti-Western and anticolonialist sentiments constituted a serious threat to regional stability. Third, the Sino-Soviet split raised tensions in this region, while China's ideological foreign policy made regional cooperation less likely. Under these conditions of Communist ideology and nationalist movements growing more volatile, it did not seem practical for Japanese leaders to initiate any regional cooperation efforts in the early 1960s. Instead, Prime Minister Ikeda Hayato reinforced Japan's position as a "free and democratic country."[29] Having been vice minister of finance in the early postwar years, Ikeda understood the importance of economic nationalism, and thus he consolidated the Yoshida Doctrine as Yoshida's true heir.

Ikeda's orientation toward the West did bear fruit. Japan's success in joining the Organization for Economic Cooperation and Development (OECD) in 1964 was regarded as a significant accomplishment.[30] Those in the Ministry of Foreign Affairs especially thought that this vindicated Japan's position as an equal member of the "free and democratic countries." Ikeda talked of the "three-pillar theory"—consisting of North America, Western Europe, and Japan—treating Japan as one pillar of the "free and democratic countries" capable of contributing to a stronger Western alliance.[31] The year 1964 also marked the success of the Tokyo Olympic Games, which advertised Japan's economic miracle. The Japanese people thought that their nation could finally become a proud member of the international community. Yet ambivalence about the widening U.S. war in Vietnam and the U.S. model of modernization left many on both the political right and the political left searching for ways to express a distinct national identity.

At this time, the Japanese government was considering whether it should develop its own nuclear weapons, especially after China tested one in 1964. Prime Minister Sato Eisaku spoke with U.S. ambassador Edwin Reischauer in December 1964, confessing that Japan had an interest in developing its own nuclear weapons because these would be cheaper than conventional weapons. Sato thought that nuclear weapons symbolized national pride and strength and that Japan had to have them in the long term as it became one of the greatest powers in the world. But the United States disagreed, asserting that the growth of national pride in Japan should be firmly associated with their bilateral relationship. It found this rising Japanese pride difficult to manage.[32]

Japan also pressed the United States for UN Security Council reform during this period. It sought a permanent seat on the Security Council, a symbol of great power status and recognition commensurate with its growing economic power. In 1968, Japan became the third-largest economy in the world, which writers celebrated as a source of national pride and cited as justifying a thirst for an appropriate international status. Considering it undesirable for Japan to be a nuclear power, the Nixon administration thought it better to support Japan's bid for a permanent seat on the Security Council.[33] America seemed to fear both Japan's militarization and the rise of anti-American nationalism in Japan. Japan's efforts failed. Only in Asia could Japan expand its horizons.

If under Ikeda Japan did not forget its identity as "a member of Asia," the contrast became clear as it started to invigorate its Asian policy from the late 1960s.[34] There are four main reasons for this. First, Japan normalized relations with South Korea in 1965. The United States played a significant role in mitigating Japan–South Korea antagonism for the purpose of allying the noncommunist countries in East Asia.[35] Although strong anti-Japanese sentiments among the Korean people limited the degree of rapprochement that could be achieved, many Japanese felt emboldened by this breakthrough. Second, the coup d'état in Jakarta in September 1965 purged Indonesia's Communists, as Sukarno was forced out and the pro-Western military elite led by Suharto seized power. Miyagi Taizo argued that this was one of the biggest turning points in the postwar history of Asia.[36] Thus, for most Southeast Asian countries, economic development became a more important goal than anti-Western nationalism or Cold War rivalry. Third and perhaps most important, Tokyo's diplomatic normalization with Beijing largely removed constraints in Japan's Asian policy. Coming on the heels of Sino-U.S. reconciliation, this opened the door to optimistic thinking about Asianism. Fourth, starting in the late 1960s, the Southeast Asia countries had initiated regional integration by establishing the Association of Southeast Asian Nations (ASEAN), and Japan was able to forge strong ties with it. This platform for regionalism became an important forum of the noncommunist countries, and Japan embraced it while rapidly expanding its economic cooperation with these states.

Japan's Asian policy became proactive in this period. With the rapid increase in trade with Asian countries and rapidly growing official development assistance, Japan sought to "Asianize" its foreign policy; however, anti-Japanese sentiments were still widespread. When Prime Minister Tanaka Kakuei visited Southeast Asia in January 1974, he encountered fierce anti-Japanese demonstrations in both Thailand and Indonesia.[37] A junior Japanese diplomat in Jakarta, Tanaka Hitoshi, who later would become a champion of East Asian regionalism, was terrified by the vehemence of anger among the Indonesian people.[38] Many Asian people feared that Japanese overt economic expansion would lead to "neocolonialism," whereby the Japanese Empire previously had tried to establish the Greater East Asian Co-Prosperity Sphere. This served as an important lesson for successive Japanese governments and became the genesis of the Fukuda Doctrine, enunciated when Fukuda Takeo, who succeeded Tanaka as prime minister, sought "to widen the framework of Japan's diplomacy." Fukuda thought that Japan "is a member of Asia, and the peace and stability of this region is indivisible with the peace and stability of the world."[39] As American forces evacuated Vietnam, Fukuda felt that it was important to stabilize Southeast Asia by boosting Japanese influence there, and, in the background, hopes grew that the quest for an Asian component to national identity could be fulfilled.

In Manila in August 1977, Fukuda made an important speech on the foundations of Japan's Asian policy, pointing out three principles.[40] He promised that Japan would never became a military giant again, offered assurances of the need for "heart-to-heart understandings" between the Japanese and the Southeast Asian peoples, and emphasized the importance of timing for creating a peaceful and stable Southeast Asia, given that the Vietnam War had just ended in 1975. The Fukuda Doctrine is regarded as an important turning point in Japan–Southeast Asian relations, mitigating anti-Japanese sentiments just as Japanese companies were rapidly expanding their business in the region. From the perspective of those heralding this initiative, this signaled Japan's genuine embrace of regional cooperation. In contrast to the 1950s initiative, Fukuda showed respect for equal, rather than paternal, relations with the other Asian countries.

In Search of a "Normal State" in the 1980s and 1990s

Japan was beginning to develop a new concept to cover the Asia-Pacific region after the Fukuda Doctrine. In January 1980, Prime Minister Ohira Masayoshi introduced the "Pan-Pacific Association" concept (Kantaiheiyo koso) during his visit to Melbourne.[41] Foreign Minister Okita Saburo, who embodied Japan's postwar Asianism for several decades, played a major role in consolidating this conception of Asia-Pacific regionalism. He was a junior official at the Ministry of Greater East Asia and moved to the Ministry of Foreign Affairs soon after the end of the war, where he established the "Postwar Affairs Study Group" (Sengo mondai kenkyukai) and published an important policy paper,[42] in which he emphasized the importance of Asia for Japan's recovery. Okita participated in both the Colombo Conference of 1954 and the Bandung Conference, and he also worked for the Economic Commission for Asia and the Far East for economic cooperation as he expanded his vision of regionalism. Claiming that it was becoming an "Asia-Pacific state" (Taiheiyo kokka) supporting "open regionalism," Japan carefully avoided alienating the United States. With UN-centered internationalism left in the shadows, Japan balanced the two remaining pillars of postwar diplomacy by promoting Asia-Pacific regionalism. The Asia-Pacific Economic Cooperation forum (APEC), which was established in 1989, conveniently avoided narrow East Asian regionalism excluding the United States, such as was seen in the East Asian Economic Caucus plan of Mahathir. Yet, as the post–Cold War era began with renewed emphasis on a single global model following the U.S. lead, many Japanese struggled anew with the absence of diplomatic balance in support of an unrealized national identity that would build on economic cooperation to conceptualize Asian regionalism.

Although Asianism and Asia-Pacific regionalism coexisted in an uneasy balance that would continue until 2010, other currents in Japan's foreign relations were influencing the struggle for diplomatic balance that was of significance for national identity. One was the rise of history issues in Japan–East Asian relations. Until the 1970s, the center of Japan's Asian policy had been the negotiations on war reparations and economic cooperation related to them. Meanwhile, Cold War tensions caused the United States to pressure noncommunist countries to cooperate with Japan, despite their anti-Japanese sentiments. Once Sino-U.S. rapprochement softened U.S. pressure, Asian countries could strengthen their claims against Japan. Especially after the conclusion of the Peace and Friendship Treaty with Japan in 1978, Beijing's voice gained more weight in East Asian international relations.

In June 1982, Japanese newspapers inaccurately reported that Japan's Ministry of Education had forced several publishers of school history textbooks to rewrite the term "*shinryaku*" (invasion) as "*shinshutsu*" (advance) in relation to the Sino-Japanese war.[43] Both China and South Korea denounced this distortion of history by the Japanese government. Although there was no evidence that the government forced a change in wording in the textbooks, Japan's Chief Cabinet Secretary officially apologized by saying that Japan would "fully listen to these criticisms for the purpose of deepening amity and friendship with neighboring countries in Asia."[44] In this way, the Chinese and Korean claims were officially accepted and would be taken into consideration when the school history textbook would be published. This marked the beginning of the difficult bilateral relationship between Japan and China concerning history issues. By admitting these criticisms, Japan gave legitimacy to China's claims on history issues. The result is "*ringoku joko*," which means that any texts must embody a spirit of cooperation with neighboring peoples.[45] China gained a new ideological framework to facilitate intraparty consolidation and strengthen regime legitimacy.

It is important to note that this history textbook issue largely reflected domestic politics in both Beijing and Tokyo, as hard-line nationalists were gaining influence within each government. When the Liberal Democratic Party (LDP) won the general election in June 1980, right-wing politicians reinforced their voice on educational issues. LDP legislators such as Mitsuzuka Hiroshi criticized education guidelines for insufficient patriotism, leading the Ministry of Education to present new ones for some textbooks.[46] This reflected growing tension between younger "neoliberals" and elder conservatives who strove to defend Japan's pre-1945 national glory. Domestic ideological tensions in both Japan and China worked to undermine the Sino-Japanese relationship on historical issues.

A similar problem could be seen in Prime Minister Nakasone Yasuhiro's official visit to the Yasukuni Shrine on August 15, 1985.[47] At first China did not express its anger, but after students at Beijing universities protested on September 19, possibly with the government's permission, a spokesman at the Ministry of Foreign Affairs severely criticized the visit for hurting the feelings of the Chinese people. This stance was related to a domestic political struggle, as this issue was used to damage the "pro-Japanese" Hu Yaobang, the general secretary of the Chinese Communist Party, who had cultivated ties with Nakasone. After hearing criticisms from China, Nakasone announced that he would make no further official visits, explaining that "he thought he had to protect Hu."[48] This abandonment, as noted by Tanaka Akihiko, gave legitimacy to the claim of the Chinese government on this issue.[49] Some conservative nationalists who were infuriated by this decision as an unacceptable concession to Beijing attacked Chinese interference in Japan's "domestic affairs." This marked the beginning of the rise of anti-Chinese nationalism within Japan.

Repercussions of the comfort women issue caused serious tensions between Japan and South Korea at the end of the 1980s. When Prime Minister Miyazawa Kiichi visited Korea in January 1992, he sincerely apologized and promised more thorough research on this issue. He and Chief Cabinet Secretary Kono Yohei, who largely accepted the fact of the army's involvement in organizing comfort women in Japan's colonies, represented a liberal group within the LDP. Again, a hawkish group of politicians and the right-wing media began a campaign to criticize fiercely Kono's comments on the comfort women issue, and their anti-Chinese as well as anti-Korean discourse grew more intense from this time as they described such apologies as "*jigyakuteki*" (self-flagellating) and insisted that to become a "normal nation," Japan should regain national pride and patriotism through its history education.[50]

In 1993, all high school history textbooks that passed the review board of the Ministry of Education included a sentence on the comfort women issue. This infuriated the right-wing political groups as well as some historians, as this issue had yet to be researched and teaching on it was not at that time common. Behind this nationalist rage was the now chronic recession and loss of national pride and hope. Unlike during the previous controversies in the 1980s, grassroots nationalism kept spreading, giving rise to a right-wing textbook group, Atarashii kyokasho o tsukuru kai.

After the end of the Cold War, international crises gave new impetus to nationalist emotions. Shocked by the impact of the Gulf War, Ozawa

Ichiro, the secretary-general of the LDP, regarded "the war as the coming of the Black Ship in the closing days of the Tokugawa period."[51]
The mishandling of the United States' requests for support was likened
by many to a "defeat" or "infamy."[52] The Japanese ambassador in
Washington, Murata Ryohei, recalled that "the time of the Gulf Crisis
and War was continuous nightmares."[53]

The North Korean nuclear crisis of 1994 also awakened Japan to serious security threats in the post–Cold War era. Tanaka Hitoshi, the
founding director of the Policy Coordination Division within the
Ministry of Foreign Affairs, felt that "he cannot bear it any more."[54]
Japan was unable to respond effectively, proving that economic policy
alone could not suffice for its international responsibility. Its immobil-
ity ignited controversy that led to an understanding in both the government and public opinion that Japan needed to transform its diplomatic
doctrine in the post–Cold War era.[55]

In response to these crises, Ozawa, who left the LDP to establish the
Hosokawa Morihiro coalition government as secretary-general of the
Shinseito (Party of New Japan), proposed that Japan become a "normal state." This required meeting two conditions: (1) "It is necessary to
do common things in international society of our own responsibility,"
especially in the field of "security"; and (2) "it is necessary to aid those
who want to live in prosperity and tranquillity, as well as to cooperate
as much as possible in the field of global agendas such as environmental
protection." Ozawa argued that "we need to free ourselves from the
Yoshida Doctrine as soon as possible," adding that "we need to create
a new strategy."[56] Both right-wing nationalists and "normal statists"
criticized this doctrine as a outdated relic of the Cold War. Likewise,
resurgent Asianists denounced United States–Japan bilateralism, pro-
posing new strategies for Asia. The theme of national identity rose to
the forefront in diplomacy, as political and cultural objectives eclipsed
economic sources of pride.

By the mid-1990s, the above-noted currents were facing an uncertain
future as Japan was reverting to a stronger alliance with America, signaled by the "Japan-U.S. Joint Declaration on Security." To meet post–
Cold War security challenges such as the crisis on the Korean Peninsula
and the rise of China, it was felt necessary to reaffirm the solidarity of
the United States–Japan alliance. The Bill Clinton administration successfully relieved anxiety about the future of U.S. commitments in East
Asia by redefining the alliance. This enabled Japan's Self-Defense Forces

to play a more proactive role in regional security. Yet the effort to find more balance continued as the Hashimoto, Obuchi, and Mori cabinets successively pursued a "Eurasian diplomacy" that tried to strengthen Japan's ties with both Russia and the Central Asian states. Togo Kazuhiko, a Russian expert at the Ministry of Foreign Affairs, wrote that Hashimoto's "Eurasian diplomacy" was based on a geopolitical calculation that improved Japan-Russia relations would strengthen Japan's position in East Asia against rising China.[57] After the Asian financial crisis, Japan also renewed its approach to East Asian regional integration. Although it tried to counterbalance the rise of China, it also decided to cooperate with China in a framework for regional cooperation. As the significance of the Asia-Pacific Economic Cooperation forum waned in the mid-1990s, this resulted in ASEAN + 3.[58]

Obuchi further explored the possibility of cooperation with the East Asian countries.[59] The ASEAN-Japan Consultation Conference, led by former vice minister of foreign affairs Owada Hisashi, submitted a report to Obuchi that resulted in Koizumi Junichiro's speech on the East Asian community two years later.[60] Japan's initiative to deepen cooperation based on the Japan-ASEAN partnership was a big step because it did not presuppose an American presence; yet Obuchi faced a difficult problem when Jiang Zemin's visit to Japan in 1998 spurred a rise in anti-Chinese nationalism, especially his harsh criticisms of Japanese militarism and the history issue during the banquet hosted by the emperor.[61] After Murayama Tomiichi had expressed his "deep remorse and heartfelt apology" at the fiftieth anniversary of the end of the war two years before, Jiang's strong demand for a further Japanese apology had backfired, making it difficult for Japan's leaders to deal with the rising tide of anti-Chinese nationalism, which was no longer limited to right-wing politicians. The end of the Cold War and the rise of China transformed Japan's national identity and diplomacy in the 1990s, but left great uncertainty as well.

Japan's Search for Balance in the New Century

In 2000 a prime minister's commission comprising forty-seven leading intellectuals outlined Japan's goals for the coming century. Iokibe Makoto chaired "Subcommittee 1," concerned with "Japan's Place in the World," which asserted that "we must develop our sense of enlight-

ened national interest, defined and built on a long-term, systematic basis, with reference to the proper shape of our nation-building efforts,"
calling for three measures: (1) global civilian power; (2) a comprehensive, multilayered security framework; and (3) neighborly relations
(*rinko*).[62] These can be understood as evolving principles first stated in
the Diplomatic Bluebook of 1957. First, for "global civilian power," it
was suggested that Japan should "devote augmented efforts to international cooperation and the use of multilateral institutions to preserve
values that the present market system cannot readily evaluate, involving
areas like culture, the environment, and human rights." It must "contribute to the creation of international public goods, such as stabiliza-
tion of the global economic system, correction of the gap between rich
and poor, environmental preservation, human security, and peacekeeping activities, through civilian rather than military means." The term
"United Nations centrism" would no longer be used, but Japan should
play a much more proactive global role.

   Second, it was reaffirmed that "the core element of Japan's pre-
paredness will be the stability and preservation of the Japan-U.S. alliance." Japan should not follow a nationalistic diplomatic course, as "a
shift to a posture of achieving national security on a completely uni-
lateral basis would entail large costs without producing a corresponding increase in our country's security." While restating the importance
of the alliance, this report took a more internationalist perspective on
national security.

   Third, and most interesting, the importance of "neighborly relations" was particularly emphasized. Although the U.S. alliance was
properly placed as the "firmest foundation of Japan's foreign relations,"
it was also written that "we should further strengthen cooperative relations within East Asia, a region of great potential for the future and
one with which we have geographical proximity and deep historical and
cultural ties." The report proposed a "Northeast Asia free trade area"
within "a pan-Asian community," at a time when establishment of an
"East Asian Community" was under discussion. In 2002 Koizumi proposed the "creation of a 'community'" in which Japan "acts together
and advances together" with other Asian countries.[63] Yet even as the
"three basic principles" of 1957 were updated with an emphasis on
Asian diplomacy and identity, balance among them would become
jeopardized by Koizumi's diplomacy along with the unexpected complications of China's rapid rise.

By singularly emphasizing the importance of the United States–Japan alliance, Koizumi unconsciously destroyed the balance of the three basic principles. Although he lent support to the idea of an "East Asian Community" in his Singapore speech in 2002, he eventually damaged Japan's relations with China and South Korea by visiting the Yasukuni Shrine every year.[64] The reason was less the strident backlash against criticisms from Asian neighbors from right-wing intellectuals than Koizumi's priority for domestic public opinion at the expense of good relations with neighboring countries.[65] *Yomiuri shimbun* described Koizumi's relations with Chinese and Korean leaders as a *"kenka"* (quarrel).[66] Watanabe Tsuneo and Wakamiya Yoshibumi, editorial chiefs of the two largest Japanese newspapers, *Yomiuri* and *Asahi,* jointly denounced Koizumi's visit to the Yasukuni Shrine.[67] Koizumi's diplomacy to maintain a strong alliance with the United States, even at the price of deteriorating relations with China and South Korea, led to an unprecedented crisis in Asian policy. Tanaka Akihiko argued that "Japan-China relations reached the most abnormal stage since 1972, when the two countries established formal diplomatic relations,"[68] adding that this deterioration of relations also affected Japan's policy toward the United Nations.

Because China occupies a permanent seat on the UN Security Council, its criticisms made Japan's bid for a permanent seat even more difficult. Kitaoka Shinichi, the Japanese ambassador to the United Nations in 2005, regretted that Koizumi could not show flexibility on the Yasukuni Shrine issue, and also could not persuade George W. Bush to listen to Japanese requests for UN reform.[69] After the United States started the war in Iraq in 2003 without clear UN authorization, Koizumi one-sidedly stressed the importance of the alliance, arguing that the United Nations alone could not defend Japan's national security.[70] At the cost of deteriorating relations with China and South Korea and the tradition of "UN centrism," Koizumi reinforced the alliance mainly through his personal amity with Bush. This left in tatters the three basic principles of postwar diplomacy, and it also raised new complications for Japanese national identity. After Bush's Asian diplomacy shifted sharply from 2006 and then Barack Obama forged a new diplomatic course, the Koizumi legacy also left Japan's diplomacy in tatters.

It is ironic that Foreign Minister Aso Taro's "Arc of Freedom and Prosperity" was launched by a grandson of Yoshida Shigeru reformulating postwar diplomatic doctrine, serving under Prime Minister Abe

Shinzo, who was a grandson of Kishi Nobusuke. The Diplomatic
Bluebook of 2007 asserts that the "Arc of Freedom and Prosperity" is
to be added "to the three pillars, namely the Japan-U.S. alliance, international cooperation, and an emphasis on neighboring Asian nations."
Aso argued that "I set forth a policy of working to create this Arc, a region that would be prosperous and stable with a foundation in universal
values, stretching from Southeast Asia to South Asia, Central Asia, the
Middle East, Central and Eastern Europe, and the Baltic states."[71] With
this emphasis on values, the intention was not just to add a "fourth pillar" to Japan's diplomacy but also to contrast Japan's national identity
with China's. Aso's initiative overlapped with Abe's "value-oriented diplomacy." Abe wrote that "today Japan and America share fundamental values such as freedom, democracy, human rights, rule of law, and
free competition—a market economy."[72] Emphasizing the importance
of values in diplomacy—and, in effect, renouncing the postwar tradition of the Yoshida Doctrine—both Abe and Aso bluntly transformed
discourse on diplomacy, which had prioritized economic strength. With
Japan's relative decline in economic power to China, these values proved
convenient as a tool for foreign policy and national identity reinvigora-
tion at a time of mounting concern about a loss of direction.

This new diplomatic doctrine, however, failed to become a "pillar."
When Fukuda replaced Abe, he ignored his rival's "arc," while striving
to restore balance between the "U.S.-Japan Alliance" and "being a
member of Asia." Then, a year later in September 2008, when Aso returned to the center of power, he strangely abandoned his own diplomatic initiative, a change criticized as incoherence in diplomatic
philosophy.[73] The Diplomatic Bluebook of 2008 also largely ignored
Aso's earlier initiative.[74]

The Democratic Party of Japan's Diplomacy under Stress: Crises on Every Front

The general election on August 30, 2009, brought a dramatic political
change. The victory of the Democratic Party of Japan marked the first
change of the Cabinet through a general election in sixty-two years. Its
leader, who would soon become a new prime minister, Hatoyama
Yukio, inherited some of his political philosophy from his grandfather,
Hatoyama Ichiro. Hatoyama Ichiro was also a prime minister in the
middle of the 1950s, and strongly criticized his predecessor's foreign

policy, or the Yoshida Doctrine, as being too much dependent on the United States. Likewise, Hatoyama Yukio pursued a more independent foreign policy.

In August 2009, Hatoyama Yukio contributed an op-ed article titled "A New Path for Japan" to the *New York Times,* stating that "I believe that the East Asian region, which is showing increasing vitality, must be recognized as Japan's basic sphere of being.[75] Although some fretted that he would be inclined to unbalance the three basic principles by promoting vigorous Asianism, others welcomed the new stress on both Asian regionalism and the United Nations as an effort, at last, to achieve equilibrium in the three basic principles by reaffirming the aspirations for national identity shared by many Japanese, despite difficult conditions for realizing them.

However, the subsequent record of Hatoyama's foreign policy indicates that he only damaged the United States–Japan relationship without reinforcing Japan's ties with East Asian countries. He unwisely promised to solve the issue of the U.S. military base on Okinawa by the end of May 2010, underestimating the difficulties of the agreement between Japanese and U.S. governments on the Futenma U.S. Marine Corps Base, and the Democratic Party of Japan had not sufficiently prepared for the solution of this difficult problem.[76] It seemed that Hatoyama's repeated insistence on more independence from the United States was partly motivated by his nationalistic stance on foreign policy.

Hatoyama was known for his anti-American political stance as well as his strong passion for regional integration based on the philosophy of "fraternity" (*yuai*). His philosophy led Japan to the "East Asian Community" in vain, because the Chinese government was then less interested in promoting regional integration based on reaching a consensus with Japan. Chinese nationalism was on the rise, and anti-Japanese sentiments were more widespread than before in China. It was clear that public opinion on both sides was not mature enough to establish solid progress for the creation of this regional community. On the contrary, Japanese public opinion showed anxiety over the deterioration of the U.S.-Japanese partnership under Hatoyama's premiership. The serious stalemate about the Futenma U.S. base issue eventually forced Hatoyama to abandon his post as prime minister in June 2010.

After Hatoyama Yukio stepped down as prime minister, Kan Naoto succeeded him on June 8, 2010. Kan's first task was to repair the damaged U.S.-Japanese relationship, and he pragmatically advocated the previous agreement on the transfer of the Futenma U.S. base. However, the biggest challenge to Kan came from China. On September 7, 2010, a Chinese trawler intentionally collided with Japanese Coast Guard ships, arousing both Japanese and Chinese nationalism. On a territorial issue, both governments could not concede to the other, due largely to nationalistic voices in their countries. This incident tells us that fierce nationalism easily damages the Sino-Japanese relationship, even though economic ties are mutually interwoven.

After Hatoyama carelessly damaged the U.S.-Japanese relationship, under Kan the Sino-Japanese relationship was frozen. Two pillars of Japanese diplomacy are under stress. At the time when the size of its economy is being surpassed by that of China, Japan has yet to find a new national identity that can replace that of the "No. 2" economic giant. The rapid rise of Chinese power has seemingly not eclipsed the importance of the three pillars of Japan's diplomacy. On the contrary, it is now widely seen among Japanese public opinion that the nation needs all three.

Dealing with the 3/11 Disaster and Redefining Japanese National Identity

One of the most powerful earthquakes in recorded history hit Northeast Japan on March 11, 2011. The ensuing tsunami swept across many cities and villages along the Pacific coast of the Tohoku district, resulting in great loss of life. The U.S. government sent more than 24,000 troops to the areas, 24 naval vessels, and approximately 190 planes, helping to make "Operation Tomodachi" a major success.[77] This reinforced the alliance, for U.S. troops have never been so appreciated by the Japanese people. On June 4, 2011, at the Shangri-La Dialogue meeting in Singapore, U.S. secretary of defense Robert Gates said that "this effort demonstrated the high-level of interoperability between the U.S. and Japanese defense forces and served to validate years of investments by both nations in combined training and capabilities." Thus, "it is clear that the alliance not only has survived this tragedy, but emerged even stronger and even more vital."[78]

International assistance reaffirmed the deep ties between Japan and the international community, which had been developed since the end of World War II. Prime Minister Kan wrote that "it has been a period during which Japan has once again realized, and once again given thanks, that we stand together with the world."[79] Japan's national identity is much more closely tied with the international community than at the time of the Great Kanto Earthquake of September 1, 1923. The Japanese people have rediscovered *kizuna* (bonds of friendship) with this community at a time when sadness overshadowed the country.

At the same time, Northeast Asian regional cooperation, which had been frozen since the Sino-Japanese split in September 2010, became possible again after the earthquake. On May 22, 2011, the leaders of Japan, China, and South Korea, who had just visited Fukushima together to see the suffering, met in Tokyo to discuss various issues. In the summit declaration, it was stated that "the incident reminded us of the essential need for trilateral cooperation, considering bonds of friendship among the three peoples as well as the geographical closeness."[80] The three countries reaffirmed the importance of regional cooperation, including disaster management, nuclear safety, and environmentally sustainable development. In this way, both "the U.S.-Japan alliance" and "Asia," two pillars of postwar Japanese diplomacy, have been reinforced through crises in Japan.

Political turmoil, however, casts a shadow on the direction of Japanese diplomacy since the Great East Japan Earthquake. The *Washington Post* and *Wall Street Journal,* among others, criticized Japanese politics as it appeared that a power struggle might delay the process of the postquake reconstruction.[81] With such a further political stalemate, it would be difficult for Japan to play an important role in international politics. Because many are speculating that this crisis will become a decisive turning point in postwar Japanese history, questions remain unanswered about what this will mean for Japan's national identity. Wishful thinking suggests that the shock will bring some much-needed clarity. Yet a reaffirmation of the "three basic principles" will not be easy when the divide between China and the United States appears to be widening, with divisive consequences for idealism about the international community. Without newfound confidence in Japan's own political and economic prospects, more groping for a diplomatic way forward is the probable outcome.

Conclusion

For a half century, we have seen the durability of the three basic principles of Japan's postwar diplomacy. Although there have been differences of emphasis, Japan could not ignore any of them. As long as the

Yoshida Doctrine prevailed and Japan pursued nationalism largely through economic growth, the principles were not seriously challenged. Despite the fact that the U.S. alliance loomed as foremost among the principles during the Cold War and remained paramount despite more serious challenges in the 1990s, the presence of the full "troika" provided reassurance that Japanese national identity was not being subsumed under some sort of U.S. universalism. Yet, in the first decade of the twenty-first century, attempts to tilt the balance closer to the United States and to raise Japan's profile as the champion of universal values were met with frustration. They did not resolve questions about realizing a "normal Japan" by clarifying its place in the international community and in Asia.

Nationalism in Japan was largely contained through the three basic principles. The Yoshida Doctrine presupposed that Japan would pursue its nationalism through economic growth. During the Cold War, nationalism was largely harmonious with Japan's alliance with the United States. As concerns intensified starting in the 1990s about the rise of China and then the threat of North Korea, the alliance regained its luster as critical to nationalism. Its vitality continued to limit any outburst of extreme nationalism. Yet it did not operate alone. The other principles persisted as a check. Recent leaders have operated within the confines of the diplomatic tradition. Koizumi hesitated to voice strong nationalist views toward China or South Korea, and Abe and Aso reinvigorated diplomatic ties with China. The three basic principles as a tandem were stronger than new ideological initiatives to transform the old tradition. They represent three aspects of Japan's national identity—Americanism, Asianism, and internationalism. Although right-wing politicians often air sentiments that cast doubt on one or another of these orientations, the history of postwar diplomacy shows how successive governments have tried to construct Japan's place in the world by striking a balance among them. Japan's direction remains muddled, however, amid a lack of clarity on how diplomacy meets the widely felt need to clarify national identity.

Notes

1. Oliver Franks, "The 'Special Relationship' 1947–1952," in *Adventures with Britannia: Personalities, Politics and Culture in Britain,* edited by William Roger

Louis (London: I. B. Tauris, 1995); Hosoya Yuichi, *Daieiteikoku no gaikokan* (Tokyo: Chikuma shobo, 2005), 284–85; Hosoya Yuichi, "Rekishi toshite no Igirisu gaiko," in *Igirisu gaikoshi,* edited by Sasaki Yuta and Kibata Yoichi (Tokyo: Yuhikaku, 2005), 15–20.

2. Tony Blair, "Doctrine of the International Community," speech at the Economic Club of Chicago, Chicago, April 24, 1999.

3. Gilbert Rozman uses a dichotomy between "internationalism" and "Asianism," pointing out interconnections between the two; see Gilbert Rozman, "Internationalism and Asianism in Japanese Strategic Thought from Meiji to Heisis," *Japanese Journal of Political Science* 9, no. 2 (2007): 209–32. Soeya Yoshihide contrasts "great power diplomacy" and "middle power diplomacy" in postwar Japan, arguing that Japan has embraced a "dual identity" between these national self-images; see Soeya Yoshihide, *Nihon no "midoru pawaa" gaiko: Sengo Nihon no sentaku to koso* (Tokyo: Chikuma Shobo, 2005), 18.

4. Recent studies on postwar Japanese diplomacy emphasize continuity with the prewar diplomatic tradition; see Inoue Toshikazu, *Nihon gaiko kogi* (Tokyo: Iwanami shoten, 2003), 118–20.

5. Although biographers—e.g., Kosaka Masataka, Inoki Masamichi, John Dower, and Kitaoka Shinichi—agree on Yoshida's significance in shaping postwar Japan and on the continuity in his diplomatic philosophy, they differ in interpreting that philosophy. Whereas Dower emphasized the importance of the "imperialist" tradition, the others stressed his "liberalist" and "pro-Anglo-Saxon" tradition. See Kosaka Masataka, *Saisho Yoshida Shigeru* (Tokyo: Chuo koronsha, 1968); John Dower, *Empire and Aftermath: Yoshida Shigeru and the Japanese Experience, 1878–1954* (Cambridge, Mass.: Harvard University Press, 1988); Inoki Masamichi, *Yoshida Shigeru,* 3 vols. (Tokyo: Yomiuri shimbunsha, 1978–81); and Kitaoka Shinichi, "Yoshida Shigeru ni okeru senzen to sengo," in *Sengo gaiko no keisei,* edited by Kindai Nihon kenkyukai (Tokyo: Yamakawa shuppansha, 1994).

6. Sheldon Garon, "Saving for 'My Own Good and the Good of the Nation': Economic Nationalism in Modern Japan," in *Nation and Nationalism in Japan,* edited by Sandra Wilson (London: RoutledgeCurzon, 2002), 109.

7. Kitaoka Shinichi, "Yoshida Shigeru ni okeru senzen to sengo," 127.

8. Iokibe divided postwar diplomacy into three courses: (1) social democrat, (2) economic oriented, and (3) traditional nationalist. Yoshida exemplified the second course, drawing criticism from both extremes. See Iokibe Makoto, ed., *Sengo Nihon gaikoshi,* rev. ed. (Tokyo: Yuhikaku, 2006), 282–84.

9. Miyagi Taizo, *Bandon kaigi to Nihon no Ajiafukki* (Tokyo: Soshisha, 2001).

10. Saito Shizuo, *Gaiko: Watashi no keiken to kyokun* (Tokyo: Simul shuppankai, 1992), 39–46.

11. Gaimusho, *Waga gaiko no kinkyo* (Tokyo: Gaimusho, 1957), 7–10. For the full contents, see http://www.mofa.go.jp/mofajlgaiko/bluebook/1957/s32-contents. htm. See also Gaimusho hyakunenshi hensan iinkai, eds., *Gaimusho no hyakunen* (Tokyo: Harashobo, 1969), 934–38. Kitaoka Shinichi first emphasized the importance of the "three basic principles" in "Furuku katsu atarashii gensoku," *Gaiko Forum,* October 1993. In contrast to his stress on the U.S. alliance, others have placed more emphasis on the "three basic principles" doctrine. See Sakamoto Kazuya, "Dokuritsu koku no joken," in *Sengo Nihon gaikoshi,* ed. Iokibe, 88–90; Inoue, *Nihon gaikoshi kogi,* 157–60; Masuda Hiroshi and Sato Susumu, eds., *Nihon*

gaikoshi handobukku: Kaisetsu to shiryo, rev. ed. (Tokyo: Yushindo, 2007), 165; and Hatano Sumio and Sato Susumu, *Gendai Nihon no Tonanajia seisaku* (Tokyo: Waseda University Press, 2007), 52–56.

12. Gaimusho, *Waga gaiko no kinkyo,* 7–10.

13. Hatano and Sato, *Gendai Nihon no Tonanajia seisaku,* 52–56.

14. Hoshiro Hiroshi, *Ajia chiikishugi gaiko no yukue 1952–1966* (Tokyo: Bokutakusha, 2008), 141–45.

15. Miyagi Taizo, *"Kaiyokokka" Nihon no sengoshi* (Tokyo: Chikuma shobo, 2008), 215–18.

16. Hatano and Sato, *Gendai Nihon no Tonanajia seisaku,* 1.

17. Hatano Sumio, "'Tonanajia kaihatsu' o meguru Nichibeiei kankei: Nihon no Kolombo puran lanyu (1954 nen) o chushin ni," in *Sengo gaiko no keisei,* ed. Kindai Nihon kenkyukai, 215–16.

18. Hatano and Sato, *Gendai Nihon no Tonanajia seisaku,* 42–43.

19. Takeda Tomoki, *Shigemitsu Mamoru to sengo seiji* (Tokyo: Yoshikawa ko-bundo, 2002).

20. Hatano and Sato, *Gendai Nihon no Tonanajia seisaku,* 44.

21. Hoshiro, *Ajia chiikishugi gaiko no yukue,* 307.

22. Hara Yoshihisa, ed., *Kishi Nobusuke shogenroku* (Tokyo: Mainichi shim-bun, 2003), 132–33.

23. On the harmony of Kishi's "Asianism" with his pro-American policy, see Hara, *Kishi Nobusuke shogenroku;* and Hoshiro, *Ajia chiikishugi gaiko noyukue,* 121–26.

24. Saito, *Gaiko,* 41–43.

25. Kase Toshikazu, *Kase Toshikazu kaisoroku* (Tokyo: Yamate shobo, 1986), 115, cited by Miyagi, *"Kaiyokokka" Nihon no sengoshi,* 55.

26. Miyagi, *"Kaiyokokka" Nihon no sengoshi,* 15–56.

27. NSC5516/1, "U.S. Policy toward Japan," Washington, April 9, 1955, quoted by Hosoya Chihiro, Aruga Sadashi, Ishii Osamu, and Sasaki Takuya, eds., *Nichibei kankei shiryoshu 1945–97* (Tokyo: Tokyo University Press, 1999), 326.

28. Otake Hideo, *Sengo Nihon no ideorogi tairitsu* (Tokyo: Sanichi shobo, 1996), 91.

29. Suzuki Takahiro, "Ikeda gaiko no kozu: 'Juyujinei' gaiko ni miru nasei to gaiko no renkan," *Kokusai setji* 151 (2008).

30. Hosoya Chihiro, *Nihon gaiko no kiseki* (Tokyo: NHK Shuppan, 1993), 19–89; Suzuki Takahiro, "OECD kamei no gaiko katei: 'Seijikeizai ittai' rosen toshi-teno juyujinei ni okeru gaikoteki chihei no kakudai," *Kokusai seiji* 140 (2005); Murata Ryohei, *Murata Ryohei kaisoroku: Tatakai ni yabureshi, kuni ni tsukaete,* vol. 1 (Kyoto: Miverva shoten, 2008), 162; Murata Ryohei, *OCED (Keizai kyo-ryoku kaihatsu kiko): Sekai saidai no shinku tanku* (Tokyo: Chuo koronshinsha, 2000), 14–19. Murata, a vice minister of foreign affairs decades later, was then a young official at the Economic Affairs Bureau responsible for OECD affairs.

31. Ito Masaya, *Ikeda Hayato to so no jidai* (Tokyo: Asahi shimbunsha, 1985), 184–85; Christopher Braddick, "Distant Friends: Britain and Japan since 1958—The Age of Globalization," in *The History of Anglo-Japanese Relations, 1600–2000, Volume II: The Political-Diplomatic Dimension, 1931–2000,* edited by Ian Nish and Yoichi Kibata (Basingstoke, U.K.: Macmillan, 2000), 271.

32. Nakajima Shingo, "'Domeikoku Nihon' zo no takan," in *Ikeda-Sato seikenki no Nihon gaiko,* edited by Hatano Sumio (Kyoto: Miverva shoten, 2004), 62–64.

33. Liang Pan, "'Keizaitaikokuka' to kokusaiteki chii," in *Ikeda-Sato seikenki no Nihon gaiko,* ed. Hatano, 167–82.

34. Tanaka Akihiko, *Ajia no naka no Nihon* (Tokyo: NTT shuppan, 2007).

35. Lee Jong Won, "Kannachi kokko seijoka no seiritsu to Amerika—1960–65 nen," in *Sengo gaiko no keisei,* ed. Kindai Nihon kenkyukai, 272–305.

36. Miyagi, *"Kaiyokokka" Nihon no sengoshi,* 178–83; Miyagi Taizo, *Sengo Ajia chitsujo no mosaku to Nihon: "Umi no Ajia" no sengoshi* (Tokyo: Sobunsha, 2004), conclusion.

37. Hatano and Sato, *Gendai Nihon no Tonanajia seisaku,* 164.

38. Tanaka Hitoshi, *Gaiko no chikara* (Tokyo: Nihon keizai shimbunsha, 2008), 20–23.

39. Fukuda Takeo, *Kaiko kyujunen* (Tokyo: Iwanami shoten, 1995), 270, 277.

40. Ibid., 278–79. On the making of the Fukuda Doctrine, see Sudo Sueo, *The Fukuda Doctrine and ASEAN: New Dimensions in Japanese Foreign Policy* (Singapore: Singapore Institute of Southeast Asian Studies, 1992), 162–85; and Hidekazu Wakatsuki, *"Zenhoi gaiko" no jidai: Reisen henyoki no Nihon to Ajia* (Tokyo: Nihon keizai hyoronsha, 2006), chap. 3.

41. For Ohira's speech, see Masuda and Sato, *Nihon gaikoshi handobukku,* 202–3. On the background of Ohira's initiative for Pan-Pacific regionalism, also see Fumio Fukunaga, *Ohira Masayoshi: "Sengo hoshu" towa nanika* (Tokyo: Chuo koron shinsha, 2008), 258–60; and Nakanishi Hiroshi, "Jiritsuteki kyocho no mosaku," in *Sengo Nihon gaikoshi,* ed. Iokibe, 178–80.

42. Inoue Toshikazu, *Nihon gaiko kogi,* 216–17; Watanabe Akio, "Sengo Nihon no shuppatsuten, in *Sengo nihon no taigai seisaku,* edited by Watanabe Akio (Tokyo: Yuhikaku, 1985), 11–15.

43. Tanaka, *Ajia no naka no Nihon,* 162–63; Yinan He, "Remembering and Forgetting the War: Elite Mythmaking, Mass Reaction, and Sino-Japanese Relations, 1950–2006," *History & Memory* 19, no. 2 (Winter 2007): 43–74.

44. For this comment on August 26, 1982, see the database "Sekai to Nihon," Tanaka Akihiko kenkyushitsu, Institute for Oriental Studies, University of Tokyo, http://www.ioc.u-tokyo.ac.jp/~worldjpn/. For more on the impact of guidance from the government, see Mitani Hiroshi, "Nihon no rekishi kyokasho no seido to ronso kozu," in *Kokyo o koeru rekishi ninshiki: Nichu taiwa no kokoromi,* edited by Liu Jie, Mitani Hiroshi, and Yang Daqing (Tokyo: Tokyo University Press, 2006), 215.

45. Hiroshi Mitani, "The History Textbook Issue in Japan and East Asia: Institutional Framework, Controversies, and International Efforts for Common Histories," in *East Asia's Haunted Present: Historical Memories and the Resurgence of Nationalism,* edited by Tsuyoshi Hasegawa and Kazuhiko Togo (Westport, Conn.: Praeger, 2008), 85.

46. Otake, *Sengo Nihon no ideorogii tairitsu,* 148–53.

47. Akihiko Tanaka, "The Yasukuni Issue and Japan's International Relations," in *East Asia's Haunted Present,* ed. Hasegawa and Togo, 119–41.

48. Murai Ryota, "Sengo Nihon no seiji to irei," in *Kokkyo o koeru rekishi ninshiki,* ed. Liu, Mitani, and Yang, 302–4.

49. Tanaka Akihiko, *Ajia no naka no Nihon,* 164–65.

50. Thomas U. Berger, "Dealing with Difficult Pasts: Japan's 'History Problem' from a Theoretical and Comparative Perspective," in *East Asia's Haunted Present,* ed. Hasegawa and Togo, 31–33.

51. Iokibe Makoto, Ito Motoshige, and Yakushiji Katsuyukii, eds., *Ozawa Ichiro: Seiken dasshu ron* (Tokyo: Ashahi shimbunsha, 2006), 30.

52. Teshima Ryuichi, *1991 nen Nihon no haiboku* (Tokyo: Shinchosha, 1993); Iokibe Makoto, "Reisengo no Nihon gaiko," in *Sengo Nihon gaikoshi,* ed. Iokibe, 239.

53. Murata Ryohei, *Murata Ryohei kaisoroku: Sokoku no saisei o jisedai ni takushite* (Kyoto: Minerva shobo, 2008), 121.

54. Tanaka Hitoshi, *Gaiko no chikara,* 70.

55. Tsuyoshi Hasegawa, "Japan's Strategic Thinking toward Asia in the First Half of the 1990s," in *Japanese Strategic Thought toward Asia,* edited by Gilbert Rozman, Kazuhiko Togo, and Joseph P. Ferguson (New York: Palgrave, 2007), 77.

56. Ozawa Ichiro, "Futsu no kuni ni nare," in *Sengo Nihon gaiko ronshu,* edited by Kitaoka Shinichi, 462–68.

57. Kazuhiko Togo, *Japan's Foreign Policy 1945–2003: The Quest for a Proactive Policy* (Leiden: Brill, 2005), 151–256; Joseph P. Ferguson, "Japanese Strategic Thinking toward Russia," and Kazuhiko Togo, "Japan's Strategic Thinking in the Second Half of the 1990s," both in *Japanese Strategic Thinking toward Asia,* ed. Rozman, Togo, and Ferguson, 206–11, 89; Michael J. Green, *Japan's Reluctant Realism: Foreign Policy Challenges in an Era of Uncertain Power* (New York: Palgrave, 2003), 145–66.

58. Munakata Naoko, "Nihon no FTA senryaku," in *Nihon no higashi Ajia koso,* edited by Soeya Yoshihide and Takokoro Masuyuki (Tokyo: Keio University Press, 2004), 144–50.

59. Yamakage Susumu, "Higashi Ajia chiikishugi to Nichi-ASEAN partnership," in *Higashi Ajia chiikishugi to Nihon gaiko,* edited by Yamakage Susumu (Tokyo: Japan Institute for International Affairs, 2003), 4–5.

60. Japan Institute for International Affairs and ASEAN-ISIS, "Towards Vision 2020: ASEAN-Japan Consultation Conference on the Hanoi Plan of Action, The Final Report with Recommendations," October 2000.

61. Ryosei Kokubun, "Changing Japanese Strategic Thinking toward China," in *Japanese Strategic Thinking toward Asia,* ed. Rozman, Togo, and Ferguson, 154.

62. Prime Minister's Commission on Japan's Goals in the 21st Century, *The Frontier Within: Individual Empowerment and Better Governance in the New Millennium* (Tokyo: Kodansha, 2000), 17–19. This report was written in Japanese and then translated into English, Chinese, and Korean.

63. Junichiro Koizumi, "Japan and ASEAN in East Asia: A Sincere and Open Partnership," Singapore, January 14, 2002. See also Tanaka Akihiko, *Ajia no naka no Nihon* (Tokyo: NTT shuppan, 2007), 308–11.

64. Tanaka Hitoshi, *Gaiko no chikara,* 169; Taniguchi Makoto, *Higashi Ajia kyodotai: Keizai togo no yukue to Nihon* (Tokyo: Iwanami shoten, 2004), xi–xx; Ito Kenichi and Tanaka Akihiko, eds., *Higashi Ajia kyodotai to Nihon no shinro* (Tokyo: NHK shuppan, 2005), 56–65.

65. Yuichi Hosoya, "Koizumi's Neglected Foreign Policy Agenda," *Japan Echo,* April 2006, 16–20.

66. Yomiuri shimbun seijibu, *Gaiko o kenka nishita otoko: Koizumi gaiko nisennichi no shinjitsu* (Tokyo: Shinchosha, 2006), 13.

67. Watanabe Tsuneo and Wakamiya Yoshibumi, *"Yasukuni" to Koizumi shusho* (Tokyo: Asahi shimbunsha, 2006).

68. Akihiko Tanaka, "Yasukuni Issue," 119–20.

69. Kitaoka Shinichi, *Kokuren no seiji rikigaku: Nihon wa doko ni irunoka* (Tokyo: Chuokoron shinsha, 2007), 243.

70. T. J. Pempel, "Japan's Strategy under Koizumi, in *Japanese Strategic Thinking toward Asia,* ed. Rozman, Togo, and Ferguson, 120–25.

71. Aso Taro, "Arc of Freedom and Prosperity: Japan's Expanding Diplomatic Horizons," November 30, 2006, Japan Institute of International Affairs, Tokyo, http://www.mofa.go.jp/announce/fm/aso/speech0611.htm; Gaimusho, *Gaiko seisho 2007* (Tokyo: Gaimusho, 2007), foreword by Aso. Aso later published a book under the same title, *Jiyu to hanei no ko* (Tokyo: Gentosha, 2007).

72. Abe Shinzo, *Utsukushii kuni e* (Tokyo, 2006), 129.

73. Yamauchi Masayuki and Hashimoto Goro, "Kono seiji katachi de norikirerunoka," *Chuo koron,* December 2008, 98–99.

74. Gaimusho, *Gaiko seisho 2008* (Tokyo: Gaimusho, 2008).

75. Yukio Hatoyama, "A New Path for Japan," *New York Times,* August 27, 2009. This op-ed article originally appeared in the Japanese monthly magazine *Voice,* September 2009. Hatoyama's anti-American tone has been largely criticized by both American and Japanese major media, and he answered that this argument had been distorted. But his main argument remains the same, and his diplomatic philosophy is less pro-American and more Asianist than that of previous LDP administrations.

76. On the problem of Hatoyama's diplomacy, see Yuichi Hosoya, "What Was Wrong with Hatoyama's Diplomacy?" *Japan Analysis,* no.19 (June 2010): 2–5.

77. Robert M. Gates, "Emerging Security Challenges in the Asia-Pacific," speech at the Tenth IISS Asian Security Summit, Shangri-La Dialogue, June 4, 2011; Yuichi Hosoya, "The Dawning of a New Age of International Cooperation," April 25, 2011, JapanEcho.net, http://japanecho.net/policy/0050.

78. Gates, "Emerging Security Challenges."

79. Naoto Kan, "Kizuna: The Bonds of Friendship," speech, April 11, 2011.

80. Ministry of Foreign Affairs of Japan, "Summit Declaration," May 22, 2011, http://www.mofa.gojp/region/asia-paci/jck/summit1105/declaration.html.

81. *Mainichi shimbun,* June 3, 2011.

Chapter 7

Korean National Identity: Evolutionary Stages and Diplomatic Challenges

Gilbert Rozman and Andrew Kim

Having been constrained in other directions, South Koreans have elevated *minjok* (ethnic identity centered on the Korean bloodline, shared history, common language, and culture) to the top rung in their discussion of national identity for a century, but it is increasingly being challenged. Progressives strove to twist it by stressing *minjung* (masses) and refocusing ethnic solidarity on North Korea. Conservative notions of ethnic purity are being tested by growing diversity at home and inclusive Koreanness abroad. Meanwhile, *gukmin* identity rooted in democracy and internationalism remains in dispute even as it advances. Tracing the evolution of the search for shared identity, we draw on South Korean rhetoric and highlight recent diplomatic challenges.

South Korean national identity formed starting in 1945 in the shadow of negative historical memories associated with dependency on China and annexation by Japan and a belligerent North Korea insistent on its legitimacy as the authentic Korea. In this atmosphere, leaders appealed to a different historical narrative and expanded integration into the international community, adjusting to stark Cold War divisions in Asia and post–Cold War regional economic integration. They were successful in forging a firm sense of national identity, and thus they overcame many handicaps even as they kept facing new, external challenges. Despite many signs of turning points in the two-thirds of a century since the second half of the 1940s, basic conditions have remained constant: North Korean determination to reunite the peninsula under its regime; dependency on the United States for defense and international support; wariness about Beijing and Moscow assisting Pyongyang in an effort to shape the evolution of the peninsula in their favor; and an awareness of Seoul's limited leverage in great power relations or even in constructing its own national identity in the midst of far-reaching changes in its economic, diplomatic, and cultural environment. At each stage of change, identity has been contested, revealing divergence that casts a shadow on what lies ahead.

At various times, South Koreans have gained confidence that their country was on the ascendancy with promise to resolve uncertainties about national identity. Under the military dictatorship, hopes centered on solidifying anticommunism in a world doomed to polarization and grounding cultural identity in a mixture of ethnic pride and economic confidence. Until the mid-1980s, leaders dismissed democratization and diplomatic diversification in Northeast Asia in the mistaken impression that they had found a lasting formula for a national identity edge over North Korea as well as an appealing image internationally. With anticommunism linked to fear of loss of solidarity and anti-Japanese sentiments sustaining fear of future loss of economic autonomy, South Korea had fertile soil for nurturing close ethnocentric cohesion.

The vulnerability of the Cold War South Korean approach to national identity was quickly exposed in the second half of the 1980s. First, it was based on top-down construction without reflecting the diversity of public sentiment. Democratization opened the door to a more vibrant civic identity, but it also made imperative a wider approach to bridging differences in thinking. The end of the Cold War removed the lynchpin of anticommunism, even as diplomatic diversification put a strain on the identity implications of one-sided reliance on the United States and growing ties to other states that were not fully trusted. Finally, globalization in its multiple respects raised doubts about homogeneous ethnic identity and narrow notions of economic and cultural identity. The choices made in the 1990s and 2000s appeared to resolve the new dilemmas, but in 2010 they were exacerbated in a manner that left in doubt all the earlier compromises and put a premium on finding clarity vis-à-vis a shifting identity.

In contrast to the pride in past glory found elsewhere, South Koreans articulate a record of resistance, enumerating a string of invasions and diminished sovereignty that leaves a legacy of suspiciousness. In these experiences, Korea saw itself as the smaller, weaker state struggling against one or another powerful neighbor. It faced China's regional dominance through most of its history and Japan's edge as the first Asian state to modernize in the half century to 1945. Then, it could not escape the shadow of the United States, as the force constraining national identity choices. The evolution of its identity and diplomatic challenges starts from these stark realities. Above all, there has been an onerous burden of living under the threat of violent attack by North Korea clothed in the rhetoric of legitimate reunification and enabled by China, whose own national identity and strategic thought lead to a permissive approach.

National Identity Up to the Time of the Korean War

Similar to Chinese and Japanese, over centuries Koreans became preoccupied with forging a strong state enmeshed in a decentralized, family-oriented society that could put behind it unsettling memories of a period of division and fraternal strife. The Chosun era satisfied concern with state stability, even as it left undeveloped the prospects for national identity formation. A half century of invasions from the 1590s to 1640s shook the long-lasting Sinocentric worldview, not dislodging it but raising a debate that showed signs of congealing into the distinct identity of a Korean state apart from the overarching Confucian civilization, and prepared, intellectually at least, to distance itself from dependence on China. Contrasting this era to the prior Koryo era when Buddhism prevailed, Koreans focused their cultural identity on Confucianism, but this could not provide much distance from China.[1] Economically, there was little trade with China and Japan, given the regional preference for tight restrictions on borders; no strong economic identity emerged either focused on substate levels, as in China and Japan, or on a central state. Given that Korea was overshadowed politically by China, under the sway culturally of a shared Confucian civilization, and economically missing a mercantilist impetus, it had a porous foundation for national identity, even if signs of autonomy were increasingly directed at constructing an identity that was distinct from China, critical of Japan, and clarifying Korean superiority in Confucianism.

As in other Confucian societies, the state claimed centrality in spreading the ethics associated with the classics of Confucianism and setting the tone for morality in social relations. Historical predecessors were faulted for failing to live by these codes. The Koryo era drew criticism for turning away from Confucian teachings, as later Confucianism refocused on utopian themes of mythical imperial eras described in the classics, and the elite set its sights on forging a contemporary version of the ideal. Yet the small aristocratic elite that gained stature by championing this cause seized upon the importance of rituals, especially in the Neo-Confucian school whose hegemony had now spread from China, to insist on strict requirements subject to their own interpretation. If Ming China was first accepted as the superior exemplar of Confucianism, later reservations led scholars to turn back to Song China.[2] When the Ming fell to the Qing under the much-scorned Manchus, more distance was put between China and the idealized Confucian civilization. Japan's militarist image disqualified it, leaving Korea as the natural core of a universal civilization. Yet the king was too constricted by the strong elite's narrow insistence on ritual obligations. Elite and reform Confucianism failed to escape the confines of the ritual orthodoxy.

Monarchical Confucianism left a foundation for national identity parallel to that of China but also setting Korea on a separate path. If in some Western states the rule of law and the rise of constitutionalism began before modernization to shape a national identity distinct from individual dynasties or leaders, Hahm Chaihark has found a similar effect from Confucian ritual in East Asian states.[3] Indeed, given the defensive authoritarianism of Manchu rule in Qing China and the rigid feudalism of the system of rule established in Tokugawa Japan, Korea was the main battleground for struggles over the power of ritual to limit the leader's authority. Debates over ritual intensifying from the seventeenth century onward served as struggles over the legitimacy of particular types of national control and even over identity. In China's shadow, notably after Manchu "barbarian" rule prevailed, Koreans struggled over narrow interpretations of ritual in an effort to situate their nation within a regional order and civilization. Confucian experts played a greater role regulating or disciplining officials than in China, while also embracing the orthodoxy of Neo-Confucianism.

Ritual observance required strict instructions on how to perform tasks linked to legitimacy. Having been founded on the claim to be establishing a proper Confucian state and overcoming the moral depravity of Koryo, the Chosun state became obsessed with ritual as the means to virtue, which in turn would be the pathway to legitimacy. Both canonical texts glorifying ancient rulers and the dynasty's founding father's edicts became sacrosanct, narrowing the options for future rulers. Factional strife at the court left a divisive legacy even as, starting in the mid–eighteenth century, autocratic control was reimposed. Because the strife and vendettas associated with orthodoxy put issues of legitimacy in the forefront and kings lacked the institutional weight of China's emperors or Japan's feudal lords to crush challenges, further preoccupation with rituals distorted the process of national identity formation. In the background was the unresolved question of how Korea could reject the cultural authority of China under Manchu rule while still showing political obeisance to the Manchus.

In the shadow of China's hegemony and Japan's impudence as awareness of more heathen Western pretenders to global power spread, Koreans were locked into a narrow peninsula with no scope for maneuvering. They hunkered down, taking comfort in their own cultural superiority through Confucian rituals. After decades of struggle over ritual purity into the eighteenth century, a fundamentalist narrowing occurred. Discourse over the king's rituals, which at times of succession threatened to become legitimacy crises, stultified elite, reform Confucianism or the sort of merchant Confucianism that was gaining ground in China and Japan. The moral authority that rested with the elite but focused on the state kept looking backward.

Similar to China and Japan, Korea faced a world of intense nationalism in the late nineteenth century armed with a Confucian outlook on civilizational identity plus elements of national identity inherent in Confucianism or given more meaning in response to claims that Korea was more Confucian than Qing China and superior to Japan, which had cruelly invaded in the 1590s and was blamed for distorting the Confucian heritage with its samurai militancy. At the end of the Chosun era, Korea was forcibly pried open by Western states, notably France in the 1860s, then faced an assertive Japan seeking a beachhead on the continent, an expansionist Russia just having acquired territory bordering Korea from

China, and a nostalgic China still claiming tributary rights over Korea. The crumbling of the Sinocentric order aroused great confusion, and many grasped for ethnic solidarity to replace their lost faith in the moral superiority of Confucianism and to find some prospect of national salvation as neighboring powers encroached ever closer.

Andre Schmid provides evidence of a shift in national identity toward *minjok*. The challenge was to break away from the long-accepted practice of conceding to China the superior culture. Recognizing that Japan had already reconstructed its early history to downgrade Confucianism, Koreans also searched for nativist forces that established the legitimacy of an autonomous culture. This gathered steam in the 1900s centered on Tangun, who according to legend founded Korea and became its first king, and whose purported descent from Heaven in 2333 BC was seen as both the outset of history and the formation of an unbroken *minjok,* though later political divisions would separate the people of an allegedly unified Korean descent.[4] This represented a shift away from Kija, the founding figure of Korea's Confucian civilization and center of Chosun court rituals. The crisis of Confucianism of the mid–nineteenth century demanded that the father of the Korean nation take his rightful place above the teacher. If Japan's colonialism erased the political entity that could have developed as the symbol of Korean national identity, it did not undercut the emerging *minjok* identity. Ethnic solidarity served as the rallying cry against Japan's humiliating attempt to eradicate Korean distinctiveness. Schmid notes that after the suppression of Korean debates right after annexation, Japan tolerated lively discussion on cultural themes in the 1920s and 1930s. Despite constraints, new attention to history, national character, and language rekindled the excitement over *minjok* that started to develop before annexation.[5] It became a "powerful, mobilizing force," forging a national history with diverse heroes sharing a common national identity and vying with an identity imposed by Japan to strip Koreanness of any potential to challenge Japanese rule, politically and culturally.[6] Owing to Japan's obsession with constructing an identity to counter Confucianism and give its people confidence in distinctiveness centered on *minzoku* (the Japanese for *minjok*), the parallel pursuit of a Korean minjok identity should have come as no surprise. Just as the Japanese claimed divine origin to suggest inherent, ethnic superiority and therefore justify their imperialistic actions on the Korean Peninsula, the Koreans proclaimed the divine superiority of their own ethnicity, traced to Tangun, to delegitimize the claims of their oppressors.

The nation acquired transcendent meaning in the context of Japan's political nihilism and cultural genocide at the end of the colonial era. Given modernization in such areas as communications, access to symbols of national identity expanded even in the midst of assimilation policies.[7] There was room for exploration of what is the authentic Korean identity, drawing on Sin Ch'aeho's 1908 essay on the history of *minjok,* which redirected "people's loyalty toward a new all-embracing identity of Koreans as a unique ethnic group."[8] Over time, the very intensity of Japan's assault on the notion of a separate Korean ethnicity entrenched *minjok* as the core identity, making it the means for national survival and later a source of legitimacy that would be contested between North and South Korea. Naturally, in an environment where Communism stood as the self-proclaimed champion of anti-imperialism and mass consciousness in a class struggle against state oppression, the thrust of resistance national identity was directed against elite collaboration and the existing world order. This legacy served North Korean legitimacy claims after 1945 and the progressive critique of the state-centered autocratic rule that kept suppressing democracy in South Korea. Yet, the legacy of anti-Japanese *minjok* also became the crux of conservative strategies to construct an identity that marginalized critics.

Koreans could not take pride in political identity under Japanese rule. The attempts by Japan to take credit for economic development and various symbols of modernization stumbled against perceived injustices in the distribution of wealth along with the disturbing integration with Japan's own economy. All that was left was a rival historiography that separated Korea from both Japan and China, whose dismal fate in the first half of the twentieth century tarnished any close association with it. When Japan pressed assimilation much more intensely in the late 1930s and early 1940s, Koreans naturally clung more ardently to their distinct cultural attributes as the sole means to ensure their nation's survival in the face of Japanese assimilation.

Another disturbingly abnormal situation occurred in the postwar era, when the division of the peninsula left South Koreans clinging to the ethnic identity that kept unity alive even as political and economic national identity forged an unbridgeable divide. South Korean leaders sought legitimacy in continuity with the movement to gain independence that was invigorated in the March 1, 1919, resistance. Sustaining the *minjok* thrust of opposition to Japan blunted North Korea's anti-Japanese and anti-imperialist vehemence. As South Korea found that its ambivalent treatment of democracy cast doubt on its commitment to a "free world" identity and its relatively slow economic advance left unclear the advantages of a "free market" identity, intense *minjok* claims filled some of the vacuum. Given the usual pattern of newly formed Communist states to disown national history apart from class warfare and victimization, South Korea gained an edge with its claim to Tangun and pride in past leaders whom Marxists perceived to be exploiters. Before North Korea changed course to self-reliance and cultural narcissism, *minjok* had served South Korea along with anticommunism as the cornerstone of a widely shared national identity.

A civil war on top of an externally imposed division of a nation preoccupied with ethnic identity put great pressure on efforts to solidify national identity. With the world convulsed by the Cold War between, on one hand, the Soviet Union and its ally China and, on the other hand, the United States and its partners in the United Nations–authorized coalition against the invasion of South Korea, anticommunism was the obvious choice to counter the identity challenge from North Korea. It was possible to demonize the North Koreans as Communists who had perverted the *minjok* identity of the Koreans living north of the 38th Parallel. Whereas Pyongyang labeled the regime in Seoul as collaborators with Japan's colonial rule and lackeys of U.S. imperialism, Seoul viewed Pyongyang as the destroyer of Korean tradition and of the elite that embodied it and also as the tool of Communist expansionism. Each side charged that the other's aggression during the Korean War constituted an attack on the entire *minjok*.[9] The line hardened between two competing *minjok*-based narratives of national identity, while in the shadows one side's Communist ideology clashed with the other's claims for the "free world."

National Identity during the Cold War

The era of the Cold War saw South Korean national identity remain fixated on *minjok* even as it faced ever more serious challenges. Because its earlier focus had been to cast off Japan's colonial rule, the anti-Japan theme remained critical. Also, in the process of constructing a distinct past rooted in Koreanness, the longtime superior status of China had to be repudiated. There were implications too for interpreting dependency on the United States and trusting the international community led by it, because ethnic exclusivity reinforces interests hostile to global integration, such as through foreign ownership. However, another notion of national identity gained ground through the contradiction between democratic ideals introduced after 1945 and betrayals by leaders bent on undermining them. Many who were angry at military coups that had defied assurances of democratization strove for greater political participation in support of *gukmin* identity. Whatever the movements they joined to defend their interests and realize their ideals, such as labor unions and student activist groups, they were reaching for a national identity not just in protest, as had been the case since 1910, but also capable of boosting civic solidarity. The United States and its long-admired ideals contributed to this quest, even as U.S. support for Chun Doo-hwan's dictatorship led to these ideals becoming disassociated from pro-U.S. sentiments.

Park Chung-hee was the most important figure in shaping national identity in the Cold War era. He strove to prioritize economic identity linked to state-centered cultural identity and a political identity on the front line in the struggle against the identity scourge of Communism. He rallied conservatives behind him and kept the progressive opposition on the defensive, primarily through coercion and censorship. Essentially, he wanted to transpose the national identity formed in Meiji Japan to his country, copying the slogan "rich nation, strong army." This involved constructing a strong vertical identity focused on a developmental state that tightly controlled society, favoring select large companies (*chaebol*) amid free market competition. Striving for agreement on the "national essence," Park proposed a combination of anticommunism as a stark choice of accepting the status quo or falling victim to North Korean designs for reunification and, belatedly, a combination of *minjok* and Confucianism as the way to remain faithful to Korea's glorious past. His notion of national identity linked statism rooted in a spirit of self-sacrifice for the nation with military values joined with authoritarianism, and harmony as a means of national cohesion in opposition to a selfish pursuit of individualism or group interests.[10] Although this choice was inspired by his Japanese background and idolization of the Japanese model, he appropriated it as a Korean, twisting the original to allow for personalized, highly centralized dictatorial rule without the bureaucratization and the consensual management style characteristic of Japan.[11]

Rapid economic growth smoothed the way to the acceptance of this identity framework, although Park proved controversial.

Park's approach to national identity was increasingly contested in the 1970s even as South Korean modernization kept bringing dividends. He was vulnerable to *minjung* and democracy identity claims, and anti-communism proved insufficient. To be part of the "free world" and depend on the United States for survival meant to tolerate some trappings of democracy, so each reversal toward repression gave an opening to progressives to press for a democratic identity. Thus, frequent U.S. disapproval and even pressure assisted the opposition to develop. The necessity of normalization with Japan—despite its refusal to offer an apology at all acceptable to the Korean people—energized Park's opponents, revitalizing the *minjung* critique.

Minjok identity capitalized on social discontent with the state-*chaebol* nexus and repression. It drew effectively on symbols of the independence movement by associating mass anti-Japanese struggles with resistance from below to injustice at the top that persists. Historians and cultural writers kept alive *minjok* themes that cast suspicion on Park's normalization of relations with Japan, failure to find a way to advance talks with North Korea, and limited appeal to sovereignty concerns. If the upwardly mobile older generation showed little concern for Park and Chun's lack of *minjok* authenticity, the democratization movement of the 1980s rallied younger Koreans behind both a broader *minjok* identity and a growing *gukmin* identity. Having long been suppressed in their expression of some themes and influenced by Marxist thinking, many in the newly confident younger generation were intent on establishing national identity clarity. Democracy served as the starting point for forging what critics of the dictatorship considered to be a moral or just nation for the majority of Koreans.

Progressives rallied support behind a civic identity, stressing democracy but extending to a notion of social justice. They criticized Park for elitist Confucianism, gaining ground in the 1960s as normalization with Japan without a proper apology opened him to *minjok* disapproval, increasingly in the 1970s as his disdain for democracy and harsh repressive measures exposed his thirst for power, and at all stages for unfair treatment of the masses caught in unbalanced modernization. Park's inept handling of a burgeoning *gukmin* identity radicalized the progressives. With Marxist-Leninist ideas informing views on the masses and lack of success in reunification fueling criticisms of how sovereignty was being handled, the lingering unpopularity of dictatorial rule allowed an alternate conception of national identity to take hold, especially in the younger generation. As memories of the Korean War faded and rapid economic growth was taken for granted, intellectuals and Christian leaders focused on values resistant to Park's narrow notion of identity.[12] After Chun Doo-hwan used the military to massacre Kwangju student demonstrators, rumors of U.S. approval made anti-Americanism an essential part of the rival identity. High levels of corruption and perceived social injustice that favored some regions over others and a small group of cronies over an expanding elite lent weight to the notion that the masses were failing to reap adequate benefits. Clinging to their dictatorial power even as they lost the struggle over identity, Park and Chun allowed time for the public to become polarized in a manner that would continue until 2011.

In the period of partial liberalization starting in 1983, the student movement was radicalized by Marxist-Leninist thought and sympathy for North Korea, as leaders punished for the Kwangju uprising re-emerged with a new vigor and individuality was subsumed in a "totalizing notion of *minjung*."[13] Repression had repercussions for national identity when it was shifting away from *minjok* and coping with strains from very rapid modernization in an abnormal context of national division and extreme dependency on the United States. The combination of democratization and the end of the Cold War removed old constraints, as identity debates intensified.

National Identity in the Post–Cold War Period

Conservatives clung to power to 1998, but they were challenged to set forth a vision of national identity that would prove more appealing to the Korean electorate than the emerging progressive narrative. Because they had been handicapped by discontinuities with the discredited era of military dictatorship and newly exposed corruption, they needed to reconstruct national identity in an era of globalization and regionalization. With anticommunism suddenly discredited by *nordpolitik* toward Moscow and Beijing and *minjok* appeals to exclusivity and homogeneity losing their attractiveness while efforts to find common ground with other states in regional and global arenas took priority, the struggle over identity took sudden turns depending especially on ties to North Korea and the United States. Already demographic changes were leading more Koreans to live abroad and return from abroad and to an influx of migrants, many being Chinese Koreans. The meaning of Koreanness defied earlier simplifications.

One conservative approach was to try to marginalize *minjok,* to develop more mature ties with the United States and Japan that would keep them from reemerging as national identity obsessions, and to reinforce state-centered claims to pride combining economic, political, and cultural identity. But the first nuclear crisis in 1993–94 exposed the limited value of recent diplomatic diversification for raising political identity, and the Asian financial crisis of 1997–98 damaged the viability of economic pride as a sustainable pillar for national identity. Dependence on the United States was highlighted in both crises. Moreover, overtures to Japan collapsed as the history issue regained the spotlight, reigniting *minjok* emotions. The failure of Roh Tae-woo and Kim Young-sam to refocus national identity left an opening for the progressives to combine *minjok* and *gukmin* ideas into a narrative with increasing appeal in the late 1990s and first half of the 2000s.

Kim Young-sam was the critical figure in the conservative effort to hold back the progressive momentum in redefining national identity. Having succeeded Roh Tae-woo—who, as a former military man handpicked by his close associate Chun Doo-hwan, continued to be the object of vilification—Kim was seen as restoring civilian rule and opening the door to the flowering of civil society. His early popularity gave conservatives a chance to solidify a worldview suitable for the post–Cold War era. Yet Kim failed to capitalize on his record of opposition to the military dictatorship when he wavered in dealing with punishment of his two predecessors for their role in the "insurrection" against democratic institutions and in massive corruption, as if this would be in the interest of "national unity."[14] After finally being tried and convicted, they were granted amnesty. As labor unions rallied support against new legislation to rein in their unruliness by rekindling marches through the streets, the Asian financial crisis undermined the crux of economic national identity. This might have dealt a powerful blow to overall national identity, but the Sunshine Policy suddenly put South Korea at the center of diplomatic ferment that raised its political identity and resuscitated *minjok* as the easy answer for solving the conundrum of reunification.

Gi-wook Shin sees *minjok,* in which shared bloodline is the primary criterion, as continuing to form the nucleus of South Korean national identity—for instance, in the intense display of national pride during the 2002 World Cup. He explains its rise as a response to Japan's colonial racism and assimilation, as Koreans kept struggling to differentiate themselves from their oppressors by insisting on their uniqueness with symbols drawn from history, language, and literature. Shin argues that leaders of South Korea in the face of a divided nation relied heavily on *minjok*—Syngman Rhee making it rather than democracy the "rhetorical basis of his anticommunist ideology"; Park Chung-hee insisting that values found in Korean history are critical to national regeneration and modernization; and pro-unification discourse under the Sunshine Policy breathing new life into it.[15] Indeed, Shin terms Kim Dae-jung's engagement of North Korea a turning point that promoted the common identity of all Koreans, reverberating in anti-Americanism when symbolic differences with the United States rose to the surface. Yet Shin's content analysis of newspapers on the left and right points to two distinct identities coming into increasing conflict.[16]

A further spurt in *minjok* came from a combination of the "Korean wave" of popular television dramas and movies at home and across East Asia and progressive moves to stir emotions—toward the United States in 2002–3, toward Japan in 2005 and afterward, and in an opposite sense toward North Korea.[17] (The Korean wave heightened pride in a distinct culture gaining popularity abroad, but it also pointed to *gukmin* themes of a mature civil society, in contrast to North Korea.) Pride was not built on a lasting foundation; the sensitivities associated with *minjok* gained new life.[18] This approach divided South Koreans in vain hopes of drawing North Koreans closer. When it lost support, progressives clung to it even in the face of Kim Jong-il's refusal to reciprocate hardly any of the overtures of Kim Dae-jung and Roh Moo-hyun. The election of Lee Myung-bak in 2007, and the North Korean belligerence over the next three years, further undermined the appeal of *minjok*. Instead, *gukmin* identity was rising, as seen in diplomatic choices that kept testing the South's leaders.

National Identity in 2010 and Diplomatic Challenges

In the 1980s, South Koreans were consumed by the abnormality of national identity. Although their shared objective was to democratize and remove the stain of failing to uphold ideals professed since the U.S. occupation and expected of a rising free market economy, many were hopeful that normality would extend to an end to anticommunism; success in overcoming the humiliation associated with Japan; and a shift in the balance of dependency on the United States, isolation from China, and, especially, dangerous hostility with North Korea. The allure of reunification drove progressive thinking compounded by a sense of injustice over elite-skewed internal policies and U.S.-skewed foreign policies. Because direct lines to Pyongyang were hard to develop, diplomacy acquired exceptional significance for a national identity imbued with *minjok* notions of brotherhood clashing with *gukmin* notions of shared values.

Progressives and even conservatives to a degree were tempted by a vision of national identity dependent on shared *minjok* emotions that would, after trust had been built, overwhelm other considerations. Once Koreans on both sides of the Demilitarized Zone started meeting in family reunions, forming Olympic joint teams, and forging economic joint ventures the barriers would naturally fall. If leaders in North Korea were too suspicious to approve such interactions without tight controls, diplomatic finesse would break the ice—as would *minjok* sincerity. The Cold War stood in the way of the diplomatic prerequisites of this shortcut to a "normal" identity. So, many assumed, had the rigid anticommunism of military dictators. Democratization from below was needed for *minjok* to flower. As it proceeded and Moscow abandoned the Cold War while Beijing normalized diplomatic relations with Seoul in search of economic regionalism, the preconditions appeared to be in place for convincing North Korea that the road to reunification was open. Assuming that the era of overdependence on the United States was ending, many pondered how best to appeal to the shared *minjok* aspirations in North Korea for normality through unification.

The budding idealism of the late 1980s gained momentum in the early 1990s with post–Cold War talks with the North Koreans; then with the Agreed Framework of 1994, in which U.S.–North Korean tensions were reduced; and finally with the burst of sympathy and optimism of the late 1990s as a famine-stricken North Korea agreed to the Sunshine Policy. The June 15, 2000, summit of the Koreas capped this uplifting transformation. It seemed only natural that both sides would share in the prospects for *minjok* fulfillment. Moreover, the diplomatic stars seemed aligned for South Korea to win the trust of the North and proceed toward reunification.

Various assumptions about the great powers undergird this reasoning. First, no matter how important the United States was in enabling South Korea to survive and prosper, its priority for the alliance and hostility to North Korea do not serve the fostering of shared *minjok* on the way to reunification. Thus, suspicions of its motives and an urge to escape its grasp, including its national identity shadow, are at the core of the search for diplomatic diversification. Distrust by the progressives of the United States was not intended to break the alliance, at least in the short run, but to free South Korea to pursue an autonomous policy toward North Korea and to leverage improved relations with China into some sort of Asian regionalism. Given the elite's expanding Americanization, to a degree without parallel in Japan or China, the *minjung* element of progressive identity mitigated against U.S. dependency.

Japan figured into the diplomatic narrative as an object of retribution but also a secondary partner in increased regional balancing. Given more options, it was now possible to criticize Japan more forthrightly while simultaneously seeking its help in persuading the United States to accept a new reality and forging a favorable regional environment for the complicated task of steering North Korea toward new objectives. *Minjok* continued to demonize Japan as it began to idealize North Korea, but conservatives were pressing for a different orientation more favorable to the United States and Japan as partners in advocating universal values. Tensions between *minjok* and *gukmin* are increasingly felt in attitudes toward Japan. The former developed in reaction to Japan and kept resentments in the forefront. The latter was amenable to finding common ground with a country that shared democratic values and opposed threats to suppress them. In 2005, Roh aggravated the emotional approach, but starting in 2008 Lee emphasized the universal values shared with Japan. As cultural ties to Japan deepened and the North Korean aura of *minjok* faded, the prospect arose that careful, joint management of Japanese–South Korean relations would shift the balance.

China served as a convenient foil for those seeking rebalancing of identity. If memories of its defense of the North in the Korean War had not faded for the older generation, younger persons were more influenced by its pragmatic economic ties to the South and the uncritical coverage of its aspirations since normalization in line with the consensus not to alienate it. The prevailing assumption was that China had become embarrassed by North Korea's brutish rhetoric and stubborn rejection of economic reform, but China would continue to coax it toward joining a regional framework for economic integration and stability. There was little mention of China's national identity or its interest in dominating the peninsula. Indeed, as the Sunshine Policy advanced, optimism was high that China was facilitating South Korean initiatives while the George W. Bush administration had started frustrating them.

In 2004, Seoul's diplomatic pursuit of a national identity fix came crashing down. China acquired more negative meaning for national identity with the Koguryo dispute. Roh Moo-hyun failed to offer reassurance about security, and his national identity narrative proved unconvincing. Above all, the dichotomy of North Korea and the United States shifted abruptly starting in 2006, as the former tested a nuclear weapon and failed to reciprocate Roh's generosity while the latter accommodated South Korean concerns and reemerged as the bedrock of national security. Shifting from *minjok* to *gukmin* identity accelerated, as conservatives regained the initiative.

The diplomatic illusion of the 1990s and 2000s was dispelled by a reawakening that North Korea is Communist with a notion of *minjok* incompatible with that of the South and that China's pursuit of Sinocentrism and even hegemony on the peninsula leaves South Korean national identity under stress. Rather than a threat from U.S. identity or just resistance to Japanese identity, South Koreans were endangered by North Korean identity and even by Chinese national identity. This reawakening was complete in 2010, when the North's acts of aggression and China's indifference cost progressives much of their dwindling support as conservatives turned more centrist in downplaying *minjok* and concerns over Japan. The transition was boosted by Kan Naoto's skillful handling of the hundredth anniversary of the annexation of Korea and Obama's fulsome support of South Korea. An alternative vision of regionalism in the broader Asia-Pacific region supplanted hopes for an exclusive East Asian community.

Looking back, one can see an obsession with *minjok* undercutting both trust in the United States and internationalism during the Cold War and then contributing to the brief North Korean spell after 2000. Continued provocations from Japan, whose ties to *minjok* emotionalism were sustained, also worked against a balanced identity. In 2010, the international environment and North Korean belligerence produced what seemed likely to be a turning point. With illusions shattered, attention could shift to less divisive domestic politics and more consensus on bolstering a shared *gukmin* identity. Instead of anticommunism narrowly defining international goals, a proud South Korea saw itself in the forefront of the international community, including the Group of Twenty, and as a active force for combining economic, political, and cultural initiatives, including Lee Myung-bak's New Asia diplomacy launched in Indonesia in 2009 and reinvigorated in his travel to Southeast Asia in 2010. China's aggressive attempt to narrow regionalism had backfired, and Lee seized the opportunity with Obama.

When anticommunism was at the core of national identity, views of the United States were favorable. When the Sunshine Policy displaced lingering anticommunism and spurred sympathy toward North Korea, anti-Americanism grew. Then, when North Korean belligerence eroded the remaining sympathy and only the U.S. alliance offered some degree of security, anti-Americanism faded rapidly. This roller coaster ride is revealing of the depth of emotions associated with bilateral ties to the United States and the power of aspirations for reunification of the peninsula. The former challenges *minjok* because the United States represents globalization with a focus on shared culture as well as a security community resistant to shared threats. Indeed, anti-Americanism was a kind of outburst to revive *minjok* after it appeared to be in jeopardy. Often conservatives are perceived as the principal supporters of the cultural identity at the core of *minjok,* but in South Korea as well as Japan strong dependence on a single ally created ambivalence among conservatives and opened the door to progressive enthusiasm for cultural defensiveness rooted in idealistic thinking about the role of the masses in history. Although there is considerable merit in correlating perceptions of threat from North Korea with positive views of the United States,[19] this perspective does not suffice to capture the impact of national identity.

Gukmin identity was incubated by the U.S. occupation and the ideals cited in the ups and downs of more than two decades of dictatorial tendencies. Both the democratization movement of the 1980s and the abrupt transfers of power to new presidents, including from conservatives to progressives and back, helped to mature the identity of a full-fledged democratic state. Progressives had reason to separate this identity from U.S. identity, criticizing U.S. leaders for standing in the way of the democracy movement. Yet their refusal to raise the human rights issue regarding North Korea and deference to China in inserting values into foreign policy revealed a distorted notion of *gukmin,* which still was laced with *minjung* anti-elitism. Finally, with the election of Lee Myung-bak and the disillusionment with both North Korea and China, the case has been strengthened for *gukmin* identity supportive of the U.S. alliance and U.S. ideals as applied to international relations.

Public Opinion and National Identity

In contrast to the dissonance between public sentiment and competing forms of national identity articulated by the conservative and progressive political elites to the end of the progressive era, public sentiment today affirms Lee's modifications to national identity, particularly as it relates to the diplomatic flashpoints of the U.S.-alliance and North Korea. *Gukmin* identity has shifted back to a conservative, anti–North Korean, anticommunist, and pro–United States orientation. Older generations nurtured in the Cold War are most supportive, middle generations coming of age in the heady 1980s are most against, and the younger generations disillusioned by failed progressive leadership at once supportive yet also less ideologically fixed. Overall, public opinion in 2010 has shown a significant increase in the willingness of South Koreans to accept the status quo of a split peninsula in the long run, subduing the mandates of *minjok* identity, such as unification, on behalf of benefits in strengthened *gukmin* identity, such as security and economic cooperation with the United States and Japan.

A study comparing public opinion in 2005 and 2010, the halfway points of both the Roh and Lee presidencies, reveals an increasingly sober and reluctant attitude toward the axiom of unification.[20] On the one hand, South Koreans have become sharply more negative toward North Korea, echoing the attitude of earlier conservative periods. From 2005 to 2010, the percentage characterizing the North as an "enemy" or "the other" doubled, while the proportion of those that see it as "a brother," "one of us," or "a neighbor" has gone down. Moreover, whereas in 2005 South Koreans felt more affinity toward North Korea than any of its most significant regional partners, in 2010, they placed North Korea last, behind the United States, Japan, and China, in that order. Affinity toward the United States and Japan notably rose, as the percentage of South Koreans showing a preference for a strengthened United States–South Korea alliance surpassed the percentage supporting "independent diplomacy."

On the other hand, though such trends reflect a return to conservative views of identity, public opinion shows a greater willingness to forgo the goal of unification, diverging from both the conservative and progressive versions of national identity. In the past five years, the proportion of South Koreans who limit sovereign territory to strictly the southern half of the peninsula nearly doubled, from 25.8 to 45.3 percent, while the proportion who do not view unification as a necessity rose sharply, from 7.9 to 19.3 percent. The most dramatic, change, however, was the increase of those "not willing to make any payments for the cost of reunification," which rose from 30.4 to 60.5 percent.

These shifts provide compelling evidence that *gukmin* identity is taking precedence in the South Korean psyche. South Koreans are increasingly tolerant of, if not satisfied with, the notion that striving for a unified state is not worth the potential costs and damage that might be inflicted on the state they already have. Koreans may be bound by blood, but South Koreans are also bound by the success of their state, which, unlike the promises of *minjok* identity, is tangibly in their hands and for them to lose. Accordingly, they are deemphasizing the role of Tangun, while preferring to use South Korean symbols, such as the national flag (*taegukgi*), to characterize their national identity. As enthusiasm builds toward the "South Korean brand" as an appealing image on the international stage, the positive tones of *gukmin* identity are replacing the negativity in *minjok* victimization.

Gukmin identity has clearly risen as a force that tempers *minjok* identity, but *minjok* identity continues to have vitality. Aspects of it, such as consanguinity, may be on the wane, but it has yet to face an existential challenge. Though the recent trend in public opinion of dwindling enthusiasm for unification is notable, the unprecedented *gukmin* identity, as it currently stands, is incapable of motivating wholesale abandonment of unification and, therefore, *minjok* identity as well. As *gukmin* identity creates a wider gulf between the two Koreas, it is still possible that there will be a resurgence in *minjok* identity, as occurred during the progressive era. One test of conservative leadership is whether it can find a balanced approach to its own *minjok* tendencies in order to make them more harmonious, in the long run, with *gukmin* identity.

Conclusion

Abnormal circumstances of national identity taking shape under conditions of peril led to a one-sided emphasis on *minjok*. A divided country in which progressive aspirations were excessively suppressed and then rebounded with democratization and post–Cold War hopes for reunification sustained *minjok* popularity, even as it was being increasingly challenged. Diplomatic diversification became focused on moves to change North Korea, but the diplomatic environment changed abruptly by 2010. Renewed reliance on the United States heightened support for shared values as well as a South Korean national identity less inclined to exceptionalism and to regional leadership. Instead, a greater global leadership role is welcomed in partnership with the United States. After two decades when progressives drove the national identity debate, conservatives regained the offensive and were building a broad consensus.

Although pragmatism toward China and remorse about North Korea linger, the shift in South Korean national identity toward pride in democracy and globalization favors a centrist approach—in contrast to the former progressive agenda. The sway of ethnic identification with North Korea and diplomatic diversification offered some appeal, but other forces have overwhelmed the ones that peaked in the period 2000–2007. Concern about a North Korean nuclear threat and an assertive China reviving Sinocentrism coincide with reduced concern about U.S. unilateralism and Japanese revisionism. As *minjok* loses ground amid globalization, *gukmin* benefits from a rejection of the progressive *minjung* theme and a reaffirmation of universal values. Conservatives can no longer capitalize on these trends to revive elements of the *minjok* identity they advocated or the elitist policies dictators favored. By recognizing the continued quest for a just society and the special vulnerability of a state dependent on China's economy and on the front line in a newly tense region, they can mitigate the danger of drifting away from centrist approaches. Given the unpredictability of North Korea and its economic dependency on China, further diplomatic challenges capable of shaking national identity assumptions are unavoidable.

Notes

1. Martina Deuchler, *Confucian Gentlemen and Barbarian Envoys* (Seattle: University of Washington Press, 1977).

2. JaHyun Kim Haboush, "The Confucianization of Korean Society," in *The East Asian Region: Confucian Heritage and Its Modern Adaptation,* edited by Gilbert Rozman (Princeton, N.J.: Princeton University Press, 1991), 84–110.

3. Hahm Chaihark, "Ritualism and Constitutionalism: Disputing the Ruler's Legitimacy in a Confucian Polity," *American Journal of Comparative Law* 57 (2009): 301–68.

4. Andre Schmid, *Korea between Empires 1896–1919* (New York: Columbia University Press, 2002), 171–98.

5. Ibid., 253.

6. Henry H. Em, "*Minjok* as a Modern and Democratic Construct: Sin Ch'aeho's Historiography," in *Colonial Modernity in Korea,* edited by Gi-Wook Shin and Michael Robinson (Cambridge, Mass.: Harvard East Asian Monographs, 1999), 349–54.

7. Michael Robinson, "Broadcasting, Cultural Hegemony, and Colonial Modernity in Korea, 1924–1945," in *Colonial Modernity in Korea,* ed. Shin and Robinson, 52–69.

8. Henry H. Em, "*Minjok* as a Modern and Democratic Construct: Sin Ch'aeho's Historiography," in *Colonial Modernity,* ed. Shin and Robinson, 342.

9. Andrew Kim, "Understanding South Korean National Identity and Its Bilateral Implications in Northeast Asia," senior thesis, Woodrow Wilson School, Princeton University, 2010, 39.

10. Chung-in Moon and Byung-joon Jun, "Modernization Strategies: Ideas and Influences," in *The Park Chung Hee Era: The Transformation of South Korea,* edited by Byung-Kook Kim and Ezra F. Vogel (Cambridge, Mass.: Harvard University Press, 2011), 117–22.

11. Byung Kook Kim, "Introduction," in *Park Chung Hee Era,* ed. Kim and Vogel, 14–20.

12. Myung-Lim Park, "The Chaeya," in *Park Chung Hee Era,* ed. Kim and Vogel, 373–400.

13. Namhee Lee, "The South Korean Student Movement: Undongkwan as a Counterpublic Sphere," in *Korean Society: Civil Society, Democracy, and the State,* edited by Charles K. Armstrong (London: Routledge, 2002), 142–56.

14. Sunhyuk Kim, "Civil Society and Democratization," in *Korean Society,* ed. Armstrong, 99.

15. Gi-Wook Shin, *Ethnic Nationalism in Korea: Genealogy, Politics, and Legacy* (Stanford, Calif.: Stanford University Press, 2006), 54, 101–9,185–203.

16. Gi-Wook Shin, *One Alliance, Two Lenses: U.S.-Korean Relations in a New Era* (Stanford, Calif.: Stanford University Press, 2010).

17. Baek Wondam, *Dongasia oe munhwa sontaek: Hanryu* (Seoul: Pentagram, 2005).

18. Gilbert Rozman, "South Korea's National Identity Sensitivity: Evolution, Manifestations, Prospects," *Academic Series on Korea 2010* (Washington, D.C.: Korea Economic Institute), 67–80.

19. Heon Joo Jung, "The Rise and Fall of Anti-American Sentiment in South Korea: Deconstructing Hegemonic Ideas and Threat Perception," *Asian Survey* 50, no. 5 (2010); 946–64.

20. "Hangukin jungchesung josa," ARI, EAI, and *Joongang Daily,* http://www.asiaticresearch.org/bbs/view.php?bbs=ari_free_01&uid=404.

Chapter 8

Unraveling National Identity in South Korea: *Minjok* and *Gukmin*

Chung-in Moon

Despite the forces of globalization, nationalism has continued to profoundly influence the dynamics of domestic politics and foreign policy behavior in South Korea. Not only have contending interpretations of Korean national history precipitated acute domestic political conflicts between conservatives and progressives;[1] intense popular sentiments also have at times tarnished otherwise friendly relations with China, Japan, and the United States.[2] Such anomalous developments can be attributed to a combination of factors—such as the continuing negative collective memory of Japanese colonial rule, the politicization of nationalist agendas for domestic purposes by contending social forces, intensified concern about how to deal with national division, and over-

The author would like to acknowledge Gilbert Rozman and David Leheny for insightful comments; the Brain Korea–21 project, Department of Political Science, Yonsei University, for research support; and Pil-young Lee and Hyun-seok Shin for research assistance.

confidence from an elevated image of the economic and political status of Korea on the world stage.

National identity is central to the nationalist discourse and continues to shape its form and content. Unraveling this identity is complicated because of its multiple and even confusing meanings in the Korean language, which mirror problems in other languages. Most scholars regard national identity as *minjok* (ethnic identity centered on the Korean bloodline, shared history, common language, and culture), but some equate it to *gukmin* (civic and political identity rooted in nation or citizenship). One also can find the notion of *gukga* (state) identity, which is closely related to *gukmin,* emerging through the contestation of elites vying to shape public consciousness and endow the state with emotional qualities. Recognizing these as discrete, contending terms within Korean discourse, in this chapter I discuss forces that shape South Korean identity and the implications of this mixture in its manifestations.

The first section of the chapter presents an analytical overview of the elements of South Korea's national identity identified just above. The second examines the basis of *minjok* identity and how it influences domestic and foreign policy. The third looks into the foundation of *gukmin* identity, exploring the civic components of identity and noting how debates over *gukga* and *gukmin* affect both domestic political and foreign policy orientations. The conclusion draws some comparative implications within East Asia.

Analytical Notes on *Minjok and Gukmin*

Samuel Huntington argues that "identity requires differentiation. Differentiation necessitates comparison, the identification of the ways in which 'our' group differs from 'their' group. Comparison, in turn, generates evaluation, . . . conflicting justification, competition, and antagonism."[3] Identity, thus, presupposes an individual or group's distinctive selfhood and solidarity, ultimately emphasizing sameness.[4] In the case of South Korea, talk of sameness has long centered upon the notion of "ethnic identity," with a focus on either shared bloodlines and ancestry or, more broadly, primordial attributes such as territory; ethnoracial origins; and common historical, linguistic, and cultural roots.[5] As Kim Byung-kook puts it, Koreans are "Tangun's daughters and sons, bound together by 'consanguineous' ties, acculturated in a unique large yearning for a common homeland."[6] This view corresponds to the ethnic-blood model proposed by Anthony D. Smith,[7] a primordial perspective that emphasizes common ancestry, history, language, and culture. To its proponents, Tangun's ancient founding of Korea is not mythology but a historical reality, and the blood ties originating from shared ancestry make all Koreans part of an extended family.[8] This view has been inspired by such pioneering historiographers as Shin Chae-ho and Park Eun-sik, who reconceptualized the past not as dynastic history but as a history of a *minjok:* "Without the *minjok,* there is no history; without history, the *minjok* cannot have a clear perception of the state; . . . a state is an organic entity formed from the national spirit (*minjok jongshin*)."[9] The popularity of this ethnic concept of national identity was pronounced during Japanese colonial rule, shaping the foundation of postwar ethnic nationalism.

After South Korea achieved national independence, *gukmin* identity became more relevant, and nationalism was seen as an instrument of realizing the goals (e.g., modernization and national unification) of a new sovereign state.[10] National identity has been increasingly identified with the *gukga,* manifested in a preferred ideology, governance mechanism, and policy orientation.[11] The Constitution that serves as the foundation of governance is one indicator of state identity; however, interpretations are often subject to intense contestation among competing political elites. Debates on *guksi* (the leading principle of the state) define the essence of this identity. Although national independence, free markets, democracy, and anticommunism have constituted the core of *guksi,* its operational meanings and manifestations have been continually contested, mostly between the conservative and progressive camps.[12] The nature of *gukga,* thus, depends on who has political power and what governing ideology they profess.

The state consists of territory, people, and sovereignty. Gellner argues that the goal of nationalism is to satisfy the principle of the congruence of the political and the national unit, but state formation alters the environment in which *minjok* and *gukmin* coexist.[13] Civic national identity is concerned with the identity of a national population, which shares a feeling of covariance, of rising and fall together,[14] but the civic nation becomes much more encompassing and influential after the creation of a nation-state. North Koreans and overseas Koreans holding foreign nationality are part of the *minjok,* but they cannot be members of the *gukmin* of South Korea. More than a million foreigners residing in Korea who have acquired South Korean citizenship are not ethnic Koreans, but they form an integral part of the national population. The civic nation is usually manifested in two forms. One is an external dimension affecting people's perceptions of outside actors. National pride, emotional attachment, and a sense of belongingness and loyalty to the state, all indicators of patriotism, can be seen as attributes of civic national identity. Loyalty to national symbols such as the national flag (*Taegukgi*), national flower (*mugungwha*), and national anthem (*Aigukga*) exemplifies this attitude. The other is an internal dimension involving the degree of unity or division over important creeds. A citizen's attitude toward these can vary according to ideological, generational, regional, and class status. External differentiation and internal harmonization characterize civic national identity. Here I argue that *minjok* has waned, whereas *gukmin* has become more pronounced. Patriotism has become more influential than ethnic nationalism in affecting behavior.

Minjok: Embedded or Diluted?

National identity in South Korea has long been understood in terms of ethnic identity, but its ethnic "embeddedness" has become increasingly questionable. As Andre Schmid persuasively contends through an in-depth analysis of newspapers in the late 1890s and early 1900s, *minjok* was invented by historiographers such as Shin Chae-ho in order to come to terms with Japan's invasion and to escape from Chinese influence.[15] In a recent study of its origin, Park Chan-seung argues that the concept did not exist before the Japanese colonial period. Japan had introduced the European concept of nation as *minzoku* in the 1870s, and this was reintroduced as *minjok* in Korea in 1906, in part, owing to Liang Qichao, who popularized the term (*minzu*) in China. According to Park, the Western concept of nation, which was predicated on equality among members of a national population, was inconceivable during the Chosun Dynasty, which was characterized by a stratified feudal class society. King Jeongjo had used the term *dongpo* (brethren or compatriots*), but its meaning fell short of *minjok*.[16]

Empirically speaking, the oneness of the Korean people based on shared bloodline and ancestry seems controversial. For example, of 275 family names in Korea, 136 are naturalized.[17] Long interaction with

China, a century of Mongolian rule, and frequent foreign invasions increased chances for interracial mixing, undercutting claims of the pure blood school. A recent genetic survey also shows that 70 to 80 percent of Koreans are of northern origin—from such places as Manchuria, Siberia, and Central Asia—whereas 20 to 30 percent originated mostly in Southeast Asia.[18]

A poll conducted by the Ministry of Gender and Family Affairs in September 2007 also reveals changing aspects of South Korean ethnic national identity. A total of 72.6 percent of 1,000 respondents answered that Korean people do not have to insist on pure blood or the oneness of the Korean race, and 79.4 percent showed a favorable attitude toward foreigners who married Koreans, marking a sharp contrast with the past.[19] A more intriguing development is the attitude of young people toward the ethnic nation. A total of 49.8 percent of 6,160 student respondents replied that they would have liked to have been born in another country rather than in South Korea, and just 52.6 percent responded that "Koreans are one nation [*minjok*]."[20] In a country where emigration is often viewed as an act of betrayal to the *minjok* and *gukga,* this response is quite astonishing.

According to proponents of ethnic nationalism, all Koreans are one in their origin, and they are brothers and sisters without any hierarchy or stratification, but such a claim is contradicted by reality. In the case of North Korean defectors living in South Korea, they have already become second-class citizens despite their legitimate legal status as citizens. They face discrimination in social status and economic opportunities because of difficulties in communications along with South Korean distrust.[21] Koreans residing in Korea stand on the top of the ethnic hierarchy, followed by overseas Koreans in the United States and Japan, Korean-Chinese (Chosunjok), overseas Koreans who do not understand the Korean language (e.g., Koreiskie in Russia and Central Asia), and finally foreigners who migrate to Korea for interracial marriages. South Koreans have a dubious attitude toward North Korean defectors, who are increasingly placed at the bottom of the hierarchy. In addition, South Korea's ethnic composition has also been changing, refuting the myth of "one ethnic nation." Those who migrated to South Korea from abroad rose from 34,710 in 2002 to 104,749 in 2007. This number is on the rise due to demographic changes, leaving a shortage of laborers. Along with this, the number of resident foreigners with permanent status had risen to 1.17 million by October 2008.[22]

Language and religion are attributes of *minjok*. The importance of language as an ethnic attribute has remained rather unchanged, although there is increasing linguistic heterogeneity between North and South Korea. Yet the South has increasingly become a multilinguistic society in which English, and to a lesser extent Chinese, are challenging the monopolistic position of Hangul; linguistic nationalism based on Hangul could soon be seriously challenged. Religion has gone through a major transformation: from Buddhism in the Koryo Dynasty to Confucianism, given a religious status in the Chosun Dynasty, and, increasingly, in the twentieth century, to a mixture of Buddhism and Christianity. As these two religions continue to compete with each other, the Confucian tradition continues to decline, albeit providing norms for social interactions. Some Christian fundamentalists express a desire to make South Korea a Christian nation, but religion can no longer serve as a common denominator underlying ethnic national identity. Excessive Christian missionary activities have recently become a source of social division.

An emphasis on ethnic identity and nationalism has recently become a subject of political contestation between conservatives and progressives. The New Right Movement has accused the previous progressive government of misusing and abusing mass nationalist sentiments for an anti-American and pro–North Korean leftist agenda. Its proponents argue that the primacy of *minjok* in favor of unconditional Korean unification during the progressive decade not only weakened the country's national security posture but also undermined the South Korean–U.S. alliance.[23] Lee Young-hoon, a professor of Korean economic history at Seoul National University and a leader of the New Right intellectuals, seeks to erase vestiges of nationalism and ethnic national identity by claiming that "*minjok* is not a concrete entity. It is nothing but an imagined community that old Koreans discovered in the twentieth century under the Japanese colonial repression" and that "nationalism belongs to the dark spiritual history of an old imperial age before 1945."[24] But this perspective constitutes a minority view, and the primordial perspective based on ethnic identity continues to be influential. Some historians even go further by claiming that the Tangun's Chosun was not only a historical entity but also was a common cradle of Northeast Asian civilization. They are now carrying out archeological field work to prove their point empirically.[25]

Of ethnic national attributes, historical identity seems still influential in affecting foreign policy on China and Japan. A majority of Koreans

believe in the perennial nature of Korean ethnic history and are sensitive to attempts to alter or downgrade it.[26] They are proud of Korea's
role in transmitting Buddhist and Confucian culture to Japan. To many,
the Koguryo Dynasty is the ultimate source of ethnic and historical
pride not only for its success in conquering most of Manchuria but also
in projecting power all the way to China's capital in AD 404.[27] Such
pride resulted in outrage over China's Northeastern Project, which
treated the dynasty as part of Chinese border history. What angered
South Koreans was the publication of their findings in the Chinese
daily newspaper, *Guangming Ribao,* on June 24, 2003. The article argued that "the history of the Koguryo Dynasty was part of Chinese
history and that Koguryo was a decentralized local government of
China."[28] It presented evidence to justify its claim: (1) Koguryo was
located in Chinese territory; (2) Koguryo's activities were delimited to
four counties of the Han Dynasty (Han si jun); (3) Koguryo maintained sovereign-subject relations with successive generations of
Chinese dynasties; (4) Koguryo subjects were incorporated into the
Chinese Han race after its dissolution; (5) and there was no historical
continuity between Koguryo and Koryo, not only because of the absence of a blood line, but also because of the 250-year interval.[29]

South Koreans were outraged. Anti-Chinese protests became widespread, and perceptions of China drastically deteriorated. According
to one survey conducted on December 13, 2006, 89 percent of respondents answered that they felt threatened by the rise of China's military
power.[30] Another survey showed that favorable perceptions of China
dropped from 65.3 to 44 percent from 2005 to 2007, whereas those of
the United States rose to 60.8 percent.[31] Although a high-level Chinese
government delegation in 2004 reached a diplomatic compromise, perceptions of China remained negative.

Preoccupation with ethnic (historic) identity was also a source of
conflict with Japan. On February 23, 2005, the Shimane Prefectural
Council introduced an ordinance designating February 22 as "Takeshima
Day," which also urged the Japanese government to recover Dokdo
Island off the east coast of South Korea from an illegal occupation.
Koreans were especially affronted by the move, believing that imperial
Japan had annexed Dokdo by force to Shimane prefecture the same
day a hundred years earlier as a trophy of its victory in the Russo-
Japanese War. Most Koreans regarded Japan's uncompromising atti-
tude as an unjustifiable assault on their territorial integrity and their
collective memory of the past.

Ethnic identity, reflected in a historical sense of the distinctiveness of the Korean nation, played a profound role in shaping responses to the way China and Japan treated their country. Ethnic identity is still embedded in Korea society, but its depth and intensity appear to vary by its diverse attributes. Although racial or blood attributes seem to be on the wane, historical identity does not show any signs of weakening. The unflagging strength of nationalism comes from this historical view of ethnic identity. Although postmodernists and even conservative intellectuals associated with the New Right Movement have been trying to deconstruct ethnic, historical, and cultural identity, all types of people on the political spectrum still support the primordial identity and even capitalize on it for their political gains. Thus, the ethnic component of national identity is likely to be a major factor affecting policy toward neighboring countries and North Korea, but its impact on domestic politics remains rather minimal.

Gukmin-Gukga: Between Consensus and Contestation

State identity took shape through Koreans' efforts to establish an independent nation-state and the termination of Japanese colonial rule. Elite visions of a new nation-state were incorporated into the Constitution as a comprehensive legal, normative, and ideological foundation. This 1948 document emphasized historical legitimacy stemming from the independence movement and the Shanghai provisional government, a democratic republican form of government, and the social democratic ideals of balanced economic development.[32] Yet the Constitution suffered from narrow support because centrists and leftists were excluded from the drafting process. Many opposed acceptance as a signal of the de facto legal division of the Korean nation, blaming a right-wing faction for the formation of a government allied with the American occupation authority.[33]

State identity has changed over time, reflecting changes in the political and social situation. The First Republic (1948–60) emphasized anti-communism, unification by expelling North Korean Communists, national security, centralization of power in the president, and the South Korean–U.S. alliance following the devastating Korean War (1950–53). In contrast, the short-lived Second Republic, which emerged after the 1960 April Student Revolution that toppled Syngman Rhee, focused on democratic governance, decentralization of presidential power through the adoption of a parliamentary system, and citizens' rights. The Third Republic (1963–72), following a military coup on May 16, 1961, restored anticommunism as the leading state ideology, while stressing state-led economic growth backed by social and political stability. The alliance with the United States was seen as the crucial safeguard for national security, despite signs of an eroding American security commitment, and Park Chung-hee sought a more independent, self-reliant defense policy. The Fourth (Yushin, 1972–79) Republic and the Fifth Republic (1980–87) maintained a similar line: the primacy of national security and anticommunism, growth over distribution, stability over democratic governance, and the central role of the U.S. alliance.

The democratic opening in 1987 and the advent of the Sixth Republic reversed the previous trend. Whereas the ideology of anticommunism and the primacy of national security waned, more emphasis was placed on democratic governance and distribution. The end of the cold war system also undermined national security as a deus ex machinae, eroding the importance of the South Korean–U.S. alliance. The progressive *nordpolitik* of the Roh Tae-woo government helped South Korea normalize diplomatic ties with China and the Soviet Union and reach the Basic Agreement on Nonaggression, Reconciliation, and Exchange and Cooperation with North Korea in 1992.

During the progressive decade (1998–2007), this trend was further accelerated. Anticommunism, national security, and growth were replaced by ideological tolerance, peaceful coexistence with North Korea, and equality and welfare. The Kim Dae-jung and Roh Moo-hyun governments attempted to harmonize inter-Korean cooperation with the South Korean–U.S. alliance. Kim was successful in this, but Roh suffered from failing to do so at times. The Lee Myung-bak government was inaugurated in 2008 and was critical of the lost decade under the two progressive leaders. Suggestions for its governing ideology (*guksi*) included a market economy, democracy and the rule of law, the U.S. alliance, "growth first," and creation of a business-friendly environment through such measures as tax reductions and extensive deregulation. In short, state identity has not been fixed; it has been oscillating between the right and the left.

Under Lee, state identity has emerged as an ideological battleground between conservatives and progressives. Progressive forces, which had taken the offensive from 1987 and became the mainstream of Korean society during the decade of Kim Dae-jung and Roh Moo-hyun's rule, were on the defensive, while the conservative forces, which had begun to strike back under Roh, grew assertive. A group of right-wing intellectuals, religious leaders, and nongovernmental organization activists, which formed a loose political and ideological coalition under the heading the New Right Movement, has undertaken sweeping frontal attacks on the progressive camp.[34] Lee explicitly rendered support to them by stating that "there is a very extensive and deep-rooted situation that damages state identity" by undermining the legitimacy of South Korea, liberal democratic order, and market economy.[35] His endorsement triggered a nationwide campaign to reestablish the state's identity, which they claim had been gravely distorted during the progressive decade.

The fiercest battle centered on the revision of Korean history textbooks. As Lee Dong-gwan, a spokesman for the Office of the President, forcefully argued, existing history textbooks are seen as incorporating anti-American, pro–North Korean, and antimarket contexts without filtering.[36] Intellectuals associated with the New Right Movement pointed to major distortions in history textbooks published during the progressive decade: a self-defeating view of contemporary Korean history, systematic delegitimization of the founding of the Republic of Korea (i.e., South Korea), glorification of nationalism and unconditional support for national unification, and an overemphasis on the exploitative nature of Japanese colonial rule.[37] They respond that South Korea is marked with a history of pride, success, and glory. Its downgrading during the progressive decade implanted a self-defeating view of Korean history in the minds of Korean youth, weakening their patriotism. For them, the real hero of the founding of South Korea is Syngman Rhee, who was its first president, not Kim Gu and, therefore, the Shanghai provisional government. Thus, they propose that the National Independence Day of August 15, 1945, should be replaced by the National Founding Day of August 15, 1948, and Rhee should be designated the founding father, despite his autocratic rule. They also place greater emphasis on Park Chung-hee for his contribution to modernization and a strong national security posture. The New Right Movement has condemned Kim Dae-jung, Roh Moo-hyun, and their followers as pro–North Korean leftists, who have defied the constitutional mandate of a market economy and liberal democracy and made too many concessions to North Korea in the name of reunification.

Contending views over Japanese colonial modernity were hotly debated.[38] For progressive historians and intellectuals as well as the ordinary public, Japanese colonial rule was the period of exploitation, underdevelopment, and national shame for Korea and Koreans. But New Right historians such as Ahn Byung-jik and Lee Young-hoon began to raise a revisionist interpretation, arguing that the Korean economy greatly benefited from investments in the industrial foundation, education, and social infrastructure that paved the way to modernization, and Korea's gross national product grew 2.7 times from 1910 to 1940.[39] Some emphasize that the South Korean economic miracle was inconceivable without colonial modernity, a view diametrically opposed to that of the progressives.

The two contending camps have also clashed over policy issues: (1) free market and small government versus regulated market and big government, (2) market-driven growth versus welfare-driven growth, (3) preservation and even strengthening versus abolition or a substantial revision of the National Security Act, (4) an emphasis on private education versus public education, and (5) the rule of law versus freedom of expression and association. The domestic terrain of South Korea is extremely divided, and ideological polarization over state identity has become a source of political instability, along with regionalism.

The question of state identity has been more pronounced in the area of inter-Korean relations and foreign policy. The New Right Movement refers to the progressive period as a "lost decade," during which national security and the South Korean–U.S. alliance were critically compromised for inter-Korean cooperation (*minjok gongjo*). Its proponents have claimed that the Sunshine Policy and unconditional giveaway to the North facilitated its buildup of nuclear weapons and missiles. They believe that because Kim Jong-il has no intention of giving up his nuclear weapons, the best way to dismantle them is to isolate and contain North Korea and to transform the Kim Jong-il regime. To achieve this goal, the South Korean–U.S. alliance should be strengthened and trilateral coordination with Japan should be enhanced. They also contend that bandwagoning with China is a mistake, and such initiatives undertaken by previous governments as the East Asian Community under Kim Dae-jung, and the Northeast Asian Community under Roh Moo-hyun, are unrealistic. Lee Myung-bak has prioritized bilateral initiatives, emphasizing the U.S. alliance.

State identity is most contested between left- and right-wing political forces, oscillating depending on the location of political power. In the midst of Lee's efforts to correct aspects of state identity allegedly distorted by the progressive governments, it is early to predict the triumph of the conservatives. The contestation is not likely to be over soon, because the progressive forces have been striking back. Both domestic politics and foreign policy may be held hostage to this protracted ideological war over state identity.

Gukmin: Divided or United?

Civic national identity refers to the identity of citizens. It began to form in conjunction with the birth of South Korea. Although an overdeveloped state prevented activation of civic national identity during the First Republic, citizens expressed strong patriotism anchored in anti-Japanese sentiments and anticommunism. The devastation of the Korean War through the North Korean invasion of the South was responsible for the rise of anticommunism as the dominant civic national identity; yet this identity was also impaired by social resignation and a lack of economic confidence amid dependence on the United States in the 1950s. Raising civic hope was the political enthusiasm that burst forward on April 19, 1960, when angry students protesting pervasive election fraud, corruption, and autocratic rule toppled Rhee and opened a brief era of democratic governance. But political divisiveness, social chaos, and economic instability following the student revolution precipitated military intervention. Major General Park Chung-hee, who staged the military coup in 1961, ruled South Korea with an iron fist for seventeen years. Whereas he was instrumental in fostering industrialization and ensuring national security, his rule brought numerous negative externalities, including authoritarianism, chronic violation of human rights, and suppression of civil society. Civic national identity during this period was tempered by compliance with authority, preference for social and political stability, and rapid industrialization and export-led growth as the means to stability with slight regard for steps to narrow widening inequalities.

Because openly criticizing the Park regime was not allowed during this period, citizens were cautious about expressing their identity. Their discontent often erupted in the form of student protests against diplomatic normalization with Japan in 1965, the constitutional amendment allowing a third presidential term in 1969, and the adoption of the Yushin Constitution in 1972. Yet the majority of citizens remained rather silent. Their external identity was no different. The indispensability of the U.S. alliance, strong anticommunism, and the primacy of national security over other sociopolitical values remained intact. Given North Korea's military provocations in 1968 and 1969 and the alarm over the Nixon Doctrine (which signaled the United States' gradual military disengagement from Asia by declaring the "Asian defense by Asians"), civic national identity remained basically unchanged.

The expansion of the middle class led to the democratic transition in 1987. As South Koreans enjoyed the double success of economic growth and democratization, they began to seek an international status comparable to their achievements, which in turn fueled patriotism. The nation's successful hosting of the Seoul Olympics heightened this pride. Social paradigms also began to show profound changes. The primacy of growth, national security, and social stability were no longer tolerated. Democratic governance, social distribution and welfare, and peace dividends from the end of the Cold War were deemed more important. The conservative establishment failed to satisfy these demands. In the wake of the financial crisis of 1997 and the protracted confrontation with North Korea, a majority of Koreans voted to give the progressive platform a chance. A decade of progressive rule, however, aroused fatigue. Engagement with North Korea, a renewed emphasis on equality and welfare, and the negation of historical achievements of past conservative regimes`backfired, resulting in another conservative government. Likewise, the way civic national identity deals with historical memory has led to discontinuities.

Korean citizens have shown multiple and sometimes conflicting identities. Kinship relationships, localism and regionalism, patriotism, East Asian regionalism, and globalism appear to coexist. According to one survey, 78.7 percent of 1,038 respondents identified themselves as citizens of the Republic of Korea, followed by the Korean race (66.9 percent), Asians (46.4 percent), members of a provincial unit (39.4 percent), and global citizens (29.4 percent).[40] A survey by Kim Min-jon also reveals strong attachment to the Korean state; 76.7 percent of respondents identified themselves with it, whereas 63.9 percent allied with *minjok* identity and 27.1 percent allied with global identity.[41] The results indicate a high degree of affiliation with the nation-state (*gukmin gukga*). Demonstrations of Korean nationalist zeal—visible in the "Red Devil syndrome" during the 2002 World Cup, anti-American protests over the death of two middle school girls in 2002, and the candlelight vigil over the importing of American beef—were manifestations of a resurgent sense of victimization.[42]

Citizens' perceptions of state identity seem diverse. According to an August 2008 survey by *Kyunghyang shinmun,* a progressive newspaper, 56.4 percent of 1,000 respondents regarded industrialization and economic development as the proudest achievement, whereas only 21.9 percent cited the preservation of human rights and democratization as the most remarkable achievement in the past six decades. A majority (76.4 percent) found the Park Chung-hee regime to be most successful, followed by Kim Dae-jung (7.1 percent), Roh Moo-hyun (4.8 percent), and Syngman Rhee (3.3. percent). A total of 45.1 percent singled out Park as the most respected leader, followed by Kim Gu (28.3 percent), Kim Dae-jung (4.6 percent), Chung Joo-young, the founder of the Hyundae Group (4.6 percent), and Rhee (3.6 percent). A total of 44.7 percent of respondents found the ideal model of future Korea in a great economic state, 32.7 percent in a welfare state, and 9.3 percent in a unified state. A total of 68.7 percent favored the primacy of national interests over personal interests.[43] The survey outcome paints a conservative portrait of Korean society.

Ideologically, the left/right divide has broadened. Growth, national security, and anticommunism have become more appealing values. The generational divide seems more complicated. In the past, the younger generation supported the progressive camp, while the older generation backed the conservative camp. An analysis of voting behavior in the 2007 presidential election reveals that an unintended alliance between older (fifties and sixties) and younger (twenties and thirties) cohorts led to Lee Myung-bak's election. Older voters chose Lee for his conservatism, such as a tough national security posture and a pro-American policy line, whereas younger persons voted for him in anticipation of an economic revival and new job opportunities. Those in their forties (known earlier as the 3-8-6 generation) still are inclined to the progressive camp.

A recent survey of Seoul National University students confirms the conservative tilt of youths. Of 660 respondents, 42 percent identified themselves as progressive, 28 percent as conservative, and 30 percent as centrists. Such figures are in sharp contrast with findings in 2002, when 63 percent of respondents chose progressive and only 11 percent chose conservative. A more surprising finding was that the ruling conservative Grand National Party was most preferred (20 percent), followed by the New Party for Progress (19 percent), the Democratic Party (10 percent), and the Democratic Labor Party (9 percent).[44] Given that Seoul National University students had been seen as the vanguard of the progressive movement, such findings clearly indicate a conservative trend.

Regionalism remains the most crucial factor in Korean politics. The breakdown of the conservative southeast Youngnam Province favoring the Grand National Party and the progressive southwest Honam Province backing the New Democratic Party (NDP) has not been broken. During the 2008 presidential election, Youngnam voters supported Lee Myung-bak, whereas Honam residents voted for Chung Dong-young, the NDP candidate. A similar pattern occurred in the National Assembly elections in April 2008. Only one NDP candidate won a seat in Youngnam Province, but no candidates from the ruling Grand National Party won a seat in Honam Province. Also, the deepening polarization of Korean society in terms of income and wealth distribution, educational opportunities, enterprise size, and type of industrial activity (export vs. domestic, high technology vs. manual labor) is fostering a new divide. The internal dimension of civic national identity seems more polarized.

An August 14, 2008, survey shows that 45.4 percent of 1,000 respondents chose the United States as the favorite country, followed by China (15.2 percent), Japan (11.7 percent), and North Korea (4 percent). In 2005, China was the favorite, but since 2006 the United States has regained that distinction. According to the same survey, Japan was the most threatening country (35.1 percent), the United States was second (23.8), North Korea was third (20.1 percent), and China was the least threatening (19.2 percent). North Korea had been perceived as the most threatening country in 2004. A noticeable phenomenon is that females, the younger generation below thirty years of age, more educated (college students or graduates) persons, white-collar workers, and housewives chose the United States as threatening.[45] As with state identity, Korean citizens are somewhat divided over the issue of North Korea and the United States. Some favor improved inter-Korean relations even at the expense of the South Korean–U.S. alliance, whereas others subordinate them to the alliance. Most believe that inter-Korean cooperation and the alliance are not necessarily contradictory. In 2010, growing alarm over North Korea and South Korea's dependence on the United States, with stress on shared values and concern about China's assertiveness, tilted the balance.

Conclusion

Focusing on *minjok* identity in this chapter, I found that its intensity varies with racial and blood attributes that are now diluted, but historical identity still profoundly affects South Korea's foreign policy toward neighboring countries such as China, Japan, and North Korea. *Gukmin* identity has been undergoing major transformation with the election of Lee Myung-bak. A conservative tone is resurgent, but progressive forces are beginning to strike back. *Gukga* and *gukmin* are affecting domestic and foreign policy as they are reshaped by ideological warfare between the two camps. *Gukmin* is divided along ideological, generational, regional, and class lines, but externally united under the rubric of patriotism. Rather than *minjok, gukmin* is likely to play a pronounced role in charting forthcoming policy.

In South Korea, ethnic identity is the foundation of ethnic nationalism, whereas civic national identity serves as the engine of patriotism, especially for perceptions of, and attitudes toward, external actors. Since the democratic transition in 1987, however, the state has become increasingly captured by civil society, and the state's identity has been contested. Whereas ethnic national identity is on the wane, *gukmin* identity has become the driving force of domestic politics and foreign policy behavior. One exception that remains influential in South Korea is historical identity centered on Japan, which is also under the shadow of the United States and has recently heavily involved China. Although it has been closely linked to *minjok* identity, it may become more easily linked to *gukmin* identity in today's changing circumstances, where historical contention with China is gaining more attention.

Notes

1. For a concise summary of the debate, see Kim Gi-hyop, *New Right bipan* (Seoul: Dolbaegai, 2009). For conservative perspectives, see Park Ji-hyang, Kim Chul, Kim Il-young, and Lee Young-hoon, eds., *Haebang jonhusahui jaiinsik,* 2 vols. (Seoul: Cahik sesang, 2006). For a progressive response, see Yoon Hae-dong et al., *Geundairul dasi ilknunda* (Seoul: Yoksa bipyongsa, 2006).

2. Gilbert Rozman, "South Korea's National Identity Sensitivity: Evolution, Manifestations, Prospects," *KEI Academic Paper Series* 4, no. 3 (March 2009): 1–8; Chung-in Moon and Seung-won Suh, "Identity Politics, Nationalism and the Future of Northeast Asia," in *The U.S., and Northeast Asia,* edited by G. John

Ikenberry and Chung-in Moon (Lanham, Md.: Rowman & Littlefield, 2008); Chung-in Moon and Chun-bok Lee, "Reactive Nationalism in South Korea," paper presented at meeting of International Studies Association of North America, San Francisco, March 26, 2008; Edward A. Olsen, "Korean Nationalism in a Divided Nation: Challenges to U.S. Policy," *Pacific Focus* 13, no. 1 (April 2008): 4–21.

3. Samuel P. Huntington, *Who Are We? The Challenges to America's National Identity* (New York: Simon & Schuster, 2004), 26.

4. Rogers Brubaker and Frederic Cooper, "Beyond Identity," *Theory and Society* 29, no. 2 (February 2000): 1–47.

5. See Gi-Wook Shin, *Ethnic Nationalism in Korea: Genealogy, Politics, and Legacy* (Stanford, Calif.: Stanford University Press, 2006); Yong-ha Shin, "Minjokui sahoihakjok seolmyong gwa 'Sangsangui Gongdongcheron' bipan," *Hanguk sahoihak* 40, no.1 (2006): 35–58.

6. Byung-kook Kim, "The Politics of National Identity: The Rebirth of Ideology and Drifting Foreign Policy in South Korea," in *Korea: The East Asian Pivot,* edited by Jonathan Pollack (Newport: Naval War College Press, 2005), 111.

7. Anthony D. Smith, *National Identity: Ethnonationalism in Comparative Perspective* (London: Penguin, 1991), 11–13.

8. Chung Young-hun, "'Dangun Minjokjuui' wa keu cheongshin sasangsajeok seongkyuk e kwanhan yongu," PhD dissertation, Dankuk University, Seoul, 1993; Ho-sang Ahn, *Minjok jungron* (Seoul: Sarimwon, 1982).

9. Requoted from Henry H. Em, "*Minjok* as a Construct," in *Colonial Modernity in Korea,* edited by Gi-Wook Shin and Michael Robinson (Cambridge, Mass.: Harvard University Asia Center, 1999), 343.

10. Yong-hee Lee, "Hanguk minjokjuui ui je munje," in *Hanguk ui minjokjuui,* edited by Yong-hee Lee et al. (Seoul: Hanguk ilbosa, 1967); Kim Hak-joon, "Tongil inyum euroseoui Hanguk minjokjuui," *Tongil munje yongu* 21 (July 1994): 43; Cha Ki-byuk, *Hanguk minjokjuui ui inyum gwa shiltae* (Seoul: Kachi, 1978); Lee Hong-gu, "Hanguk minjokjuui reul boneun sae shigak ui mosaek," *Asea yongu* 27, no. 1 (January 1984): 38-62.

11. Kang Won-taik, ed., *Hangukinui gukga jungchesung gwa Hanguk jungchi* (Seoul: East Asian Institute, 2006).

12. Kim, "Politics of National Identity," 111.

13. Ernest Gellner, *Nations and Nationalism* (Ithaca, N.Y.: Cornell University Press, 1983), 6.

14. Karl Deutsch, *Nationalism and Social Communication* (Cambridge, Mass.: MIT Press, 1966), 97.

15. Andre Schmid, *Korea between Empires 1895–1919* (New York: Columbia University Press, 2002).

16. Park Chan-seung, "Hangukaeseoui 'minjok' gaenyomui hyongsung," *Gainyom gwa sotong,* June 2008.

17. *Hangyeoreh,* April 7, 2008.

18. *Wolgon Chosun,* January 11, 2009.

19. *Yonhap News,* September 5, 2007.

20. *Munwha ilbo,* December 20, 2008.

21. Chun Jae-sung, "Segye, Dongasia, minjok, gwa Nambukhan jungchae-sung," paper presented at Yonsei University, December 2008.

22. Kang Hui-won, "Hanguk damunhwa sahoiui hyongsung yoin gwa tonghap jungchaek," *Gukga jungchaek yongu* 20, no. 2 (2006): 5–34.

23. Park Ji-hyang et al., *Haebang jonhusaui jaiinsik,* vol. 1, 13–14.

24. Lee Young-hoon, *Daehan minguk iyagi* (Seoul: Giparang, 2007), 20, 45.

25. *Donga ilbo,* September 27, 2007.

26. See Chung-in Moon and Chunfu Li, "Reactive Nationalism in South Korea: Domestic Discourse and Impacts on Relations with the Neighboring Countries," paper presented at meeting of International Studies Association of North America, San Francisco, March 26, 2008.

27. *Wolgon Chosun,* March 27, 2009.

28. *Guangming ribao,* June 24, 2003. This article was written under the pen name Bian zhong, which represented three historians from the Research Center for the Historiography of the Borderland at the Chinese Academy of Social Sciences.

29. *Shin Dong-a,* September 1, 2003, 332–45.

30. *Joongang ilbo,* December 13, 2006.

31. *Hankook ilbo,* September 22, 2006.

32. Shin Ju-baek, "Lee Myung-bak Jungbuwa New Rightui wiheomhan hyundaisa insik," *Kyunghyang shinmun,* August 19, 2008.

33. Another critical factor affecting the formation of the founding Constitution and state identity in South Korea was national division and the existence of North Korea as a rival. See Myong-lim Park, "Honbop, gukga, minjok, geurigo Nambukhanui jungcheisung hyungsung," unpublished paper, College of Law, Yonsei University, Seoul, 2009.

34. In support, see Ahn Byung-jik and Lee Young-hoon, *Daehan minguk, yoksaui giroae seoda* (Seoul: Giparang, 2007); Lee Young-hoon, *Daehan minguk iyagi;* Park Ji-hyang et al., *Haebang jonhusaui jaiinsik.* In opposition, see Kim Gi-hyop, *New Right bipan;* Yoon Hae-dong et al., *Geundairul dasi iknunda.*

35. *Joongang ilbo,* December 24, 2008.

36. Ibid.

37. Chun Jae-ho, "21segi Hangukui nashionalism: Gyogwaseo forumui yoksainsikeul jungsimeuro," paper presented at a conference on "East Asian Regional Order and Nationalism," Sungkyungwan University, January 2009.

38. For an earlier debate on this issue, see Stephan Haggard, Chung-in Moon, and David Kang, "Japanese Colonialism and Korean Development: A Critique," *World Development* 25, no. 6 (June 1997): 867–81.

39. Ahn Byung-jik and Lee Young-hoon, *Daihan minguk, yoksaui giroae seoda,* 144.

40. Kang Won-taik, "Hangukinui gukga jungchesunggwa minjok jungchesung: Daehan minguk minjokjuui," in *Hangukinui gukga,* ed. Kang, 23.

41. Kim Min-jon, "Jibdan jungchesung, sahoi gyunyol, jungchi gyunyol," in *Hangukinui gukga,* ed. Kang, 59.

42. Another result in this study by Kang shows a paradoxical outcome: A total of 65.8 percent of respondents found Korean national identity in ethnicity-related symbols (white-cloth-wearing nation, 26.4 percent; one nation, 17.3 percent; Tangun, 11.7 percent; Korean language, 10.4 percent), whereas those who related Korean national identity with symbols related to the Republic of Korea were merely 32.1 percent (national flag, 26.9 percent; national anthem, 4.1 percent; national

flower, 1.1 percent). Kang Won-taik, "Hangukinui," in *Hangukinui gukga,* ed. Kang, 19–20.

43. *Kyunghyang shinmun,* August 15, 2008.

44. *Chosun ilbo,* July 14, 2009, a survey conducted by Hong Du-seung.

45. See the special feature on national identity in *Kyunghyang shinmun,* August 14, 2008.

Chapter 9

China's National Identity and Foreign Policy: Continuity amid Transformation

Jin Linbo

China's foreign policy was long defined by the values of Confucian tradition rather than oft-changing external circumstances—where it was almost always compelled, but reluctant, to react. This feature of China's isolationist and inward-looking tendency contrasted with Japan's timely adaptability to changes occurring in the outside world. The contrast was best exemplified in the responses to the West before and after the Opium War. Although much has changed, the challenge remains of drawing on China's cultural legacy, minimizing the negative effects of remnants of its traditional international system clashing with the Western system, while boosting the positive aspects of the Confucian tradition as a force for peace and stability. This chapter reviews the role of this tradition in the premodern, modern, and contemporary periods and its potential impact ahead.

As one of the oldest civilizations, China has an exceptional basis for continuity in its national identity. For more than two thousand years officials and scholars alike were reluctant to reconsider the principles of

Confucianism that defined the role of China's state and its place in the known world. Yet, after the May Fourth Movement repudiated the Confucian ideals and practices following the 1911 collapse of the Qing Dynasty, and leadership after 1949 rejected this tradition, doubts were raised about the degree of continuity that still existed in national identity. Once contemporary reform was launched in 1978, however, the focus began to shift to how to draw on the tradition in order to achieve a synthesis of old and new—a reaffirmation of elements of the Confucian heritage and support for the elements that can be conducive to a peaceful and harmonious international system.

Backed by unparalleled cultural achievements in early history, China developed a strong sense of Sinocentrism and established the "tributary system," an international order with China as the superior, central power and its neighbors—including the countries on the Korean Peninsula, in Southeast Asia, and in Central Asia, as well as Japan at various times—as peripheral, tributary states. Under this Confucian-based system, ethnocentrism and universalism, egotism in cultural superiority, and altruism coexisted, but China's national economic interests as a whole were basically unattended, and the search for knowledge beyond the system itself seemed unnecessary and, consequently, neglected. The traditional passive attitude toward foreign affairs left China unprepared to face the abnormally strong "barbarians" of Western nations in the nineteenth century. Yet China's reluctance to deal with this unprecedented challenge, which stemmed from its sense of cultural superiority, remained basically unchanged even after the Opium War. In form, as Immanuel C. Y. Hsü put it, the Confucian universal empire had metamorphosed into a nation-state, but in spirit the old Middle Kingdom' worldview lingered.[1]

China was forced to recognize the collapse of its tributary system and adopt, unwillingly, the Westphalian international system, which in its eyes demonstrated despised militarism rather than cultural superiority, of which it had been highly proud for more than two thousand years. Under such a power-based system, China was unable not only to keep an equal footing with the Western imperialist powers but also to maintain its independence and territorial integrity, due to intensified external intrusions and internal troubles caused by corrupt government. As a result, the century-long national sentiment of humiliation and victimization generated strong resentment against imperialism and Confucianism, and a powerful inclination to modern nationalism, which facilitated the rise of Communism. Although the establishment of the Republic of China provided a loose environment for introducing Western civilization—including modern nationalism, liberalism, and individualism—the weakness of the central government left China unable to block the intensified foreign invasion led by Japan. Victory in the eight-year war of resistance was not sufficient to offset the tremendous war damage on both China's physical strength and historical prestige.

The founding of the People's Republic of China (PRC) gave China a chance to establish a new identity under an effective central government led by the Chinese Communist Party. For several decades under Mao Zedong, the new China tried to discard as much as possible of its Confucianism-based cultural tradition and build a political and economic independent power that could serve as a revolutionary center for the developing world. Such efforts peaked in the Cultural Revolution, but resulted in the most disastrous turmoil (socially, politically, culturally, as well as economically) in the history of the PRC. Although in the early 1970s China succeeded in improving relations with the United States and Japan, its two main enemies after 1949, its self-reliance and isolationist orientation were not seriously changed. Its national goals were not clearly redefined, affecting its identity.

It was not until the start of China's reform and open door era—led by Deng Xiaoping, a pragmatic political leader rarely seen in Chinese history—that perceptions of the outside world changed dramatically, reflecting a shift in national identity from a pure socialist country, the overwhelming emphasis in Mao's era, to a country that is "socialist with Chinese characteristics." Economic development was prioritized for the first time, and many capitalistic international standards, especially in trade and finance, were eventually adopted. In the process of establishing a "socialist market economy," China was, consciously or unconsciously, internationalized, bringing unprecedented changes to its views of the world. Many perception gaps with other nations, especially the developed countries, were greatly narrowed. Although there were fewer changes in China's political system, with its one-party dominance, than the outside world had expected, Deng's bold pragmatism toward economic development, implemented in China's foreign as well as domestic policies, refocused the national identity as well as international relations.

Propelled by the positive results of reform and opening during three decades, China now has much more confidence about finding a proper role for itself through revitalizing its Confucianism-based traditions, while striking a balance between them and its status as a socialist nation. The slogans of constructing a "harmonious society" and a "harmonious world" well reflect new efforts to forge an identity that fits a rising China. Domestically, given the reduced effectiveness of socialist ideology and increased need for national solidarity, the pursuit of these harmonious goals raised the need to forge a combination of Confucian traditions, universalism, modern nationalism, and patriotic internationalism. This was the context in which the Beijing Olympic Games came to serve as the perfect stage for China to demonstrate simultaneously enthusiastic nationalism and internationalism. Yet it is premature to conceptualize this pattern as the culmination of the transformation, politically and economically, initiated by Deng Xiaoping. In foreign policy, given the active campaign over decades against hegemonism and the reluctance since the 1980s to seek political leadership in what was then known as the "third world," the search for a new identity may suggest that China wants to be a substantive member of the "second world," though officially it will continue to present itself as a member of today's developing world.

The Premodern Chinese Concept of the World

The term "Tianxia" (All-under-Heaven) has long been associated with the worldview looking out beyond China's borders. Although this term was used more frequently during the Qin and Han dynasties, which established a unified and strong state, its origin can be traced back to the preceding Zhou Dynasty, when the *Shijing,* one of the classics of Chinese thought, referred to it in the following words: "Under the wide heaven, there is no land that is not the emperor's, and within the sea-boundaries of the land, there is none who is not a subject of the emperor."[2]

As an ode titled *Beishan* explicitly states, ancient Chinese held that Tianxia was the whole known world, and the emperor (the Son of Heaven) was the sole legitimate ruler, who reigned supreme over all humankind with the "Mandate of Heaven." Theoretically, there were neither foreign states outside the wide universe that China governed without regard to boundaries nor any other emperor who could be regarded as Son of Heaven. Although in the Warring States period many feudal principalities had fought against each other while conducting interstate diplomacy, they were nominally under the rule of the Zhou emperor and not independent states engaged in foreign policy.

Even early in their history, the Chinese people had generated a strong ethnocentric worldview analogous to nationalism, supporting an unchallenged cultural superiority combined with a sense of political, military, and economic preeminence. This unique philosophy put China at the center of the entire known world as the "Middle Kingdom," which gained credibility after Emperor Qin Shihuang first unified the country. Perceiving their state as the center of the world, the Chinese saw their search for identity as defining the universally applicable truth for all of humankind, a mission that had enormous influence on thinking throughout history. Throughout the remainder of the premodern period, the Chinese continued to perceive their country through a civilizational lens as the only cultural center of the entire known world.[3] This was a kind of universalism,[4] which along with Sinocentrism and nationalism proved to be an enduring force in modern China.

Although there were other schools of thought, the ideas advocated by Confucius and his disciples became the basic worldview, holding significant sway over all aspects of Chinese society thereafter. When it was embraced by the Han Dynasty, it began to enjoy the strong state patronage that would persist until the twentieth century. With its emphasis on state benevolence and morality, it led to a record of writing the history of each dynasty after its fall, explaining the virtues that allowed it to endure and the moral failings that accounted for its fall. Assessing the character of the state against an idealized moral standard became fixed in Chinese thinking, adding an element of national identity to the civilizational identity associated with Tianxia. Confucianism was so deeply embedded that it not only survived the catastrophic Cultural Revolution but was also revitalized in the following decades as a factor in social life and politics, including foreign policy.

Confucianism became associated with peace, order, and harmony. It favored the maintenance of stability, linking self-identity through personal cultivation; following the proscribed conduct in the five major relationships (emperor-subject, father-son, husband-wife, elder brother–younger brother, and friend-friend) that would lead to proper order in the family and society; and imperial conduct to ensure harmony with nature and, thus, the universe. If the state were properly run, adhering to the right identity, success would be ensured at all these levels. A strong and unified China, even under dynasties such as the Yuan and Qing whose rulers were ethnically not Chinese, was a source of pride and an example for the future. Dynastic identity set a precedent for modern state identity.

Although making much of peace, order, and morality as state responsibilities that must permeate society, Confucianism had contempt for the unfettered pursuit of economic interests and scorn for militarism. It saw the former as promoting greed that unavoidably leads to immorality, disorder, and conflict, eventually resulting in wars and dynastic collapse; and it saw the latter as rule by coercion, which was treated as the opposite of rule by moral suasion. The contempt for militarism had significant implications for China's attitude toward the West after the Opium War. Not only was it unworthy for the Chinese ruling class to pay attention to the British victory by military force rather than cultural superiority, but also this aroused antiforeign sentiment among the Chinese populace, retarding positive adoption of Western civilization and the process of modernization. It was not until the Guomindang established the Huangpu Junxiao, the party-led national army academy in 1924, that national contempt for military affairs began to change.

Chinese enriched the content of Tianxia with a hierarchical approach to handling relations with neighboring peoples. Because under this concept the emperor claimed to rule over all under heaven, his domain naturally included non-Chinese ethnic groups and even those who did not fall directly under Chinese governance. If they did not accept Chinese civilization, they were called "barbarians." Although superiority was manifested in many ways, Chinese self-identity relative to other peoples, centered above all on cultural pride. This was not a matter of race, religion, or national origin—criteria for feelings of superiority in other states around the world—but of cultural achievement and confidence in the utility of established rituals and beliefs for a more just and stable society guided by the imperial state.

This orientation was reflected in a benevolent, noninterventionist, nonexploitative approach to outsiders. After all, strictly speaking, barbarians were not foreigners but just "uncivilized" peoples awaiting assimilation into the Chinese orbit, not through coercion or proselytizing but through cultural awakening. Expecting that these peoples would seek transformation on their own, China generally followed a laissez-faire policy. This was accompanied by a lack of attention to the benefits of borrowing from the outside world or focusing on particular states as "significant others" for national identity. In the absence of such contrasts, civilizational identity could persist without turning into true national identity, as was occurring in Europe during centuries of internecine warfare. Facing the Western "barbarians," old methods of responding to powerful barbarians—appeasement, intermarriage, or using one barbarian to check another (*yiyi zhiyi*)—did not suffice. China's response was slowed by an identity gap, which combined a lack of appreciation for the way another state could pose an existential challenge and failure to realize the urgency of a nationalist upsurge centered on the Chinese state in this era of imperialism.

In treating other nations along a continuum from "barbarian" to largely civilized by virtue of their emulation of China's Confucian orthodoxy, the Chinese were unprepared for "barbarians" who were insistent on their civilizational superiority with unprecedented knowledge as well as military and economic prowess. There was no alternative but to follow Western ways in agreeing to treaties and striving to secure sovereignty at a time when treaty ports and other intrusive measures raised concerns about colonialism, which was widespread around the globe. China was obliged to recognize the collapse of the tribute system and adopt, if reluctantly at first, an international system, which, in its eyes, served to justify despicable militarism rather than cultural superiority. In this environment, it was unable to secure equal footing with the imperialist powers, suffering losses to its independence and territorial integrity blamed both on the unjust behavior of these powers and the incompetence of its corrupt and insufficiently nationalistic government. Sentiments of humiliation and victimization spread, infusing a surge of self-criticism directed against the Manchu-led dynasty and, after its fall, the Confucian heritage that permeated thinking about the state, society, and the outside world. Modern national identity was shaped by nationalism in other states and perceived insults against the Chinese nation.

The Tianxia concept evolved into the "tributary system," which served as an early type of international order in East Asia. Relations centered on the status of China as paternal head, offering ritual recognition to new tributary kings and assistance to them when necessary. The junior members of this system paid homage to China in the form of periodic tribute, which brought no net benefit to China because return gifts were substantial as proof of China's benevolence. Yet the ceremonial affirmation of status differentials was what mattered, especially for China's incipient cultural and political national identity. Within this system, China as the central power played no role in dealing with disputes or conflicts among member states. This made tributary relations ceremonial and ritualistic rather than exploitative. Foreign trade was an unworthy objective for high policy. Emperor Qianlong clearly expressed the view that China had no need to have trade relations with the Britain in his famous letter to King George III of England in 1793.[5] From the Chinese perspective, this regular confirmation of the correct hierarchical order offered proof of continuity of a world order that was complementary to the domestic order, which was also highly ritualized and supportive of state authority.

National identity, though still more a manifestation of civilizational pride than of a competitive orientation toward other nations, became clearer through the tribute system in the Ming and Qing dynasties. This Sinocentric international order placed China in the center as the dominant power, while treating its neighbors, whether they were formally part of it or not, as peripheral. They were tributary not because they supported China economically or militarily but through ritual deference and acknowledgment of the Confucian order that confirmed China's superior status in a hierarchical system radiating out to the Korean Peninsula, Southeast Asia, Central Asia, and Japan. If a nation far enough away to escape retribution opted out of this system, as Japan did by the late Ming and throughout the Qing, this was no cause for reconsideration of assumptions about both China's superiority and its benevolence. In this way, the Chinese could be both ethnocentric by doubting the value of what they could learn from others and cosmopolitan, assuming that they were bestowing favors on other nations, such as assisting their stability.

Korea provides a case in point. Whereas Koreans came to view relations with China through the pejorative lens of *sadae,* serving the senior in a dependent relationship, China saw this as a nominal association, which gave it no reason to meddle in Korean politics and left it little prepared to exert control over its foreign relations. At no time did Korea challenge China's cultural superiority, including the elevated status of the emperor when he granted an audience or exchanged messages, thereby sparing China any need to question whether its identity, based on cultural superiority, was being questioned. In the 1880s, in the face of foreign assertiveness, China strengthened its political and military position, but it refused to make any claim to suzerainty in Korea in response to efforts by Japan and the Western powers to cut a diplomatic deal as they pursued their own political and economic interests. In 1911, Liang Qichao pointed to this refusal as the worst mistake China had made in its relations with Korea and the way other states were treating it.[6]

Modern Chinese Nationalism and Cosmopolitanism, 1895–1949

The power of the Western states and, before long, also of a modernizing Japan, was increasingly felt by China as it was exposed to their military and economic prowess as well as their advanced scientific and technological knowledge. They gave an impetus to focus on the nation in the struggles that preceded and followed the 1911 Revolution and again in the decades when state power was fragmented and unified resistance to foreign pressure was elusive. A critical element in the emerging Chinese national identity was consciousness of other states, as villains in victimizing the Chinese people or possible models for a new Chinese state able to modernize and to hold its own. After the Sino-Japanese War, Japan was the most significant "other" in debates over how China should respond. Following the Bolshevik Revolution, the Soviet Union set an example that drew increasing attention. The United States was also important. Under Japanese occupation, the Chinese grew ever more resentful of their country's inability to establish a powerful state. The search for national identity was inconclusive for several decades, when Western ideas spread widely but traditional concepts also were revived.

One influential idea that represented an extension of the Tianxia theme was *datong*. Kang Youwei, struggling to bring reform to the Qing Dynasty, interpreted this concept of a universal commonwealth as a utopian world in which all nations would dismantle their national borders as soon as possible. Also advocating cosmopolitanism was Sun Zhongshan, the founding father of the Republic of China. While turning against "barbarian" Manchu rule as well as imperialism, his interest in *datong* as an aspect of the traditional worldview showed the importance he attached to reviving universality with China not merely one nation in pursuit of narrow interests in a relentless struggle against other nations. In this quest for a broader community of nations, reestablishing the link between civilization and nation, the Chinese were showing discomfort with the Westphalian international system as incompatible with the tributary system and its basic assumptions.

Kang's Hundred Days' Reform in 1898 was the first bold action in this direction. He had attempted to take the Meiji Restoration as a model for a modern nation-state without abandoning Confucianism as the guiding philosophy. Liang Qichao, Kang's disciple who had escaped to Japan, was moved by its fanatic nationalism to also try to forge a modern nation. Whereas Kang enthusiastically advocated cosmopolitanism, Liang embraced the ideas of modern nationalism. Deeply moved by Japan's nationalism, Sun zealously absorbed it into his plan for overthrowing the Qing Dynasty and establishing the Republic of China. Unlike Liang, however, Sun not only advocated Pan-Asianism, an idealistic version of East Asian regionalism, but also affirmed a belief that all nations should make sincere efforts to accomplish *datong shijie,* the cosmopolitan world.

After the Sino-Japanese War, a series of moves by Japan—including intensified activity in China's northeast provinces, colonial rule in Taiwan, the annexation of Korea (1910), and the notorious "Twenty-One Demands" in 1915—contributed to fixing an image of Japan as a militaristic enemy. The Manchurian Incident (1931) and the Marco Polo Bridge Incident (1937) decisively turned the long-standing resentment against foreign encroachment into an unprecedented surge of resistance against Japanese aggression.

China's image of persistent stagnation and disorder as well as weakness proved a source of embarrassment. A major source of humiliation was cultural, rather than military or economic. The fact that the Western world order applied the "law of the jungle" and depended on military coercion made it less civilized and deprived it of legitimacy as a model. In contrast to the tributary system, with its emphasis on cultural prerequisites of international relations, this order left China victimized without any obvious recourse. A nation with superior culture such as China was forced against its will to sign a series of unequal treaties. Even during China's most eager adoption of Western civilization starting in the 1920s, its distrust toward the international system imposed by the imperialist powers remained strong. Li Dazhao, a founder of the Chinese Communist Party (CCP), condemned the outcome of the Paris Peace Conference as nothing more than "dividing the spoils among the imperialists."[7]

The lingering influence of China's distinct cultural identity made its embrace of the usual type of modern nationalism difficult. Chen Duxiu, a famous scholar and another founding father of the CCP, in 1915 recognized three fundamental differences between nations in the East and the West: (1) Whereas the former were warlike, the latter were pacific; (2) whereas the former were individual-based, the latter were family-based; and (3) the former were based on legalism-utilitarianism, in contrast to the emotionalism of the latter.[8] Whatever we might make of these simplifications today, they are indicative of the tendency to make a sharp distinction between China's national identity and the identities attributed to Western civilization, however much efforts to borrow from the West had intensified. Efforts to pit one imperialist state against another failed when Japan invaded, arousing more intense nationalism and an even stronger rejection of the existing order.

The May Fourth Movement signified a "literary and cultural renaissance" among intellectuals in China. Many school of thought—including liberalism, individualism, social Darwinism, and Marxism-Leninism—aroused interest. This ferment produced the most important period during which the ideas of both Chinese and Western civilizations were eagerly introduced or reexamined, leaving uncertainties about national identity and perceptions of the world. Meanwhile, dissatisfaction with the results at Paris and repeated frustration over the negotiations with foreign countries over the revision of the unequal treaties exacerbated feelings of national victimization and humiliation. Anti-imperialism and Communism gained widespread support in the younger generation starting in the 1920s. It was against this background that the CCP was founded in 1921. The Soviet socialist model was attractive to many young Chinese, in contrast to imperialist models, including that of Japan. Despite the fact that the Guomindang could not accept Soviet ideology, the Soviet offer to abolish the unequal treaties and assist with military training, among other things, appeared attractive to Sun and others. With Soviet support, Sun founded the first modern national army. Later, the formation of a revolutionary party army brought further rethinking of the traditional contempt for force and military affairs, as reflected in Mao Zedong's famous remark that "political power grows out of the barrel of a gun."

Socialism and Its Transformation

After its defeat in the Opium War, China began to search for a new national identity under which it could retain not only its territorial integrity and political and economic independence but also its Confucian cultural tradition. The new Republic of China appeared to provide an answer and a direction for modernization, but internal political disunity caused by uncontrolled warlordism and intensified foreign expansion left the central government too weak to maintain China's independence and obtain a satisfactory international position. As the search for a strong national political identity intensified during the war of resistance against Japan, the attractiveness of the Soviet socialist model rose, contributing to the founding of the People's Republic of China.

Guomindang rule had sought to revive elements of Confucianism in support of a strong state, while also claiming to rally the Chinese people in defense of sovereignty. However, boycotts against foreign goods, student demonstrations, and Communist-led strikes and guerrilla movements stirred a nationalist upsurge that the still-shaky state could not bring under its control. During the war of resistance to Japanese aggression, opinion coalesced around the importance of a strong state able to restore national pride and to defend sovereignty. The CCP won the support of many who rallied against Japan's brutal occupation and also favored a centralized state capable of mobilizing resources on behalf of Chinese sovereignty. The founding of the PRC gave China a chance to establish a clear national identity under an effective central government. It leaned to the side of the Soviet Union, accepting Stalin's leadership of the international Communist cause in pursuit of world revolution, while also, under Mao's leadership, concentrating on inculcating a strong sense of Chinese patriotism centering on the CCP's rule.

In contrast to the conservative emphasis on maintaining the proper social order in Confucian thought, the consequences of successful revolutions in 1911 and 1949 justified social violence, which served calls for a shift in national identity. Against this historical background, the Chinese justified the decision to follow the Soviet model. Although the two countries enjoyed relatively good relations in the 1950s, their ideological differences and border disputes soon became unmanageable. This deterioration of bilateral relations had much to do with the personality differences between the two nations' leaders, along with their different nationalities. Mao had a strong revolutionary and independent spirit. Disavowing the Confucian stress on maintaining proper order in society, he asserted the importance and inevitability of overthrowing the existing order through political and social revolution.

The first decades after 1949 produced many symbols of national identity. In the period of the Korean War, the United States was vilified as the evil imperialist heir to all the aggressors that had subjected liberation movements and oppressed social classes. U.S. support for Guomindang rule served as a reminder, reinforced at times of shelling offshore islands occupied by the forces based on Taiwan, that China's history of division and humiliation was not yet over. Attacks on Soviet revisionism, linked to a history of Tsarist imperialism, expanded the image of a beleaguered China struggling against many enemies. In striving to establish a revolutionary center for the developing world, in the midst of anti-imperialist and class struggles, China sought to cast its national identity as the true heir to Lenin and Stalin's leadership of the international Communist movement. But the main struggle over national identity was domestic. One part of this was the intense effort to discard as much as possible of the Confucian-based cultural tradition, reaching a peak in the Cultural Revolution; however, this resulted in disastrous turmoil, casting grave doubt on the political, cultural, and economic character of Chinese national identity.

The 1949 revolution gave China a chance to discard its Confucian cultural tradition; however, as a socialist country, it was in a difficult position to clarify its national identity. The top priority in the Cultural Revolution was to uproot the deeply embedded Confucian ideology and newly formed bureaucratic social order, even before a new order had taken shape. In foreign relations, Mao had learned a great deal from the traditional Chinese ruling wisdom. Regarding the Soviet Union, he believed its leadership was "revisionist" and had less enthusiasm for promoting an anti-imperialist revolution in the world. In return, the Soviet leaders criticized Mao as a bellicose leader whose policies, both internal and external, were counterproductive and dangerous.

Confronted with worsening relations with both the Soviet Union and the United States, China began to work out an independent foreign strategy in the 1960s focusing on the developing world. This presumed an independent socialist model, discontinuous with the Confucian tradition and Stalinism while making China the revolutionary center of the world. Ideological priority replaced national economic interests, sometimes even national security needs, in foreign policy. To win political support against the superpowers, especially the Soviet Union, China increased its economic aid to countries in Asia and Africa. Although this improved its bilateral ties, especially in Africa, it paid a big price, as shown in the dramatic worsening of its relations with Vietnam and Albania in later years.

Further uncertainty about national identity arose when China succeeded in improving its relations with the United States, the state long
demonized for its imperialism, and Japan, the villain from which China
had to be liberated in the 1940s. This created a disconnect between
normalization with these two capitalist countries and retention of an
orientation to national identity stressing self-reliance, class struggle,
and recovery from a history of humiliation. Efforts to reconcile domestic and international policies remained contradictory until Deng
put forth his concept of "socialism with Chinese characteristics," along
with his reform and open door policies, which abandoned criticism of
"revisionism."

The history of the three decades after Deng introduced his reforms
shows the moves by China's leaders to leave their imprint on an independent national identity, drawing on the gradually expanded reper-
toire of Mao Zedong thought, Deng Xiaoping theory, Jiang Zemin's
three represents, and Hu Jintao's scientific development. The central
question remains how to blend support for the international system, of
which China has become a leading beneficiary and in which it has
played a constructive role, with memories of victimization and rising
nationalism. This requires reconciling its enduring Confucian legacy,
its clear commitment to retain a socialist identity, and its growing stake
in globalization with its demands for an international identity. China's
continuous emphasis on state sovereignty and noninterference in domestic affairs, even as its global reach expands, raises international concerns about its future behavior. But one of the important tasks for the
Chinese government is to keep nationalist emotions under control by
leading in a constructive direction, both in selecting policies and in
shaping discussion on what is the core of national identity.

Conclusion

What has been the impact of China's half century of intellectual struggle
over how to manage its Confucian legacy, of the next three decades of its
government-led eradication of that legacy's remnants, and of the past
three decades of its breakneck economic globalization that normally
would be expected to undermine traditional thinking? Focusing on national identity, which was incipient in premodern times and then became
an obsession in a nation struggling to assert its place in the world, this

chapter has considered the challenge of finding a balance between continuity and transformation. Indicative of continuity is awareness that Chinese perceptions of the outside world have been fundamentally affected by the strong sense of unparalleled Chinese cultural superiority, which had its origin in Sinocentrism and Confucianism. The multicentury persistence of the tributary system not only endorsed China's culturalism but also made the principles of the system virtually fixed in the Chinese worldview. When Western civilization arrived with military expansion and colonialism, it was doomed to fail to obtain Chinese understanding. Military defeat brought national humiliation to the Middle Kingdom, but it did not uproot China's deeply rooted culturalism.

Transformation did occur, however, as the need for national survival after the unexpected defeat in the Sino-Japanese War propelled China to begin embracing Western nationalism and the modernization process. Failed political reform in 1898 suggested that the creation of a new national identity entailed more radical measures, paving the way for the nationalist revolution led by the Guomindang and the socialist revolution led by the CCP, each changing Chinese perceptions of the world. In addition, the dramatic transformation wrought by reforms and globalization since 1978 has given rise to a national identity now much more confident of China's capacity to shape its own destiny and play a large role in international society.

Notwithstanding significant changes, continuation of the Confucian worldview can be found in the linkages between past Sinocentric universalism, modern nationalist cosmopolitanism, and contemporary socialist internationalism. The continuation of positive aspects of Confucian tradition, such as stressing peace and harmony, is conducive to maintaining stability not only within China but also in the international community. Of course, the negative effects of the Confucian cultural legacy and the clash between China's traditional international system and the Western system should also be taken into consideration. Those positive aspects of Confucianism can be promoted in today's world only through cultural exchanges and diplomatic efforts, but when China's "soft power" as well as "hard power" are both on the rise, the aggressive promotion of the Confucian tradition may be regarded as "cultural imperialism" in international society. Striking a balance between the traditional Chinese worldview and modern Western perceptions will remain important for China and the international community in the decades to come.

Economic national identity has gained prominence in the thirty years since Deng led China into a reform era. This served to prioritize capitalist international standards, especially in trade and finance, causing China, consciously or unconsciously, to become internationalized in the process of establishing its "socialist market economy." Building symbols of ultramodernity, including skyscrapers and high-speed railroads, China seeks to present itself as in the forefront of the global economy. With this change in thinking on economic matters came unprecedented adjustments in views of the world, narrowing the perception gap with other nations. Although there were fewer changes in the PRC's political system than many in the outside world expected, development-centered pragmatism had strong spillover effects on both foreign and domestic policy. This gave China more flexibility in dealing with diverse challenges.

Cultural national identity has also intensified with growing confidence during the past thirty years. In revitalizing its Confucian cultural tradition and striving to strike a balance between this tradition and its contemporary socialist cultural orientation, China has turned to new political slogans, seen in Hu's call to construct a "harmonious society" and "harmonious world." Given the reduced effectiveness of socialist ideology and the much-increased need for national solidarity and social cohesion, the Confucian cultural tradition as well as modern nationalism combined with calls for "patriotic internationalism" was viewed as a means for forging a harmonious society. The Beijing Olympic Games served as a perfect stage to combine these themes, demonstrating simultaneously enthusiastic nationalism and internationalism, while showing pride in China's cultural history. With its spectacular contemporary architecture for Olympic venues, Beijing also presented itself as in the forefront of modern culture.

Of course, political national identity draws the closest attention. Much discussion revolves around whether China's current pattern of development could be conceptualized as a new model, representing the culmination of the transformation process initiated by Deng Xiaoping at the end of the 1970s. When outsiders raise the prospect of a "Group of Two" or a "Beijing Consensus," they suggest that the PRC's active campaign against hegemonism is now taking shape as an assertive pursuit of leadership in a reestablished "second world," where it will compete with the United States. Although China was reluctant to pursue leadership in what was then known as the "third world" in the 1980s after earlier endorsing that community in its worldview, China is now officially continuing to denominate itself as a member of this grouping without claiming to organize it or become its leader. It appears more comfortable rejecting the path of hegemonic global power while serving as the head of some sort of "second world," in rivalry with the United States, while depicting itself as an East Asian regional power with global influence.

This debate over China's self-image is important for its national identity, even if it may not diminish rising expectations within the international community for China to assume a greater role. It has become difficult for China to remain reluctant to articulate its position on regional and global matters that may have little to do with its core national interests. If it wants to be regarded as a "responsible stakeholder," then on matters viewed as important by other great powers, its input will be considered a test of its national identity. Thus, its identity could be increasingly affected by external elements, shaping its perceptions of a world with which it is becoming increasingly interdependent.

Notes

1. Immanuel C. Y. Hsü, "Late Ch'ing Foreign Relations, 1866–1905," in *The Cambridge History of China, Volume II, Late Ch'ing, 1800–1911, Part 2*, edited by John K. Fairbank and Kwang-Ching Liu (Cambridge: Cambridge University Press, 1980), 70.

2. Immanuel C. Y. Hsü, *China's Entrance into the Family of Nations: The Diplomatic Phase, 1858–1880* (Cambridge, Mass.: Harvard University Press, 1960), 6.

3. Banno Masataka, *Kindai Chugoku seiji gaikoshi* (Tokyo: Tokyo daigaku shupankai, 1973), 77.

4. In his work examining the history of early Chinese political thought, Liang Qichao referred to cosmopolitanism (*shijiezhuyi*) as most important, along with populism (*pingminzhuyi* or *minbenzhuyi*) and socialism (*shehuizhuyi*). *Yinbinshi heji* 9 (Beijing: Zhonghua shuju, 1989), vol. 50, 1.

5. Guo Tingyi, *Zhongguo jindai shigang* (Hong Kong: Xianggang Zhongwen daxue chubanshe, 1980), vol. 1, 41.

6. Liang Qichao, *Yinbinshi heji 6* (Beijing: Zhonghua shuju, 1989), vol. 21, 23–27.

7. Li Dazhao, *Li Dazhao wenji* (Beijing: Remin chubanshe, 1984), vol. 2, 1.

8. Chen Duxiu, *Duxiu wencun* (Hefei: Anhui renmin chubanshe, 1987), 27–31.

Chapter 10

China's National Identity in Diplomacy: Noninterference in Internal Affairs

Ming Wan

This chapter discusses China's cardinal principle of noninterference in internal affairs and traces back how Chinese national interests, national identities, and global rules of the game at a given historical moment define this principle and explain how it has been practiced. I argue that this principle has reduced the tremendous uncertainties resulting from transitions in Chinese domestic politics and world affairs by providing a stable institution, defined as a rule of the game that constrains human interaction.[1] Self-interest aside, the principle has also been shaped by Chinese national identity informed through traditions and interactions with the outside world. Thus, national identity is treated as both independent variable for the noninterference principle and a dependent variable explained by social values and interactions. This chapter delves into one piece of the larger puzzle of Chinese national identity in thinking about international relations.

The Chinese government likes to say that its foreign policy is principled. All Chinese diplomats and many educated Chinese have been socialized about the Five Principles of Peaceful Coexistence (hereafter the Five Principles): (1) mutual respect for each other's territorial integrity and sovereignty, (2) mutual nonaggression, (3) mutual noninterference in each other's internal affairs, (4) equality and mutual benefit, and (5) peaceful coexistence.[2] Of these, arguably the most important is noninterference in a country's internal affairs. Why is China so attached to this "Western," Westphalian principle? And what does this say about China's perception of national interests and identity?

Insistence upon noninterference is not uniquely Chinese. Almost all developing countries view sovereignty as protection of their interests, particularly survival, and developed countries also normally guard their sovereign rights. Whether one jealously guards sovereignty is also often framed as a modern/postmodern divide. The current world sees a coexistence of a premodern world, with failed or failing states, which are sovereign only in name; a modern world, with functional states with strong adherence to sovereignty; and a postmodern world, with mainly European developed countries that shift part of their sovereignty to the European Union.[3] China has gone through traumatic transformations since the mid–nineteenth century. Thus, we need to understand how the principle of noninterference has changed in Chinese thinking and practice, informed by an evolving national identity.

The Chinese are not insisting on historically unique concepts such as the Middle Kingdom. One may argue that these traditional notions still matter, and I think they do, but they work at most on the subconscious level for most Chinese. They are certainly not institutionalized foreign policy principles on a par with that of noninterference.

This chapter examines three periods: the mid–nineteenth century, when the modern conception of sovereignty was introduced into China; the early 1950s, when the People's Republic of China had been recently established; and the present post–Cold War period. Not surprisingly, the noninterference principle has always been contested in China, as it has been elsewhere in the world. To better illustrate this, the chapter also touches on other periods. In looking at the Chinese conception of noninterference, it helps to understand the continuity and discontinuity in Chinese national identity—from the Qing Empire to the Republic of China to the People's Republic of China. Discussion of the past has implications for the present, because current Chinese foreign policy is informed by sharp shifts in national identity.[4]

This chapter does not engage social science debates over sovereignty in detail, given the focus here on national identity; but the discussion here of the Chinese principle of noninterference in domestic affairs is influenced by Stephen Krasner's work, which frames sovereignty as "organized hypocrisy," noting that the enduring principle of sovereignty in the international system has always been contested and violated.[5] Krasner did not address how the Chinese tributary system and some other past international systems were replaced by the modern international system. In his comprehensive study of sovereignty in Chinese foreign policy, Allen Carlson distinguished four areas: territorial sovereignty, jurisdictional sovereignty, sovereign authority, and economic sovereignty, which are consistent with recent international relations studies.[6] Although this chapter cannot sharply separate these four areas, particularly in the early years of China's interactions with the West and neighboring Asian countries, it essentially covers the issue of sovereign authority, namely, the state's control over its internal affairs. To understand the evolution of sovereignty, it is helpful to show the ideas that shaped it,[7] but to narrow the focus, I concentrate on the complex interaction of modernity versus tradition and identity versus interest.

Noninterference and Premodern China

To understand China's current adherence to the noninterference principle, one needs to understand how the Chinese accepted sovereignty, a principle established with the 1648 Treaty of Westphalia. Article 64 of this treaty established territorial sovereignty, without using that term, and noninterference in internal affairs over religious matters. That legally ended the Catholic Church's domination in much of Europe. Article 67 also emphasizes noninterference in internal affairs. China was not part of that Western international system until powerful sovereign Western states came into contact with it.[8] Yet China and Japan had every component needed to be a sovereign state and were at similar stages of economic development as recently as the mid–eighteenth century.[9] This made it possible, but not easy, for them to transform into modern states.

China had engaged in a balance-of-power game in Central Asia after signing the Treaty of Nerchinsk with Russia in 1689, the first treaty with a European power that determined part of the border between the two empires, and limited conflicts for about a century. However, China had played balance of power games throughout its history; so the competition with Russia did not imply the introduction of new principles of international relations.[10] In fact, as noted by Peter C. Perdue, at

Nerchinsk "neither empire's rulers believed in equal-status negotiations between sovereign states. Both acted from hierarchical assumptions of tribute, vassalage, and deference."[11] Official recognition of state sovereignty came in 1861, the year that saw the emperor's decree that England was an independent sovereign state enjoying an equal status to China, acceptance of Western diplomatic missions in Beijing, and establishment of its foreign affairs office (Zongli yamen, or Office for the General Management of Affairs and Trade with Every Country).[12]

China's acceptance of sovereignty took place under duress, as the immediate result of the Second Opium War (1857–60). The government's policymakers were reluctant to comply with what they viewed as unequal treaties—until British and French troops attacked and occupied the Chinese capital. To send a strong message, the British and French looted and burned the imperial summer palace, Yuanmingyuan, leaving a scar that helps to sustain an image of Western powers continuously bullying and humiliating China, which still serves as the core of national identity in support of the government.[13]

Much has been said about why Japan was more successful in modernization than China, but one little-noticed difference was China's systemic burdens. Japan and Vietnam had their own tributary systems, but China had the ultimate tributary system in East Asia and needed to resolve its legal relations with tributary states under Western pressure and intervention. Hypocrisy on all sides was the rule of the day. On the Western side, the sovereignty principle applied mainly to other Western states, while non-Western societies were largely colonized. Moreover, the Western clarification of the legal status of Chinese tributary states such as Vietnam often served to separate them from a weakened China and put them into their own orbit. At the same time, support for China's sovereignty in the later years by some Western powers like Great Britain and the United States also served China's interest in self-preservation and its claims to regions that could have been problematic from a legal perspective. For example, Britain's imperialism helped to script Tibet's modern geopolitical identity because it was driven by Britain's imperial interests in India. The script was "Chinese suzerainty / Tibetan autonomy," which facilitated China's shift of relations with Tibet into jurisdictional sovereignty, a legal status accepted by all sovereign states.[14]

A major contradiction lay in the fact that the Han Chinese, who controlled the agenda of forming a modern sovereign state based on growing Han nationalist identity, laid claim to areas such as Tibet and Xinjiang based on the conquests by the now-minority Manchus (and the Mongols who first administered Tibet).[15] Where China did not claim sovereignty, as in Korea, it arguably copied a page from Western imperialism, namely, informal empire and unequal treaties.[16] Having engaged in massive expansion by the mid–eighteenth century, China was often extraordinarily brutal toward border peoples,[17] at a time when other Asian countries such as Japan, Vietnam, and Burma also engaged in their own imperial expansion.[18]

The Qing Empire began to introduce legal reform to remove extraterritoriality, which compromised its sovereignty, and the only way to do this was to introduce modern law.[19] Ironically, an understanding of international law was one reason that the Chinese were so indignant about unequal treaties; they realized immediately the conflict between the spirit of international law and the actual practice of Western powers in China. Studies of law also reinforced a conviction that China must become strong. As a Qing official commented, "International law is . . . reasonable but unreliable. If it is a case of right without might, then right will not prevail."[20] But China had no choice but to turn to international law for whatever leverage it could get. If international law did not prevent Japan's seizure of Manchuria in 1931 or the establishment of a puppet state there, it did portray Japan as an aggressor, which triggered a chain of events that led to Japan's defeat in 1945 and China's recovery of the lost territories. Nationalists realized the power of sovereignty for helping to maintain territoriality and independence. But a national identity that had emerged based on victimization at the hands of the West and Japan in contrast to past glory added a sharp emotional edge and commitment to resisting perceived foreign intervention in China's domestic affairs. Any perceived offense to Chinese sovereignty triggered an immediate nationalist reaction, a trend that continues to this day.

Noninterference and Modern China

To best understand the notion of sovereignty, we look to the formative years of the People's Republic of China (PRC), when thinking was informed by patterns of China's foreign relations developed over millennia, lessons learned from one hundred years of humiliation, and the Chinese Communist Party's (CCP's) foreign affairs dealings before 1949.[21] The sovereignty principle was not the only "alien" principle that came to be reified, as the PRC introduced Marxist ideology, however inexactly it was understood. The Five Principles came into existence in the context of China-Indian negotiations over Tibet in the years 1953–54. Premier Zhou Enlai proposed them, and they were incorporated into the preamble signed by Zhou and Prime Minister Jawaharlal Nehru. The key component of the agreement was for India to recognize Tibet as part of China and to relinquish extraterritorial rights in Tibet inherited from Great Britain. Called Panchsheel in India, the principles were not emphasized there, because they did not prevent a border war in 1962 with China, and Nehru came to be criticized as a naive politician who failed to stand up to China.

The special importance of the noninterference principle can be seen in Mao Zedong's emphasis on it. In January 1949, Mao added the following item to the CCP Central Committee's instructions on foreign relations: "As the last but the most important item, no foreign countries or the United Nations will be allowed to intervene in China's domestic affairs because China is an independent country. The affairs within China's territory will be decided by the Chinese people and the Chinese government alone."[22] Announcing to the world the founding of the PRC on October 1, 1949, Mao specified equality, mutual benefit, and mutual respect for territoriality and sovereignty as principles for diplomatic relations. He defined noninterference as follows: A country takes care of its domestic disputes, which are not the business of another country. A country can only recognize the government selected by the people of another country.[23]

Adding China's own stamp with the principles of equality and mutual benefit differentiates this from the Western conception of sovereignty. An analogy would be "socialism with Chinese characteristics." Remarks by leaders such as Mao Zedong, Zhou Enlai, and Deng Xiaoping serve as sources of legitimacy.[24] The Five Principles are indeed reified cardinal principles, which have outlasted other principles such as class struggle that were adopted in the PRC's early years. Through them, China puts its spin on existing tenets rather than creating a different set of principles for structuring international order. This reveals China's national identity as part of the modern world. It has often been argued that China only rejoined the international system in the early 1970s and continues to experience difficulty in being part of today's world. In fact, the PRC has always wanted to be part of the world, albeit specifying its own terms.

One should also keep in mind the legal status of the PRC from 1949 to 1971. Although China was sovereign in the Westphalian sense, it was not sovereign in the international legal sense, because it was not part of the United Nations or recognized by most developed countries. In his book, Krasner differentiates sovereignty in its four meanings: domestic sovereignty, which entails public authority within a state and effective control; interdependence sovereignty, which entails authority over transborder movements; international legal sovereignty, which entails a mutual recognition of states and other entities; and Westphalian sovereignty, which entails the exclusion of external actors from domestic authority arrangements. The PRC did not have complete international legal sovereignty until 1971,[25] but, as reflected in Mao's remarks in 1960, for a long time it was not eager to join the United Nations because there were no obvious benefits, and China is like its own United Nations with provinces bigger than some countries.[26] As Mao recognized, the United States had organized many countries to block China's entry into the UN. But at the same time, Mao expressed discomfort about being bound by too many UN rules.

The sovereignty principle has always been contested in China's foreign policy practice, mainly in three areas. First, how could the CCP reconcile noninterference with Communist internationalism and alliance with the Soviet Union in the 1950s? Mao and the Chinese leadership turned to Moscow for instructions and had to accept Stalin's insistence on resuming Russia's special rights over the Chinese Eastern Railway, Dalian, and Port Arthur, secured in the Yalta Secret Agreement for the Soviet Union to participate in the war against Japan. The railway was returned to China only in 1952, and Dalian and the port in 1955. Mao started with a Communist international orientation, which pitted the Communist camp against the capitalist one. That reflected his decision to "lean to one side." Yet, when Mao's ideology differed from the de-Stalinization at the Twentieth Party Congress in 1956, the Sino-Soviet alliance was undermined. The history of humiliation since the Opium War was an important reason for insistence on independence and noninterference in China's domestic affairs. As the Five Principles were gradually applied to relations with other socialist countries, the principle of noninterference prevailed over the principle of socialist brotherhood, and the identity of an independent modern state prevailed over that of a fellow socialist country.

The Chinese felt particularly alarmed by the Brezhnev Doctrine, which was announced in late 1968 to justify the Soviet invasion of Czechoslovakia that August. The doctrine stated clearly that if hostile forces try to turn a socialist country to capitalism, it becomes not only the problem of the country concerned but a common problem for all socialist countries. This appeared to lay the "legal foundation" for the Soviet Union to intervene in the domestic affairs of other socialist countries, including China. Growing concern for its independence was part of the reason for adopting a realist foreign policy to the United States. Mao's successors saw him defending the Chinese national interest, as revealed in his firm stand against the Soviet Union, even when they repudiated many of his leftist domestic policies.

The second source of tensions lies in China's relations with developing countries. Ironically, the Five Principles did not prevent the 1962 border war between the two Asian giants. China supported various insurgencies and guerrilla movements in the developing world, which was of course an extreme expression of interference in another country's internal affairs. Mao believed firmly that China had responsibility to support world revolution. But actual foreign policy was more nuanced. Peter Van Ness showed that whether Beijing treated a particularly developing nation as a target for revolution depended largely on whether that country adopted a friendly or hostile policy toward China.[27]

Third, in later years, China would also compromise on its principle of noninterference in its arguably most important foreign policy issue: Taiwan. Beijing has always argued that Taiwan is China's internal affair, but it knows that the Republic of China had international legal sovereignty, as a UN member, until 1971, and that it continues to have Westphalian sovereignty (effective control over a population in a defined territory) and to enjoy support from the United States. Thus, Deng Xiaoping in later years balanced the principle of sovereignty and interest in maintaining a good relationship with the United States by telling Americans during his visit to the United States that China would stop using the slogan of liberating Taiwan and pledge not to use force first, a concession to the United States.[28] And China continues to discuss the Taiwan issue with the United States, urging it to help restrain Taiwan's moves toward independence despite the fact that the United States is a foreign power from the Chinese perspective. Geopolitical realities constrain how much China's principle of noninterference can be practiced.

Noninterference, Modern China, and Postmodern Values

The Tiananmen Square turning point in June 1989 preceded the end of the Cold War. Framing tension as Western interference in China's domestic affairs, Deng declared to former Canadian prime minister Pierre Trudeau in July 1990 that China will never accept such interference and that the most important principle in a new international order is that of noninterference in other countries' internal affairs, particularly in their choice of social system.[29] China's concern was heightened by realization of its identity of having a different political system in an environment where major Communist countries like the Soviet Union had fallen. Leaders also saw the West using human rights as an excuse to damage China.[30] Recalling invasions since the Opium War, Deng claimed that countries steeped in hegemony were not qualified to talk about human rights, adding that China's identity as a victim of Western imperialism warrants its resistance to Western pressure, which he linked with adherence to the Five Principles.[31] Deng continued to believe in the importance of maintaining the rule of the CCP.[32] Yet, continued economic reform and the open door policy made nonconfrontation with the West a necessity.

Foreign Minister Qian Qichen, who played a central role in orchestrating foreign policy to break free of Western isolation and to enhance relations with the developing world, echoed Deng's thoughts. A strong socialist identity in contrast to Western capitalism was clearly the basis for his emphasis on noninterference. He said that "the easing of tension [between the two superpowers] . . . does not mean an end to conflicts and is not tantamount to stability. With the general trend towards détente, the struggle between different social systems and different ideologies will become more complicated and acute." Qian concluded that "the reality is the coexistence of countries with different social systems, and the norm for such coexistence is the Five Principles of Peaceful Coexistence."[33]

China made a significant adjustment by appealing for support from developing countries, arguing that it shared with them a past of colonialism and humiliation. If the West could intervene in China's internal affairs, it could also easily pick on other developing nations. An enhanced identity as a non-Western, developing country identity factored in this shift.

There has been a rising tide of nationalism since the early 1990s.[34] Despite the country's rise, some still feel humiliated by the West. The accidental bombing of the Chinese Belgrade embassy on May 7, 1999, confirmed to the public that Western humanitarian intervention against the Serbs was a brutal intrusion into other countries' internal affairs, which had now also caused damage to China and a direct violation of

China's sovereignty. The critics are often driven by a strong sense of national identity as they draw a sharp contrast to the West in terms of race and cultural traditions.

As Xu Jian argued, China solved its international legal identity problem of needing to be treated as an equal by founding the PRC and winning a seat at the United Nations, and it began to solve its international economic identity problem by joining the World Trade Organization (WTO) and by having its market economy status recognized by more and more countries. However, the Chinese were surprised by severe Western media criticism over Tibet and human rights before the 2008 Beijing Olympics, in which the Chinese took great pride. This cultural clash is much harder to overcome than the more material differences that have been confronted.[35]

China's insistence on noninterference in its domestic affairs has not changed much since the early 1990s. China has become more active in multilateral human rights diplomacy and has allowed discussion of human rights issues and legal reform since the early 1990s, but its "new diplomacy" amounts to "active defense" in handling human rights disputes rather than a changed position on the principle of noninterference. After all, it has not given greater freedom to international organizations to monitor the human rights situation in China, as it continues to use the noninterference principle against what it views as Western attempts to influence the domestic politics of developing countries, particularly those in which it has strategic or commercial interests. Alarmed by the "colored revolutions" that took place in Georgia, Ukraine, and Kyrgyzstan, China tightened control over foreign nongovernmental organizations that promote human rights and democracy. This reaction was similar to its post-1989 assessment of America's conspiracy to undermine the CCP internally.[36]

With China's rise, it is being pressured to improve human rights situations in countries such as Burma and Sudan, and it made some technical adjustments before the 2008 Beijing Olympics due to high-profile protests from Hollywood figures such as Mia Farrow and Steven Spielberg and also from human rights organizations due to diplomatic persuasion from the United States and other Western governments. Beijing reduced assistance to Zimbabwe's president, Robert Mugabe; pressured the Sudanese government to accept a large international peacekeeping operation; and urged the Burmese military government to talk to Aung San Suu Kyi. China even appointed a special envoy who expressed "grave concern" about the situation in Western Darfur.[37] But soon it was clear that these were just tactical moves meant to ensure a successful Olympics.

Wang Yizhou argued recently that China now has a richer definition of the noninterference principle as part of its new diplomacy. Citing China's greater involvement in regional and global security issues such as peacekeeping in East Timor and policing for Haiti as well as a modified approach toward Darfur, Wang suggested that China has developed from the noninterference principle a "constructive involvement" notion—which is still different from the "brutal, counterproductive" intervention of the West, because China does not want great powers to impose their will on others and limited intervention must be authorized by the United Nations Security Council, while respecting the wishes of the government and public of the country in question.[38] Yet Wang's argument is about the emerging standards for greater involvement in another country's internal affairs rather than relaxation of the noninterference principle. Involvement only when the UN Security Council—where China has a veto power—and the target country accept it would not violate the noninterference principle in any meaningful fashion.

Moreover, China has certainly not changed its position on noninterference in its own internal affairs. It is still largely hiding behind the noninterference principle because of its national interests and its perceived distinct identity from that of the West. Given its own record on human rights and minority rights, it is concerned that intervention in other countries' internal affairs would invite criticism of its domestic problems. As a nondemocracy, China does not see the wisdom in helping the West push for better human rights in developing countries, which would jeopardize its commercial interest in acquiring natural resources and its political interest in seeking allies against Western pressure. Moreover, the truth of the matter is not that China does not intervene.[39] Its very presence is at least an unintended intervention. Rather, China does not want to intervene in the way the West wants it to intervene. This is fundamentally a question of national identity.

Although China's position on noninterference has not changed much, its position on some other expressions of sovereignty has moderated since the 1990s. It has continued economic reform and integration into the global market, joining the WTO. Its membership in binding international institutions such as the WTO means that it cannot do whatever it wants domestically in areas governed by these institutions. This partial relaxation results from its growing national identity as a successful emerging power within the global economy.

The issue of sovereignty is being reimagined in a varied but distinct way in China right now. For example, although the "Tianxia" (All-under-Heaven) discussion so far has not explicitly addressed the issue of sovereignty,[40] arguments that have already been advanced should logically lead to a discourse that is not about whether one should intervene but about the very justification and methods of involvement in other countries' business. Noninterference in a modern international system is based on a differentiation between self and the other. By contrast, the Tianxia removes this difference. A reconciliation of noninterference with a "Chinese world" as imagined is possible, but severe tensions would arise.

China's revolutionary legacy lives on as well. Because of a growing income gap and a perceived erosion of Chinese values through Western influence, a school of thought called the New Left has become active in recent years. These thinkers reject the notion that Maoism is all wrong and the West has all the answers and instead want China to pursue a unique path of development. Thus, they are particularly sensitive to what they perceive to be Western interference in China's political, economic, and social development.

The opposite—and the target of the New Left—are those swayed by Western thinking, notably scholars who have a more subtle understanding of human rights and humanitarian intervention. Zhang Zhizhou, for example, recognized that legal international intervention for human rights as a mechanism of the UN Charter compensates for an insufficient protection of human rights in a sovereignty-based international order, but this order still cannot be replaced, and the international protection of human rights and the domestic protection of human rights are related.[41] This line of thinking actually can be traced back further. Wang Yizhou understands the limits to sovereignty and the reality that sovereign states are not equal in the contemporary international system, arguing that China should adopt a conception of sovereignty with a world perspective that is also consistent with its national interests.[42] More recently, Jia Qingguo made a similar subtle point: Although China should oppose interference in its internal affairs, improved human rights and a progressive political system would be the fundamental guarantee of its peaceful rise.[43] One may make an inference from these arguments that, logically, a sovereign country cannot do whatever it wants in its internal affairs because insufficient domestic protection of human rights inevitably invites foreign attempts to intervene, which is actually consistent with the UN Charter.

Joshua Cooper Ramo coined the term "the Beijing Consensus" in 2004 to summarize the Chinese approach to development—in contrast to the Washington Consensus, which advocated a sort of neoliberal, market-friendly system, with intervention by multilateral institutions as needed. He suggested that the Beijing Consensus is attractive because "China is forging a path for other nations around the world who are trying to figure out not simply how to develop their countries, but also how to fit into the international order in a way that allows them to be truly independent, to protect their way of life and political choices in a world with a single massively powerful center of gravity."[44] Some commentators contrast the Chinese approach to the American and European approaches, using noninterference as a crucial indicator—the United States engages in aggressive military and political intervention in the world; the European Union annexes neighboring countries into its supranational institutions on a voluntary basis; and China advances its interests pragmatically based on principles of mutual noninterference and sovereignty.

Conclusion

This chapter has focused on one specific Chinese foreign policy principle to illustrate how China's national identity has factored into its foreign policy since the mid–nineteenth century. After repeated defeats at the hand of European powers, China accepted the modern conception of sovereignty under duress, but the modern state system was disadvantageous to China in two important ways. First, it meant that China had to clarify its traditional influence in tributary states from a weak position against Western powers that sought to wrest these states from it. Second, China itself ended up being subject to unequal treaties that compromised its sovereignty just when it was accepting this concept, which was a principal source of the Chinese national identity of humiliation. At the same time, the sovereign norm also served China's interests in important ways. It allowed China to use the legal cover of sovereignty to protect what was left of its empire.

The People's Republic of China fervently accepted the norm of non-interference, which continued to serve its interest in national independence. It could also embrace this norm because it added a new twist, putting it within the framework of the Five Principles, which also emphasized equality and mutual benefits. Given its struggle for diplomatic recognition with the rival Chinese government in Taiwan, the stakes for national identity were high. China's emphasis on noninterference since the end of the Cold War has reflected its heightened concerns for regime survival in an international environment in which liberal democracy is prevailing. One important theme in this chapter is that there has been incongruence between China and the West. The modern Western international system coincided with a stable Chinese empire, a premodern failed state, and a Communist regime seeking alternative modernity. When China finally began modernizing in a fashion somewhat similar to the trajectory of noncommunist Asian countries, the West was moving toward a postmodern stage. The chapter also shows that the norm of noninterference is contested beneath the surface, where there often are evolving Chinese national identities based on Chinese traditions and interaction with the outside world. China's adherence to the nonintervention principle will now be further tested, given its rising power status and higher stakes in other countries' "internal affairs."

Notes

1. Douglass C. North, *Institutions, Institutional Change and Economic Performance* (New York: Cambridge University Press, 1990).

2. These principles are written into every training manual or text for Chinese officials, including *Lingdao ganbu waishi zhishi duban* (Beijing: Zhongguo duiwai jingji maoyi chubanshe, 1999), 52–53.

3. Robert Cooper, *The Breaking of Nations: Order and Chaos in the Twenty-First Century* (New York: Atlantic Monthly Press, 2003).

4. Lowell Dittmer and Samuel S. Kim, eds., *China's Quest for National Identity* (Ithaca, N.Y.: Cornell University Press, 1993).

5. Stephen D. Krasner, *Sovereignty: Organized Hypocrisy* (Princeton, N.J.: Princeton University Press, 1999).

6. Allen Carlson, *Unifying China, Integrating with the World: Securing Chinese Sovereignty in the Reform Era* (Stanford, Calif.: Stanford University Press, 2005).

7. Daniel Philpott, *Revolutions in Sovereignty: How Ideas Shaped Modern International Relations* (Princeton, N.J.: Princeton University Press, 2001).

8. Yongjin Zhang, *China in the International System, 1918–20: The Middle Kingdom at the Periphery* (New York: St. Martin's Press, 1991), 6–21.

9. Kenneth Pomeranz, *The Great Divergence: China, Europe, and the Making of the Modern World Economy* (Princeton, N.J.: Princeton University Press, 2000); R. Bin Wong, *China Transformed: Historical Change and the Limits of European Experience* (Ithaca, N.Y.: Cornell University Press, 1997).

10. S. C. M. Paine, *Imperial Rivals: China, Russia, and Their Disputed Frontier* (Armonk, N.Y.: M. E. Sharpe, 1996).

11. Ibid., 30.

12. Yongjin Zhang, *China in the International System*, 19–21.

13. David Scott, *China and the International System, 1840–1949: Power, Presence, and Perceptions in a Century of Humiliation* (Albany: State University of New York Press, 2008), 35–46.

14. Dibyesh Anand, "Strategic Hypocrisy: The British Imperial Scripting of Tibet's Geopolitical Identity," *Journal of Asian Studies* 68, no. 1 (February 2009): 227–52.

15. Dru C. Gladney, *Muslim Chinese: Ethnic Nationalism in the People's Republic* (Cambridge, Mass.: Council on East Asian Studies, Harvard University, 1996).

16. Kirk W. Larsen, *Tradition, Treaties, and Trade: Qing Imperialism and Choson Korea* (Cambridge, Mass.: East Asia Center, Harvard University 2008).

17. Evelyn S. Rawski, "Reenvisioning the Qing: The Significance of the Qing Period in Chinese History," *Journal of Asian Studies* 55, no. 4 (November 1996): 829–50.

18. Ming Wan, *The Political Economy of East Asia: Striving for Wealth and Power* (Washington, D.C.: CQ Press, 2008), 103–4.

19. Jonathan K. Ocko and David Gilmartin, "State, Sovereignty, and the People: A Comparison of the 'Rule of Law' in China and India," *Journal of Asian Studies* 68, no. 1 (February 2009): 88–91.

20. Dong Wang, *China's Unequal Treaties*, 117.

21. Michael H. Hunt, *The Genesis of Chinese Communist Foreign Policy* (New York: Columbia University Press, 1996).

22. Chinese Foreign Ministry and Central Committee Documents Research Office, eds., *Mao Zedong waijiao wenxuan* (Beijing: Zhongyang wenxian chubanshe, 1994), 78.

23. Ibid., 181.

24. Ye Zicheng, *Xinzhongguo waijiao sixiang cong Mao Zedong dao Deng Xiaoping* (Beijing: Beijing daxue chubanshe, 2001).

25. Krasner, *Sovereignty*, 3–25.

26. Chinese Foreign Ministry and Central Committee Documents Research Office, *Mao Zedong waijiao wenxuan*, 450–54.

27. Peter Van Ness, *Revolution and Chinese Foreign Policy: Peking's Support for Wars of National Liberation* (Berkeley: University of California Press, 1970), 166–80.

28. Ye, *Xinzhongguo waijiao sixiang*, 59.

29. Deng Xiaoping, *Deng Xiaoping wenxuan* (Beijing: Renmin chubanshe, 1993), 359–60.

30. Ming Wan, *Human Rights in Chinese Foreign Relations: Defining and Defending National Interests* (Philadelphia: University of Pennsylvania Press, 2001).

31. Deng, *Deng Xiaoping wenxuan,* 348, 363.

32. The CCP leadership drew lessons from the fall of the Soviet Union to ensure the survival of the CCP. David Shambaugh, *China's Communist Party: Atrophy and Adaptation* (Berkeley: University of California Press, 2008), 45–86.

33. "Qian Qichen on the World Situation," *Beijing Review,* January 15–21, 1990, 15.

34. Yongnian Zheng, *Discovering Chinese Nationalism in China: Modernization, Identity and International Relations* (Cambridge: Cambridge University Press, 1999); Peter Hays Gries, *China's New Nationalism: Pride, Politics, and Diplomacy* (Berkeley: University of California Press, 2004); Xu Wu, *Chinese Cyber Nationalism: Evolution, Characteristics, and Implication* (Lanham, Md.: Lexington Books, 2007).

35. Xu Jian, "Zhonghua minzu fuxing de guoji rentong wenti," China Institute for International Studies, December 1, 2008, http://www.ciis.org.cn/index-news. asp?ClassName=%D7%EE%D0%C2%D1%D0%BE%BF&NewsID=20081201133702117&d=3.

36. Shambaugh, *China's Communist Party,* 87–92.

37. Robert L. Rotberg, "China's Quest for Resources, Opportunities, and Influence in Africa," in *China into Africa: Trade, Aid, and Influence,* edited by Robert L. Rotberg (Washington, D.C.: Brookings Institution Press, 2008), 12–13.

38. Wang Yizhou, "Zhongguo waijiao shitese," *Shijie jingji yu zhengzhi,* no. 5 (2008): 14–15.

39. While China talks about noninterference, its diplomatic practice has also demonstrated that it is a determined power balancer that does not want to give its rivals any advantages. See Gilbert Rozman, *Chinese Strategic Thought toward Asia* (New York: Palgrave, 2010).

40. Zhao Tingyang, "Tianxia tixi de yige jianyao biaoshu," *Shijie jingji yu zhengzhi,* no. 10 (2008): 57–65; William A. Callahan, "Chinese Visions of World Order: Post-hegemonic or a New Hegemony?" *International Studies Review* 10, no. 4 (2008): 749–61.

41. Zhang Zhizhou, "Renquan de guoji baohu yu guonei baohu," in *Renquan yu waijiao,* edited by Zhou Qi (Beijing: Shishi chubanshe, 2002), 63–85.

42. Wang Yizhou, *Dangdai guoji zhengzhi xilun* (Shanghai: Shanghai renmin chubanshe, 1995), chap. 2.

43. Jia Qingguo, "Jiyu yu tiaozhan danji shijie yu Zhongguo de heping fazhan," *Guoji wenti luntan,* no. 1 (2008): 73.

44. Joshua Cooper Ramo, *The Beijing Consensus* (London: Foreign Policy Centre, 2004), 3.

Contributors

Yuichi Hosoya is associate professor of law at Keio University in Tokyo, focusing on Western diplomatic history and international politics.

Andrew Kim is a student in the Master's in Public Affairs Program at the Woodrow Wilson School of Princeton University.

Jin Linbo is a research professor at the Chinese Institute of International Studies in Beijing.

Chung-in Moon is professor of political science at Yonsei University. He was formerly ambassador for international security affairs at the Ministry of Foreign Affairs and Trade and head of a presidential commission on Northeast Asian regionalism in Seoul.

Gilbert Rozman is Musgrave Professor of Sociology at Princeton University. In 2010 and 2011, he was a fellow at the Woodrow Wilson Center.

Kazuhiko Togo is professor of international politics at Kyoto Sangyo University. Previously, he was Japanese ambassador to the Netherlands and director-general of the Eurasian Department of the Ministry of Foreign Affairs.

Ming Wan is a professor at George Mason University. In 2002 and 2003, here was a Luce Fellow in Asian Policy Studies at the Woodrow Wilson Center.

Index

abductions, 4, 36, 163
Abe Shinzo, 104, 162–66, 185–86, 190;
  views of, 19, 35–36, 92
Afghanistan War, 37
Africa, 251, 266
agreed-on framework, 210
agriculture, 56, 122, 148, 166
anti-Americanism: and Bush, 6; and
  Japan, 116, 161, 165, 177, 187; and
  South Korea, 54, 66, 69, 209–13,
  224, 228, 231
anticommunism: in Japan, 155–57,
  173, 176; in South Korea, 50–53,
  118, 198, 204–14, 226–27, 230–32
antinuclear thinking, 26, 83
anti–spiritual pollution campaign, 84,
  94. *See also* spiritual pollution
arc of freedom and prosperity, 162,
  185–86

ASEAN (Association of Southeast
  Asian Nations), 144, 178, 183
ASEAN + 3, 94, 120, 122, 144, 163, 183
AsiaBarometer survey, 56–57
Asian financial crisis, 14, 48, 94, 122,
  163, 183; and South Korea, 56, 61,
  65, 68, 104, 111, 208, 231
Asianism, 5, 18–19, 27, 36–38, 139,
  144, 163–65; in Chinese history,
  159; failure of, 41–42, 118–20; in
  Japanese history, 32, 34–35, 143,
  152, 159, 173–77, 182, 187; romanti-
  cism of 23, 190
Asian values, 65, 69, 94, 121; appeal of,
  22, 80, 104, 108, 111, 142
Asia-Pacific community, 30, 39, 41,
  179, 212
Asia-Pacific Economic Cooperation
  (APEC), 160, 179, 183

Perry, Commodore Matthew, 27
Persian Gulf War, 15
public opinion, 91–92, 96–97, 123, 187, 225; and polls, 65, 214–15, 231–33
Putin, Vladimir, 62

Qian Qichen, 265
Qing, 200–201, 240, 245–48, 261

racism, 15, 32, 153, 209, 244
rare earth metals, 29
Reagan, Ronald, 37–39
regionalism: foundation for, 3; and globalization, 35, 68, 120–23, 207; leadership of 14, 30, 34, 144–45, 173, 178–79, 213; priority of, 18, 58, 127, 130, 211, 233
religion, 5, 9, 30, 33, 114, 207, 224, 228; in China, 79, 83, 86–88, 244
revisionism: of Japan, 3, 5, 19–24, 36, 89, 104, 109, 122, 129, 216; of the Soviet Union, 12, 81, 83–84, 88, 90, 94, 139–41, 251–52
revolution, 15, 85, 90, 96, 247–53, 265, 268
Rhee, Syngmun, 53, 226, 228, 230, 232
rice, 56, 148
Roh Moo-hyun, 51, 62, 65–70, 104, 115–18, 143, 209, 227–29, 232; on history, 4; and the United States, 55, 110
Roh Tae-woo, 54, 208, 227
Russia, 38, 151, 201, 259; war with Japan, 32, 96, 109, 152

sacred torch relay, 5, 93
sadae, 60–61, 143, 246
samurai, 52, 108, 114, 152, 131; and bushido, 20–27, 31–32, 107, 111, 127, 149–51
San Francisco Peace Treaty, 23, 40, 122, 129
Sato Eisaku, 158, 176–77
Schmid, Andre, 202, 222

Self-Defense Forces, 33, 158, 160, 182
Senkaku/Diaoyu Islands, 4, 93
sensoron, 24, 41, 89
September 11, 2001, terrorist attacks, 43, 161
Shanghai Cooperation Organization, 120, 144
Shidehara Kijuro, 171
Shigemitsu Mamoru, 154–55, 172–73
Shin, Chae-ho, 221–22
Shin, Gi-Wook, 208
Shinto, 29, 149–50, 152
Sichuan earthquake, 5
Sinocentrism, 57, 95–96, 130, 216, 240–43, 253; as objective, 17, 34, 79, 106, 120, 143; as regional order, 147, 150, 199–203. *See also* Southeast Asia
Sino-Soviet split, 87, 92, 96–97, 139, 143, 176, 263
six-dimensional framework, 2, 9, 19–20, 68, 74, 101–2, 130
Six-Party Talks, 4, 65, 144
Smith, Anthony D., 221
socialism with Chinese characteristics, 97, 139, 241, 252, 262
socialist spiritual civilization, 85, 139, 141
soft power, 84, 93, 162, 253
Southeast Asia, 153, 159, 162, 173–78, 186, 213, 223; and Sinocentrism, 96, 144, 240, 246
South Korea: bashing and passing of, 14–15, 57, 119; as brand, 215; dictatorship in, 3, 49–51, 54, 87, 103, 198, 205–7, 230; as normal country, 54, 62, 209; presidential power in, 8, 48, 58–60, 115, 226–27; socialist thought in, 49, 206–7; and summits with North Korea, 10, 210. *See also* Korea
sovereignty, 4, 7, 116, 117, 120; and China, 85, 87, 91, 95–97, 144–45, 245, 250, 259, 261; failure to defend, 24, 91; and Japan, 34, 114–15; and